ADVANCE PRAISE

CM00740713

"Most of humanity's forthcoming challenges will depend for [...] relatively few American youth seem to be interested in careers in engineering. How could this be? It is in part because engineering basics as taught in most schools, if taught at all, frankly, seem B-O-R-I-N-G. Sam Stier offers an altogether new hands-on approach to teaching engineering that draws upon the excitement of living things that are all around us in the world. He transforms the subject into what it really is: not just fascinating but truly exhilarating. I only wish that some of my K–12 teachers would have read this extraordinary book."

—Norman R. Augustine, Retired Chairman & CEO,
Lockheed Martin Corp.

"As a 30-year veteran of STEM education, I consider *Engineering Education for the Next Generation: A Nature-Inspired Approach* among the best resources I have ever seen. It combines engineering—an area given more attention in the Next Generation Science Standards—with sustainability—an area demanding more attention in modern society. Further, it connects students with nature through biomimicry, and teaches them how to think analogically and creatively—engaging them and empowering them as learners."

—Brett Criswell, Ph.D., Assistant Professor of Secondary Education,
Science, West Chester University

"Sam Stier's book provides a welcome balm for a generation inheriting the harsh realities precipitated by our historically cavalier relationship with Nature. Biomimicry reminds us how connected we are, how balanced we stand, and how much promise we hold. With Stier's work, our students leverage their astonishment and amazement of Nature towards ambition and activism in tackling the immense challenges ahead. Blending solid science with infinite possibility, Stier reminds us that we are not yet finished evolving."

—Robert Gilson, M.A., Med, STEAM Specialist, Blue School, NYC

"*Engineering Education for the Next Generation* illuminates the intersection between the engineering feats that have changed the world and planning the educational experiences for our students who will inherit it. As Stier unpacks how nature has provided an inspiration for innovators and inventors, he creates a compelling case as to why STEAM educators should utilize nature-inspired examples as students first examine the engineering process and engage in engineering experiences."

—Christine Anne Royce, Ed.D., Professor of Science Education,
Shippensburg University and 2018-2019 NSTA President

"It is such a wonderful book that I wish I were a K–12 teacher ready to jump into this. Truly inspiring and grounded in facts. Sam Stier has brought in many advanced concepts and handled them masterfully. The chapter on structural engineering is what we teach to second-year engineering students. My initial thought when I started reading was, why introduce this topic so early to K–12 students? And when I finished, my thought was, why not?"

—Mariappan Jawaharlal, Ph.D., Professor of Mechanical Engineering,
California State Polytechnic University, Fellow, Biomimicry Institute

ENGINEERING EDUCATION FOR THE NEXT GENERATION

NORTON BOOKS IN EDUCATION

ENGINEERING EDUCATION FOR THE NEXT GENERATION

A NATURE-INSPIRED APPROACH

SAMUEL CORD STIER

W. W. NORTON & COMPANY

Independent Publishers Since 1923

Note to readers: Models and/or techniques described in this volume are illustrative or are included for general informational purposes only; neither the publisher nor the author can guarantee the efficacy or appropriateness of any particular recommendation in every circumstance.

About the cover design: The two main images on the front cover of this book, the flying fish and the octopus tentacles, are whimsical Victorian illustrations, conjuring up an age that was both the grand Darwinian era of natural history and a time of immense technological change. (Vintage Nature images form a visual thread throughout the book, as well.) Notice only the body of the fish is shown, which makes a big difference in how we look at it—being naturally empathetic toward Life, we seem to be able to pay more attention to the design of an organism when we aren't distracted by its face. The wooden gears symbolize engineering and also subtly suggest air bubbles rising from the fish. Thus, here as always, engineering and Nature are intertwined.

Copyright © 2020 by Samuel Cord Stier

All rights reserved
Printed in the United States of America
First Edition

For information about permission to reproduce selections from this book, write to Permissions, W. W. Norton & Company, Inc., 500 Fifth Avenue, New York, NY 10110

For information about special discounts for bulk purchases, please contact W. W. Norton Special Sales at specialsales@wwnorton.com or 800-233-4830

Manufacturing by Versa Press
Book design by Vicki Fischman
Production manager: Katelyn MacKenzie

Library of Congress Cataloging-in-Publication Data

Names: Stier, Samuel Cord, author.
Title: Engineering education for the next generation : a nature-inspired approach / Samuel Cord Stier.
Description: First edition. | New York : W. W. Norton & Company, Independent Publishers Since 1923, 2019. | Series: Norton books in education | Includes bibliographical references.
Identifiers: LCCN 2019014876 | ISBN 9780393713770 (paperback)
Subjects: LCSH: Bionics—Study and teaching (Elementary) | Engineering design—Study and teaching (Elementary) | Activity programs in education.
Classification: LCC TA164.2 .S85 2019 | DDC 372.35/8—dc23
LC record available at https://lccn.loc.gov/2019014876

W. W. Norton & Company, Inc., 500 Fifth Avenue, New York, NY 10110
www.wwnorton.com
W. W. Norton & Company Ltd., Castle House, 75/76 Wells Street, London W1T 3QT

1 2 3 4 5 6 7 8 9 0

TO TEACHERS AND CHILDREN EVERYWHERE,
and the human-built world
your admiration of Nature will foster.

CONTENTS

1 WHY A NATURE-INSPIRED APPROACH?   5

Makes the case that engineering education is broadly relevant to all students, not just those who may become engineers, and highlights the value of a Nature-inspired approach in terms of meeting Next Generation Science Standards, integrating STEM/STEAM subjects, enhancing college and career preparation, generating student interest, fostering a connection with Nature, re-energizing teachers and their practice, and more.

2 GETTING STARTED   27

Offers practical and effective ways to introduce the fascinating subject of engineering and Nature-inspired engineering to students of all backgrounds.

3 SHAPE AND STRENGTH: LEARNING STRUCTURAL ENGINEERING FROM SCHOOLYARD TREES   55

Demonstrates how to unpack fundamental concepts in material science and structural engineering by going no further than the schoolyard. Among other activities, students make models to see physical stress effects using plastic from the garbage bin and learn how professional engineers borrow ideas from trees to improve the safety of buildings and bridges.

4 ENLIGHTENED BY BONES   85

Explores how professional engineers and designers learn from bones how to make designs lighter without sacrificing performance. Students apply what they've learned to their own redesign of a common household object.

ACKNOWLEDGMENTS

There are probably easier things to do than write a book; by the time this one was done, my computer was literally held together by packing tape. Writing it wouldn't have been possible without the support of many people and organizations, not least of which include my agent, Grace Freedson, and editor, Carol Collins, and her amazing team at W. W. Norton & Co. I especially thank my spirited children, Julio and Kestrel, and my wife, Tammy. I also thank Janine Benyus, who changed forever how I see the natural world and the possibility of a sustainable human way of life. I would also like to thank the many educators, too numerous to list here, that I have been fortunate enough to work with over the years. A very special thanks goes to Dr. Ziheng Sun, at the Center for Spatial Information Science and Systems (George Mason University), a complete stranger who generously fixed a chapter file of this book that had become corrupted and unopenable, and without whose big heart I would now have many, many more gray hairs. Finally, I'd like to thank the board of directors of The Center for Learning with Nature, Ken Blum at the Dean Witter Foundation, Cynthia Loebig of the Kalliopeia Foundation, the Clif Bar Family Foundation, the United Engineering Foundation, the National Science Foundation, and the European Commission for supporting much of the curriculum development and pedagogical theory discussed in this book.

. . . to the eyes of the person of imagination,
nature is imagination itself.

–William Blake, 1799

ENGINEERING EDUCATION
FOR THE
NEXT GENERATION

When I heard the learn'd astronomer,
When the proofs, the figures, were ranged in columns
    before me,
When I was shown the charts and diagrams, to add,
    divide, and measure them,
When I sitting heard the astronomer where he lectured
    with much applause in the lecture-room,
How soon unaccountable I became tired and sick,
Till rising and gliding out I wander'd off by myself,
In the mystical moist night-air, and from time to time,
Look'd up in perfect silence at the stars.
                         –Walt Whitman

In God's wildness lies the hope of the world.
                         –John Muir

INTRODUCTION:
HOW TO MAKE SURFERS INVISIBLE

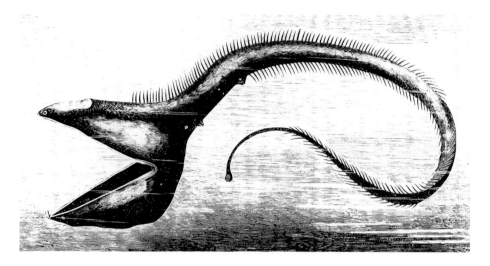

To be blunt, sharks sometimes eat surfers. It's considered an accident, which is sort of reassuring I guess, but sharks sometimes mistake the dark outline of surfboards for seals, a favorite snack, floating on the surface of the water.

Let's call that a "problem."

Some creatures in the ocean have a remarkable ability: they can generate light, which they direct below them. This ability to glow has the effect of blending the body in with the sky above. A form of camouflage, this neat trick obscures one's silhouette and makes it harder for predators lurking below to see you. Firefly squid (*Watasenia scintillans*) can do this, as well as Hawaiian bobtail squid (*Euprymna scolopes*). There are octopuses that do it, and fish, even crustaceans. There's also a shark that does it to sneak up on prey, the velvet belly lanternshark (a great name for an animal . . . though who was feeling this shark's belly?) as can the unnervingly-termed "cookiecutter shark" (*Isistius brasiliensis*).

Biologists call this ability to match the sky using light *counterillumination*—it sounds like a feature in your kitchen, but it can be a big help to ocean creatures: researchers found that midshipman fish using counterillumination are preyed upon half as much as midshipman fish who don't. Organisms with this ability not only can match the light intensity of the sky above but also can match the color wavelength of the water around them. Creatures achieve this astonishing feat through various means: some produce light themselves, like marine versions of fireflies; others maintain partnerships with bioluminescent bacteria that reside inside them (and presumably share the same motivation to get the camouflaging just right).

Let's call counterillumination one of Nature's many wonderful talents.

Now, what if I asked you to stop reading for a moment and think of a novel idea from Nature for how we might address the problem of surfers on surfboards getting attacked by sharks from below? . . .

What likely just happened in your mind is the subject of this book. Making a counterilluminating surfboard is a terrific idea and an example of Nature-inspired engineering. It's also known as biologically inspired innovation, biomimicry, or biomimetics, and it's a fascinating and hopeful approach that professional engineers, designers, and architects today increasingly use to imagine and innovate for a better world. Nature-inspired engineering includes inventing shoes that grow along with the children that wear them, designing roads that fix their own potholes, unleashing the body's immune system to take out tumors, and addressing the sweeping perils of climate change (e.g., by learning how human lungs remove CO^2 from our bodies). The basic idea is how Nature, with its seeds journeying on the wind, singing whales, carnivorous plants, and flying snakes—what poet William Blake called "imagination itself"—can spur our own creative species to invent technological breakthroughs to address the many challenges facing humankind, and to pursue untapped opportunities that abound in plain sight to make our lives better. This book is about teaching engineering and innovation to young people using this captivating and promising approach.

If you are an educator looking for ways to engage your students in STEM/STEAM (science, technology, engineering, art, and math), prepare students for college and career, or reconnect kids with Nature through education, this book was written for you.

1

WHY A NATURE-INSPIRED APPROACH?

*I think the biggest innovations of the twenty-first century
will be at the intersection of biology and technology.*

—Steve Jobs

How should we teach engineering to young people?

This question is more relevant today than ever. If there were a movie theater devoted to K-12 education, this is the question that likely would light up the marquee much of the year. To begin with, new education standards include engineering for public schools for the first time in U.S. history. Similar standards requiring the same now exist in many other countries. Meanwhile, the maker movement continues to grow in popularity, and teachers find themselves in need of learning activities that incorporate basic principles of engineering design. Since entirely new subjects rarely join long-time staples of public education (such as reading, writing, math, and more recently science), the somewhat abrupt prescription to teach engineering with large-scale K-12 educational standards has rightfully pushed the question of *how* to the front of contemporary education discussions.

Fortunately for us, this question has an uncommonly stellar answer.

This is a book about teaching engineering to young people using a Nature-inspired approach. *Nature-inspired engineering* means addressing design questions and opportunities by looking to the living world for ideas. Known by a number of terms (such as biologically inspired engineering, biomimicry, and biomimetics), Nature-inspired engineering today is at the cutting edge of professional engineering practice. It is responsible for many of the biggest technological advances in the daily news, as well as many existing technologies that define the modern world. Nature-inspired engineering is also the educational approach taken by many of the most prestigious engineering colleges and university programs around the world, producing engineers with the kinds of backgrounds today's most successful companies seek. At a time when parents are increasingly concerned about their children's connection to the natural world, it is also an exceptionally powerful way to reconnect students with the living world of which we are part, even when they can venture no farther than the classroom or schoolyard each day. Nature-inspired approaches to engineering education have a demonstrated record of success for educators who have already adopted it, engaging young people from all backgrounds, rural to inner city, Memphis to Mumbai. Last but not least, Nature-inspired engineering is an exciting and inspiring approach for teachers to learn about, reinvigorating their classroom practice and reminding them why they chose teaching as a profession in the first place. For these many reasons, Nature-inspired engineering continues to spread and to attract advocates and practitioners. It deserves to be in your educational tool belt too.

At first blush, a Nature-inspired approach to engineering education may seem surprising, if not downright strange. After all, some would say, isn't engineering and technology what distinguishes humans from the rest of Nature? From that perspective, Nature-inspired engineering seems like an oxymoron. But it's easy to forget just how similar the practice of engineering is to the functions of biology. To begin with, both use design to address opportunity. Ever since our ancestors shaped their first stick or chipped away at their first rock to make tools, humans have been designing things to make our lives better. That's what engineers do: they strive to generate effective solutions to design challenges. The rest of Nature has been doing something very similar, for several billion years. Who can look at a seagull soaring above the planet and fail to see a superb solution to the hassle of getting around? Or at a spindly vine and not be impressed by its resourcefulness in using other plants to reach the light? Or at your own hands, holding this book, and not see a masterly tool for manipulating objects? Engineers use cognitive processes to solve design challenges; engineering in the rest of Nature is accomplished through the ever creative, ever optimizing, ever restless process of evolution. The means differ, but the result is the same: the production of effective solutions to the struggles and possibilities of Life. And Nature is full of answers to unnoticed

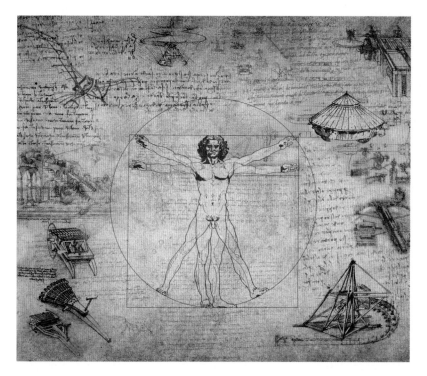

ONE OF THE BEST-KNOWN ENGINEERS OF THE WESTERN WORLD, Leonardo da Vinci (1452–1519) was a great observer of Nature, borrowing ideas from the living world for many of his designs. He is also a superlative example of someone who successfully integrated science with art.

questions. The breathtaking ability of an octopus to camouflage the texture of its skin to mimic surrounding coral, even the housefly in your kitchen doing stunts a jetfighter pilot would envy, shows that we already live in an exceptionally well-engineered world. And that's a world human engineers can learn from.

No wonder, then, that so many of our world's most famous engineers, architects, and creators throughout history have drawn inspiration for their work from the living world. Leonardo da Vinci, the best-known engineer in the Western hemisphere, astutely observed Nature and reflected what he saw in his inventions as well as his art. His anatomical drawings of the human heart educate and inspire surgeons and medical students to this day. And his famous fifteenth-century sketches of flying contraptions based on the wings of birds and bats are considered some of the earliest clear examples of bio-inspired engineering we have.

The practice of looking to Nature for design inspiration continued to pick up steam in the 1800s, when Alexander Graham Bell, fascinated by the structure and function of the human ear, had an epiphany that changed modern communication as we know it. In 1874, while experimenting with an ear from a cadaver, Bell began conceiving the fundamental architecture of the modern telephone. Observing the way the tympanic membrane mechanically activated the middle ear bones, he wrote: "It occurred to me that if a membrane as thin as tissue paper could control the vibration of bones that were, compared to it, of immense size and weight, why should not a larger and thicker membrane be able to vibrate a piece of iron in front of an electro-magnet?" Here was the mechanical blueprint of the modern telephone laid out for the first time, inspired by the structure of the human ear he so admired. Certain he was now on the right track, Bell scribbled in his notebook: "Make transmitting instrument after the model of the human ear. . . . Follow out the analogy of nature." The diaphragms and connected magnets in today's cell phones, which make the speakers and microphones generate working electric currents, are the direct result of Bell appreciating and understanding the architecture and mechanisms of the mammalian ear. He translated what he observed and abstracted what he understood into the metal, wire, and other materials of human industry. Your cell phone works, fundamentally, because it contains an abstract model of the mammalian middle ear in it. Engineering inspired by Nature is right in our pockets.

Every time we soar around the planet on an airplane, we're also enjoying the fruits of Nature-inspired engineering. For a thousand years or more, people strapped feathered appendages to their limbs and jumped to their deaths, flapping in futile mimicry of birds in the hopes of flying. Then, in the 1800s, an English baron named George Cayley figured out that, while flapping like birds wasn't the answer to human flight, soaring like them was. The Wright brothers built on Cayley's work and from watching birds discovered the secret to controlling roll in aircraft, the last obstacle to building workable airplanes. Turkey vultures, for example, control roll by twisting their

wings, which the Wright brothers copied faithfully through their "wing warping" technique. On modern aircraft, rolling is controlled by the same principle using ailerons, small movable flaps at the ends of wings. Birds first planted the very aspiration of flight in our imagination and then showed us how to achieve it.

The computers that run an aircraft's navigational systems and help you book a flight through the Internet are also products of Nature-inspired engineering. The heart of the machine, the central processing unit (CPU), is as much a biological model as the critical parts of a cell phone. In the 1930s Claude Shannon, a Michigan graduate student, had the epiphany that relay switches (the precursors of today's silicon transistor switches) could be arranged in sequences that modeled human logical reasoning. This single, wildly creative idea, which Shannon detailed in his graduate thesis (widely considered the most influential master's research project of all time), opened the door to the kind of sophisticated automated "thinking" that computers do on a routine basis, from figuring out whether it will be raining six days from now to enabling me to write this book using a word processing computer program. Shannon's flash of genius is why the electrical wiring in a computer's CPU is known, literally, as a logic circuit. Computers can perform the logical operations that make them work because the mind of a university student drew an improbable analogy between how humans reason and the design of electrical circuitry.

Another monumentally consequential example of Nature-inspired engineering comes from the origin of modern antibiotics, which Alexander Fleming discovered in 1928. The story of Fleming's discovery is legend: he returned from holiday to a messy lab to find mold growing on the petri dishes of the cultured bacteria he studied. But noticing unwanted mold growing on his research project was not what earned Fleming a knighthood or a Nobel Prize (I discover as much whenever I venture into the recesses of my own refrigerator). Fleming is celebrated because he saw the relevance of the fact that the mold on one of his petri dishes appeared to be stopping the bacteria he studied from spreading. From there the world's first human-made antibiotic, penicillin, was engineered, a medical revolution that has saved millions of lives. Many of you reading this book owe your lives to this one Nature-inspired innovation, either from taking life-saving antibiotics yourself at some point or because your direct ancestors did.

These are standout historical examples, of course, but Nature-inspired innovations are anything but a thing of the past. Many of the technologies filling today's headlines are the result of engineering inspired by Nature. These include ongoing breakthroughs in genetic engineering, inspired by a virus's ability to alter host DNA; the current revolution in artificial intelligence, a.k.a. machine learning or "neural networks," modeled on the processing architecture of human neurons; and the burgeoning field of robotics, whose mechanics, sensors, and control systems draw heavily from biological models as varied as elephants, vines, geckos, and locusts. Lesser known technologies also important to society today are inspired by the natural world as well. These include programs for computer-assisted design, or CAD, a principal tool used by professional designers and engineers to model their ideas, which incorporate algorithms inspired by how bones grow. This software allows engineers to minimize the material required to design everything from airplanes to skateboards without sacrificing safety. Redesigning everyday products using bone-inspired light-weighting software is estimated to save millions of dollars for companies, as well as over one billion pounds of material each year, reducing annual carbon dioxide emissions by nearly one million tons in the aerospace sector alone (see Chapter 4).

INNOVATORS EVERYWHERE LOOK TO THE NATURAL WORLD FOR INSPIRATION, which informs both their technological research and their teaching. *Top left*: For Dr. Frank Fish (Dept. of Biology, West Chester University), studies of marine life have resulted in a completely new kind of energy-efficient rotary blade, based on the hydrodynamics of humpback whales. *Top right*: Dr. Paula Hammond (Dept. of Chemical Engineering, MIT) develops ways to fight cancer inspired by the microbiology of the human cell. *Left, second image down*: Dr. Zhenan Bao (Dept. of Chemical Engineering, Stanford University) develops electronics that can biodegrade. *Middle right*: Dr. John Dabiri (Dept. of Mechanical Engineering, Stanford University) discovered that, by arranging wind turbines together, he could boost their overall efficiency, much like the schools of fish that inspired the idea. *Left, third image down*: Dutch designer Lilian van Daal designs recyclable furniture inspired by the versatility of cellulose. *Bottom*: Inspired by the byssus threads that enable marine mussels to adhere to rocks in pounding surf, Dr. Kaichang Li (College of Engineering, Oregon State University) developed a toxin-free adhesive now used in plywood.

Because companies and organizations like Airbus, General Motors, Verizon, Apple, Facebook, Google, the New York Stock Exchange, and NASA are all relying on Nature-inspired technology to operate, it should come as little surprise that colleges and universities everywhere are following this trend as well as helping shape it. In the last few decades, dozens of prestigious postsecondary educational institutions have established Nature-inspired approaches to train their engineering, architecture, and design undergraduate and graduate students. This includes Harvard's Wyss Institute for Biologically Inspired Engineering, Georgia Tech's Center for Biologically Inspired Design, and the Imperial College of London's Centre of Bio-Inspired Technology, to name a few. Every state in the union today has one or more colleges or universities that employ Nature-inspired innovation as a component of teaching, research, or both. Whether at a public state school or an expensive private university, Nature-inspired engineering is how today's college students and tomorrow's professionals are being trained, coast to coast and around the world.

Such approaches to engineering and design are so historically important, so contemporarily relevant, and now so widespread across colleges and universities that using this approach in K-12 schooling will undoubtedly help prepare students for college and careers. One economic impact study projected nearly two million jobs resulting from bio-inspired innovation in the United States alone and the addition of $1 trillion in gross domestic product. In fact, so firmly established is Nature-inspired innovation that it's probably easier to make the case that *not* teaching engineering through a Nature-inspired approach is likely to leave students ill-prepared for the future.

AN APPROACH WITH THE POWER TO
ENGAGE STUDENTS AND TEACHERS

None of this would matter much if students didn't find Nature-inspired engineering fascinating. But they do. Educators using Nature-inspired approaches to teach engineering have known this for years. Just one example comes from a pilot study of students at a public high school in California, who were asked about their interest in the field of engineering after completing a Nature-inspired engineering course. Nationally, only about 14 percent of high school students in the United States report an inter-

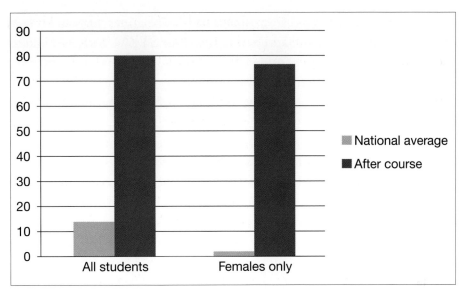

PERCENTAGES OF HIGH SCHOOL STUDENTS REPORTING AN INTEREST IN ENGI-NEERING: nationally (light gray) and among students who took a Nature-inspired engineering course (dark gray).

est in engineering, and just 2 percent of female students. But among students who took a Nature-inspired engineering course, 80 percent reported greater interest in engineering afterward—five times the national average. For female students, this rate was even more dramatic: 77 percent—*over 38 times* the national average.

More impressive than the numbers are what students say after experiencing Nature-inspired engineering. Here's just one typical example out of dozens, from Ashlynn, a high school junior:

> *This course has been, without a doubt, my most absolute favorite course we've had at school so far! I wish we could have it all year like we have math. The lessons were so unbelievably fascinating! I loved getting to learn about so many amazing, remarkable creatures and learning how certain things work. I've noticed that I'm more aware of the products and technologies we use and the way things, human-made and in nature, function. Overall, I enjoyed the class immensely and took so much away from it.*

How often do high school students speak so enthusiastically about their classes?

From a teacher's perspective, Nature-inspired engineering can serve as a unifying, integrating, and authentic context for STEM/STEAM education. This is an important consideration given the value and importance of interdisciplinary education, as well as practical time constraints. As I detail throughout this book, engineering inspired by Nature brings in the life sciences, of course, which underpins the entire approach. It also relates to chemistry and physics, the sciences that help us understand the biological abilities of organisms, while math is the language often used to describe and explore all of these branches of science. Engineering also relates directly to technology. And one need go no further than Leonardo da Vinci to see how engineering and art go hand in hand. The upshot is, no other approach to a school subject comes remotely close to Nature-inspired engineering as a way to unify and integrate all of STEM/STEAM learning.

> I cannot tell you how excited I am to integrate this curriculum into my classes. . . . This curriculum ticks so many boxes for me: critical thinking skills, project-based learning, engineering design, creativity, interdisciplinary, STEM/STEAM, environmental sustainability, prototyping, and so on. This curriculum is a perfect example of twenty-first-century education.
>
> –Mr. Brian Hoover, Technical Design,
> Hellgate High School, Missoula, Montana

A Source of Fascination and Hope

At least two features of Nature-inspired engineering make it so engaging to students and teachers alike. First, Nature-inspired engineering is a unique blend of natural history and compelling technological advances. Every Nature-inspired technology—from materials inspired by geckos that enable people to scale sheer glass walls (see below) to plastics inspired by trees, made of atmospheric carbon dioxide (see Chapter 6)—joins a fascinating natural history story with a story about human creativity that results in a brilliant technological fusion of natural and human design. That's a package that is hard to beat.

Second, these technologies are hopeful. Many of the scenarios we imagine about the world's future are not very optimistic—just consider movies like *Terminator* and *The Matrix* and the dystopic novels so popular with young people today. Many of the trends we all sense in modern society seem to lead to an unpleasant logical conclusion; perhaps art helps us process our complex feelings about the matter. Nature-inspired engineering is a powerful countercurrent to these subterranean concerns. What other approach to technology shows us, for example, ways of creating carbon-negative cement you can make out of car exhaust (inspired by coral reefs; see Chapter 6), productive and sustainable farming systems like permaculture (inspired by how natural plant communities function), or ways for billions of humans to live on Earth while actually *increasing* biodiversity and access to Nature, through urban planning strategies inspired by ants (see Chapter 6)? While human society can seem hopelessly destined to increasing misery and self-destruction, we are yet surrounded by a world with millions of flourishing populations of creatures, full of light and color, billions of years old, and noticeably absent of pollution and waste.

By drawing inspiration from such a world, by reimagining and recreating our technologies through Nature's mentorship, we can start to glimpse a human-built world that works as well as the rest of Nature, a world without toxins, blight, or poverty. The truth is, the future is not at all predetermined: it can be as terrible as we often imagine, or more extraordinary than we ever dreamed. All that's certain is that, to a very large extent, which future we'll end up with has to do with which future we pursue. Right now too many young people don't believe they or this world has much of a chance. A recent, large-scale study of one million students across the United States found that less than half of these young souls feel hopeful about the future. Giving young people a vision of a future worth inventing can make all the difference in what they think is possible, all the difference to their aspirations, and, ultimately, all the difference in what they achieve with their lives. Nature-inspired engineering can be that hopeful, solution-oriented vision of the future we all sorely want and need.

A Connection to the Natural World

There is an additional way in which Nature-inspired engineering can be transformative for students: through nurturing a bond with the living world around us. Many young people today never form such a connection. A recent study—this is no joke—actually found incarcerated *prisoners* spend more time outside today than do our children. How can our children enjoy the full experience of what it means to be alive while living a Nature-less existence? Not only does this lack of connection profoundly wither the full experience of being alive for young people, but it also severely limits the choices they will make over their lifetimes, including what products to buy or not buy, what political leaders to elect, and what activities to pursue in their lives. Since at the heart of Nature-inspired engineering is a greater awareness and appreciation for the myriad, superlative abilities of Life around us, greater admiration and love for the natural world readily results from a deep engagement with Nature-inspired engineering.

Getting kids outdoors is a laudable goal but challenging to achieve. Some children don't have much of an outdoors nearby to experience: most U.S. children today now live in urban areas, and the trend is growing world-wide. Can we labor to get more children outside more often and to green our schools and cities? Yes, we can, even if progress is slow and expensive. But in the meantime, a readily achievable strategy for reconnecting most of the world's children with Nature already has the funding and necessary infrastructure in place: schools. Millions of children go to school for over seven hours each day, for over a decade of time during the most formative period of their lives. All that's missing is a Nature-oriented curriculum and teachers ready to implement it. Engineering can be the perfect subject with which to start this process of healing the rift between children and Nature and instilling hopefulness about the future.

AN APPROACH THAT MEETS CURRENT STANDARDS

Does a Nature-inspired approach to engineering education work with new educational standards that require engineering be taught in the first place? To begin answering this question, let's take a look at these standards, at least those in the United States. Table 1.1 summarizes what U.S. K–12 students are expected to be able to do to demonstrate their engineering competence, according to the Next Generation Science Standards (NGSS). In the parlance of the NGSS, these are the "Performance Expectations," that is, the end-point metrics used to assess student learning in engineering, not the foundational practices, core disciplinary ideas, and crosscutting concepts that underlie them.

TABLE 1.1.

NGSS engineering performance expectations for K–12

Grades K–2

Ask questions, make observations, and gather information about a situation people want to change to define a simple problem that can be solved through the development of a new or improved object or tool.

Develop a simple sketch, drawing, or physical model to illustrate how the shape of an object helps it function as needed to solve a given problem.

Analyze data from tests of two objects designed to solve the same problem to compare the strengths and weaknesses of how each performs.

Grades 3–5

Define a simple design problem reflecting a need or a want that includes specified criteria for success and constraints on materials, time, or cost.

Generate and compare multiple possible solutions to a problem based on how well each is likely to meet the criteria and constraints of the problem.

Plan and carry out fair tests in which variables are controlled and failure points are considered to identify aspects of a model or prototype that can be improved.

Middle School

Define the criteria and constraints of a design problem with sufficient precision to ensure a successful solution, taking into account relevant scientific principles and potential impacts on people and the natural environment that may limit possible solutions.

Evaluate competing design solutions using a systematic process to determine how well they meet the criteria and constraints of the problem.

Analyze data from tests to determine similarities and differences among several design solutions to identify the best characteristics of each that can be combined into a new solution to better meet the criteria for success.

Develop a model to generate data for iterative testing and modification of a proposed object, tool, or process such that an optimal design can be achieved.

High School

Analyze a major global challenge to specify qualitative and quantitative criteria and constraints for solutions that account for societal needs and wants.

Design a solution to a complex real-world problem by breaking it down into smaller, more manageable problems that can be solved through engineering.

Evaluate a solution to a complex real-world problem based on prioritized criteria and trade-offs that account for a range of constraints, including cost, safety, reliability, and aesthetics, as well as possible social, cultural, and environmental impacts.

Use a computer simulation to model the impact of proposed solutions to a complex real-world problem with numerous criteria and constraints on interactions within and between systems relevant to the problem.

What Do the Standards Say Students Should Be Able to Do?

Whew! Table 1.1 is a lot to read, and even more to do, but remember, it's something students are supposed to learn how to accomplish over a thirteen-year period. Let's break it down a bit. Fortunately, some themes are quickly evident, so we might be able to boil things down to their essence and (mostly) ignore the rest. Looking across the standards, you might notice the following motifs:

- Some form of **defining design challenges** is part of every grade band's standards. K-2 students "gather information about a situation people want to change." Upper elementary students "define a simple design problem reflecting a need or a want." Middle school students must understand a design problem in order to "define its criteria and constraints." And high school students "analyze a major global challenge." All these variations reflect a theme, involving *clearly identifying and describing a challenge* that one is attempting to address through engineering.
- **Generating and representing solutions** is also a part of every grade band's standards. Whether it's illustrating how a solution functions (K-2), generating and comparing solutions (3–5), developing models of solutions (middle school), or designing and evaluating solutions (high school), the idea that students *create something solution oriented* runs throughout the standards.
- Finally, **testing potential solutions** is part of every grade band's standards. In K-2 and middle school, that means "analyzing data from tests"; in grades 3–5, "planning and carrying out fair tests"; and in high school, testing potential solutions by simulating their effects using a computer.

The small number and continuity of these motifs across K-12 are noteworthy. I return to these motifs on occasion, because they are the skeleton running through the NGSS engineering standards. You can think of these as the raisons d'être, evidently, for the NGSS engineering standards to exist. They represent the skill set students are to learn. This summary of the performance expectations at each level of schooling can help translate the potentially overwhelming verbiage of the NGSS into something more concise, capturing their essence.

What Do the Standards Not Say?

Something else useful is also highlighted in Table 1.1 or, rather, not high-lighted. That's because what is *absent* from these performance expectations is also important and instructive—perhaps even more so. Notice that there is no mention whatsoever of any content knowledge for specific types of engineering in these standards, no mention of concepts particular to mechanical or electrical engineering, for example, or architecture or computer science. That doesn't mean one shouldn't bring specific engineering content knowledge into the classroom curricula once fully manifested (more on this later), simply that it is not mandated by the standards. No particular type of engineering is preferred above any other.

Second, there is no mention of domain-specific mathematical or physics knowledge, what we normally think of when we think of pre-engineering curricula. The NGSS engineering standards are not standards for a pre-engineering education. The emphasis, instead, on defining problems, creating solutions, and testing ideas adds up to a set of standards with a much greater emphasis on *design process*. Engineers do many things, and the NGSS can't cover it all. In fact, these standards are not even actually called engineering standards. Instead, they're referred to in the NGSS specifically as engineering *design* standards. A careful read of what's in and what's not in the standards makes why abundantly clear: kids are supposed to understand problems, make things to fix them, and test what they make. The NGSS are design-oriented engineering standards, full stop.

That makes good sense, when you think about it. There are just too many engineering subdisciplines to address in educational standards, as mentioned, but the aspects addressed here—defining challenges, generating solutions, and testing them—are things pretty much all engineers in every subdiscipline do. So the standards demonstrate great wisdom here, to their credit. If you're going to address engineering in K-12, you want students to come away with what is essential across as many of the engineering fields as possible. It's not that Young's Modulus of Elasticity isn't an important concept in materials engineering; it's just that not every kind of engineering-related curriculum needs to cover it. But figuring out what you're trying to fix, coming up with solutions for fixing it, and testing whether your solutions are any good *are* relevant to every form of engineering, irrespective of engineering subdiscipline. These standards, then, have succeeded in the difficult and vital task of being relevant, irrespective of what kind of engineer a student might become. They capture engineering's essence.

AN APPROACH WITH RELEVANCE FOR ALL STUDENTS

Of course—and this is key—some students might not become engineers at all. In fact, *most* won't. Do the engineering standards still need to be relevant to them? *Of course they do!* This is a mistake many K-12 engineering curricula make: they are designed on the assumption that students will (or should) become engineers. Thus, they are developed based on the implicit question, what should every engineer know? And, adapted to the K-12 context, they become something like a pre-engineering curriculum.

But this makes no sense: we don't teach math to students because we think they should all become mathematicians, or art because we think all students should become artists. We teach these subjects to young people because we think there is something valuable about them *no matter what* students do with their lives. Identifying problems, coming up with solutions to them, and testing solutions are not just central to what engineers do; they are worthwhile abilities for *all* people to have. And the process of acquiring these abilities is a valuable educational opportunity to explore and learn all manner of topics.

Here's how Sonia Dhingra, a wise high school sophomore, put it in a recent article in *Scientific American*:

> *A lot of people in my age group ask, why do engineering activities if you don't think you will be an engineer? . . . I love painting, but my motivation is not to become a professional artist. Similarly, I do not play the piano because I think I am going to grow up to be a concert pianist. I do these things because they are both enjoyable and help me unwind; they relax and carry me to a place where my mind can try different things without judgement. So why not engineering? Engineering is also creating.*

This imperative, that K-12 engineering standards be relevant to *all* students, no matter what careers they end up pursuing, is a profoundly wise K-12 educational philosophy, evinced in the NGSS's language. And when we consider the most important reason teachers select a specific curricular approach to engineering education, the importance of relevance understandably comes up again. An engineering curriculum—or any curriculum, for that matter—that fails to be relevant to students will simply not be successful. That's because student engagement is the number one prerequisite for a successful curriculum of any kind. The positive connections among student engagement, intrinsic interest, learning, and achievement (not to mention student satisfaction and happiness) are not only self-evident but also have been confirmed through extensive educational research. Strong student engagement is an essential feature of any successful curriculum. It's got to feel relevant to students—not to mention teachers, too.

Unfortunately, the track record thus far for K-12 engineering education, at least in terms of generating interest, leaves a lot to be desired. Based on surveys of schools with existing K-12 engineering programs (one prominent program has been operating since the 1990s), student interest in engineering is not high. Moreover, it generally declines over time. That means the longer students learn engineering in these programs, the less they become interested in it! In one study, for example, interest in engineering plummeted from a high of 63 percent in elementary school to 20 percent by the end of high school. As mentioned above, nationwide student interest in engineering averages a measly 14 percent overall at the end of high school, and a scarce 2 percent for girls. Weak interest in engineering continues into college and careers, especially for certain groups. Only 14 percent of the professional engineering workforce in the United States is made up of women, for example, despite women making up half the population.

What gives? Is engineering just inherently boring? That's unlikely, to say the least: humans have been making things ever since we became human, if not before. Making stuff is part of who we are, and that inclination has led us to where we are today. I've yet to meet a young child uninterested in how things work or in making stuff, and you probably haven't either. The truth is, the process of making things can be utterly fascinating, both in and of itself and as a window on many topics of equal interest: explorations into human creativity, stories of invention, how things are manufactured, the impact of technology upon ourselves and the environment, and the reaches of human possibility itself.

Advocates for K-12 engineering education often point to the need to prime the workforce pipeline and keep our competitiveness up with other countries. But that preoccupation may be shortsighted, and counter-

MAKING THINGS IS PART OF WHO WE ARE. From this masterfully shaped spear point to this extraordinary telecommunications and pocket computer tool, some 73,000 years of nearly nonstop human ingenuity and engineering have addressed human needs and wants.

productive besides. Perhaps we should focus less on turning young people into future engineers and more on how engineering education can turn young people onto the world around them—more attentive, that is, to the benefits engineering education can provide students regardless of their eventual professions. In K-12, we err when thinking engineering education is primarily vocationally motivated; it isn't, and shouldn't be, for it offers much more valuable benefits still.

The real question is, how can engineering education be a means of enriching the lives of young people and, in the process, society overall? The potential benefits to young people of an engineering education are enormous, potentially the largest of any STEM subject. In part that's because we largely live in a human-built world: an engineering education is an opportunity to better understand, appreciate, and participate in the world in which we live. Why are the things we make designed the way they are? Where do the materials we make stuff out of come from? How are these materials processed? What happens to these things when they're disposed of? How do the things we make have an impact on us and on the environment we depend on? How were the things that define our human-built world invented in the first place? How can we improve on what we make, innovate and optimize their design? These are the kinds of questions from which a great engineering education is shaped.

Undeniably, the need to produce young people interested in these questions, as well as these pursuits, is more important than ever. Every aspect of human technological development today has been put into question by our current circumstances. Humankind's current technological practices strain Earth's resources, strain the quality and functionality of the environment, and strain our personal health and well-being. This pressure worsens on a daily basis at an exponential rate, making a vibrant and engaging engineering education of appropriate scope and scale for all children an imperative for our continued and ideally improving way of life.

A Nature-inspired approach to engineering provides this vibrant and engaging education, and it has much greater educational and social value than more myopic concepts of K-12 engineering education. Since most children will not grow up to become engineers, even in the best K-12 engineering program possible, an engineering curriculum has to have value that extends beyond a vocational orientation toward college and career. A Nature-inspired approach to engineering, with its propensity to reconnect children with Nature and its capacity to raise their hopes, skills, and aspirations to invent a better human-built world, has the kind of enhanced value educators should seek for the diversity of children we serve. And a Nature-inspired approach to engineering education also can provide the fundamentals needed for preparing students for life beyond graduation, in the most pragmatic sense.

ORGANIZATION OF THIS BOOK

A Nature-inspired approach to engineering education also offers ample opportunities to not only teach engineering but also meet the NGSS engineering requirements and other standards (such as the Common Core math standards) and generally support and integrate learning across all STEM/STEAM subjects. This book explores this approach in detail. The sequence of Chapters 2–8 correspond to sequential steps in an engineering program: introducing students to engineering inspired by Nature (Chapter 2), exploring a variety of engineering topics (Chapters 3–7), culminating in student-led projects where students employ Nature-inspired design processes for innovation and problem solving using their own ideas and skills (Chapter 8). And while kindergarten students are very different from seniors in high school, the chapters explore these topics in a cohesive way applicable to all grade bands, so as to be interesting and relevant to all teachers, across primary and secondary education.

Each chapter is not intended to provide the material for an entire curriculum. Could you do an entire course on Nature-inspired computer science or Nature-inspired product design? Of course, and it would be cool! But I'm not trying to squeeze all of that into any single chapter within this book. This is intentionally a broad, moderately deep, survey-like introduction to K-12 engineering education using a Nature-inspired approach. While what follows is structured differently than a series of lesson plans, nonetheless a goal of this book is to provide you with a practical understanding of Nature-inspired engineering education and its implementation, with a range of student activities clearly identified throughout. If I can show you some concrete examples of how to use Nature-inspired approaches to engineering topics, then perhaps you'll want to take your teaching to the next level and start to seek or work out an actual curriculum. This book is not that curriculum itself but its ambassador.

Finally, a note of humility: Nature-inspired engineering is not new, but teaching engineering using a Nature-inspired approach is. These are still early days in the practice of Nature-inspired engineering education in K-12. I'm not claiming this is the only way to approach Nature-inspired engineering education, or that this is the best way to do it. But we definitely can get started with what we have now, and we shouldn't wait. We'll figure out more as we go along. There are more people who still have a lot to contribute to this field. So, while I want to provide you with state-of-the-art content, I know we're just getting this party started. In my writing this book, and in your reading it, we're doing something new together. It's a beginning.

Additional Resources

Video introductions to innovation inspired by Nature

Michael Palwyn's TED talk, "Using Nature's Genius in Architecture": https://www.ted.com/talks/michael_pawlyn_using_nature_s_genius _in_architecture?language=en

Janine Benyus's TED talk, "Biomimicry's Surprising Lessons From Nature's Engineers": https://www.ted.com/talks/janine_benyus_shares_ nature_s_designs

Books on Nature-inspired engineering

Benyus, J. M. 1997. *Biomimicry: Innovation inspired by nature.* Harper Perennial.

Forbes, P. 2005. *The gecko's foot.* Fourth Estate.

Harman, J. 2013. *The shark's paintbrush: Biomimicry and how nature is inspiring innovation.* Nicholas Brealey.

Khan, A. 2017. *Adapt: How humans are tapping into nature's secrets to design and build a better future.* St. Martin's Press.

Excellent online magazine about Nature-inspired design

Zygote Quarterly: https://zqjournal.org/

K-12 curricula on Nature-inspired engineering

The Center for Learning with Nature: www.LearningWithNature.org.

Good introduction to the subject of biology

Hoagland, M. B., and Dodson, B. 1998. *The way life works: The science lover's illustrated guide to how life grows, develops, reproduces, and gets along.* Three Rivers Press.

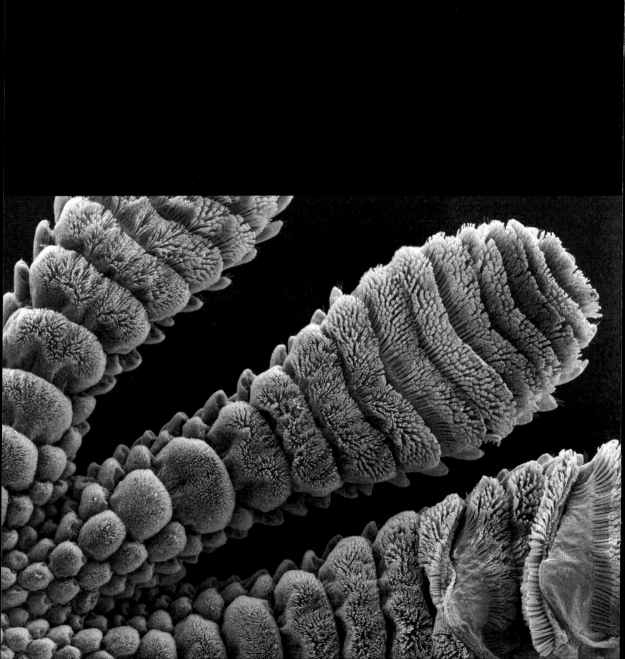

2
GETTING STARTED

If we did all the things we are capable of doing, we would literally astound ourselves.

–Thomas Alva Edison

So, now that you're more familiar with engineering inspired by Nature, you're eager to get started. Great! How do you introduce Nature-inspired engineering to your students?

DEFINING ENGINEERING

A good first step is to get everyone on the same general page about what engineering is. The dictionary definition will only get you so far, of course. Dictionary.com defines *engineering* as "the art or science of making practical application of the knowledge of pure sciences, as physics or chemistry, as in the construction of engines, bridges, buildings, mines, ships, and chemical plants." Not terrible, considering how hard it is to define *engineering* in a single sentence. The other definition given is "the action, work, or profession of an engineer." This might seem uselessly circular, but there is actually value in it—after all, engineering is whatever it is that engineers *do*, and engineers do a huge variety of things. This is an important point: we want to define *engineering* broadly. Anyone who spots and defines problems or opportunities, generates innovations to make Life better, and tests them to optimize their design is an engineer for our purposes. For us, *engineer* is shorthand to include not just mechanical engineers, electrical engineers, chemical engineers, and civil engineers but also software programmers, industrial designers, fashion designers, product designers, architects, inventors tinkering away in their garages, and more. Fortunately, we don't require an exhaustive definition of engineering any more than we need an exhaustive definition of the color blue—we generally know it when we see it.

This might confuse or even annoy some people who are used to thinking of the term *engineer* in more restrictive ways. But don't forget: the Next Generation Science Standards addressing engineering are actually called *engineering design* standards, already a much more inclusive term. And the term *engineering* itself is hardly static—far from it. Its first recorded use in 1325 referred to someone who made mechanical weaponry. We would be pretty antiquated if we limited today's engineering education to the subject of catapults. With its routine inclusion in postsecondary schools in the 1900s, the subject came to be associated with one of four branches, mechanical, chemical, electrical, and civil, but this has quickly evolved into a much more diverse range of engineering activities, a bush rather than branches, if you will.

For our purposes, it makes more sense to think about the activity of engineering in terms of its Latin root, *ingeniare*, a verb meaning "to contrive, to devise." The point is, applications of engineering will change. Yesterday it was about how to drop hot oil on marauding armies storming the castle wall; today it includes programming software to run video games. And tomorrow, who knows? But the abstract process of designing and innovating—of identifying challenges and opportunities for improving the world, generating solutions, and optimizing them through testing—is as relevant today as it was in the Middle Ages, and it will be just as relevant in the future. So, take a broad, historically informed view of what engineering is and what engineering education should address and be ready to defend it against more myopic conceptions if need be.

By the time you approach the subject of engineering with your students, they will undoubtedly have encountered the term before; they'll already have some preconceived notions about what engineering is and what it is engineers do. Since whatever you do with your students will be understood within your students' implicit concept of engineering, it's useful to know what that implicit concept is. Of course, children's craniums aren't made of glass. But a few years ago, researchers Meredith Knight of Tufts University and Christine Cunningham of the Boston Museum of Science cleverly borrowed the well-known "draw a scientist" methodology for studying student conceptions of science to better understand what students think of engineering. In a written survey portion of the study, given to several hundred students in grades 3–12, the single largest response about what engineers do is that they "build" things, followed by "fixing," "creating," and "designing" things. Fortunately, this is not a difficult preconception to work with, because it's already pretty broad and fits the Nature-inspired approach, but be aware that not all students' conceptions of engineering may conform to these notions.

> **ACTIVITY: The Deconstruction Project**
> An especially effective way to engage students with what engineering is involves having them undertake some engineering-related project straight away, that is, define engineering experientially. By giving students a personal, hands-on example of doing something engineering-related themselves, early on, the conclusions they draw will be richer and more meaningful, even while their ideas continue to evolve over time with more experiences.

This can be surprisingly simple to pull off. Consider, for instance, having your students take something apart—a radio, a cell phone, a computer, virtually anything will do. That way students can examine the object's insides and appreciate its many components and their connections to one another, as well as use tools and figure out by themselves how to deconstruct something. This simple activity is peculiarly engaging for students. Most have never taken anything apart in their lives. One teacher at a public school in Boston had students take apart things to kick off her Nature-inspired engineering class and reflected how "one of the girls completely took apart one of the cell phones and none of the boys could duplicate what she had done—she's still walking a few inches off the ground!" Another student remarked that it was "the best project I've done at school," and he was a senior in high school.

I still enjoy the memory of how, one Saturday morning, I took my nine-year-old son to a second-hand store and let him select any old gizmo he wanted. He selected a used clock radio that cost all of $2.50. I set him up on our living room carpet on top of a lily pad of newspapers, handed him a flight of screwdrivers, and let him go to town. He spent the next four hours taking every little piece of that clock radio apart (never to wake up another soul again, I'm afraid). When my son was finally done, his arms literally shot into the air like a Tour de France bicyclist crossing the finish line. He was in heaven.

I'm still unpacking why this simple activity is so engaging and satisfying. Part of it, I believe, is the thrill of getting to peek inside the black box of human technology that surrounds us. Also, the unstructured effort involved in figuring something out is appealing, in this case how to disassemble a relatively complicated piece of technology. It's like a puzzle but in reverse. In this way, it's an example of self-directed problem solving and generates a strong sense of accomplishment. This activity likely exercises what today are seldom-used human abilities that evolution has spent perhaps millions of years refining and rewarding in us.

ACTIVITY: The Marshmallow Tower Challenge
In addition to taking things apart, another natural way to have students explore what engineering is involves having them put something together. Probably the best-known activity of this kind is the marshmallow tower challenge, where teams of students are given the same set of materials (e.g., twenty sticks of dried spaghetti, a meter of string, a meter of tape, and one regular-sized marshmallow) and a limited amount of time (e.g., 18 minutes) to create a self-standing tower topped by a marshmallow. The goal is to have the tallest tower fitting these conditions when the time is up. (For more information, see the Additional Resources section at the end of this chapter.)

INSTRUCTING BY DECONSTRUCTING. Boston students take apart a
copy machine (top). A deconstructed electric typewriter (bottom). Like a
reverse puzzle, the act of deconstructing something can be a surprisingly
engaging entrée into the world of engineering.

Not only is such a "lit-fuse" type of activity instantly engaging for
students (exhilarating for some, harrowing for others), but it also fur-
nishes them with a decidedly nonabstract, personal example of what engineering is—perfect for a subsequent classroom discussion about what it is
that engineers do. Students quickly see that engineering involves aspects
of solving specific challenges, under material and time constraints, using
design, trial and error, teamwork, and more—addressing several staples of the Next Generation Science Standards (criteria for success and

MARSHMALLOW TOWER. The author's son and friends building an original example.

constraints on things like time and materials show up regularly in the NGSS Engineering Design standards).

This is a much broader and fuller conception of what engineering actually entails than the clinical notion captured in the Dictionary.com definition given above. Having students describe what engineering is from recently acquired personal experience is far more valuable than any dictionary definition they might hear or recite. (I also like the fact that the towers are topped by marshmallows. Adults put clocks on top of their towers, a symbol, presumably, of the importance we place on Time . . . what could be more apt for a child's tower than a marshmallow? Definitely plan on handing out some marshmallows at the end of the activity!) Incidentally, Peter Skillman, a designer credited with inventing the marshmallow tower challenge, has conducted this activity with hundreds of people, from little kids to professional engineers. The people who most consistently make the tallest towers in the allotted time? Kindergarteners.

WHY STUDY ENGINEERING?

Let's back up for just a second. Why cover engineering in school? your students might reasonably wonder. Who cares about engineering, anyway? Part of introducing the subject of engineering to your students should also include feeling comfortable legitimizing its presence in their curriculum in the first place.

This is actually easier to do than with most other standard school subjects, such as math or science. Students can easily come to appreciate the importance of engineering owing to its obvious prevalence all around them. Everything in their classroom—the desks, the chairs, the computers, everything—all of these are products of engineering. Zoom out a touch: the very school itself is a product of engineering, the walls and windows, electrical wiring and plumbing pipes—all designed, manufactured, and maintained by engineers. Scale out further: have students look out the windows; better yet, take them to the edge of the schoolyard or on a neighborhood walk. They will see that engineers shape nearly *every* aspect of the world we live in: the streets, the cars, the houses, indeed the entire city and surrounding farm fields--all the work of engineers.

As such, engineers design and build not only *products* but also *places*, the venues in which we live out our lives, in which we work, eat, and play, in which we react, in which we have feelings, in which we decide our dreams and ambitions. Engineers have a strong say in every part of our daily lives: how healthy the water we drink is, the kinds of chemicals released into the air by manufacturing, how long we spend in traffic, even how roomy the sidewalks feel. The impact engineers have on people, both physically and mentally, is massive and is global in scale. Just have students turn to a classmate next to them and check the tag on the back of their partner's shirt: the clothes on our backs are highly engineered objects, textiles whose raw materials are grown, dyed, and sewn together in such far-flung places as India, Vietnam, the Philippines, and Guatemala.

For the vast majority of the billions of people living on this planet, our lives play out in a human-built world. I don't mean we just *inhabit* a human-built world; rather, we *experience* what it means to be alive in these engineered places, both materially and emotionally. And these human-built worlds are defined by the vision and capabilities, and limitations, of engineers. That should give us pause. This makes the subject of engineering at least as important and worthy of deep educational examination and exploration as learning our ABCs and multiplication tables, much less grammar and calculus.

ENGINEERING INSPIRATIONS

Given the pervasive impact engineers have on our lives, a central question about engineering emerges: where do engineers get their ideas for what to make and how to make it? There is probably no more important question than this. Certainly much that is called *engineering* is simply remaking what has been made before, but we are more interested in new ideas, in innovation. How do engineers innovate? In Steven Johnson's book *Where Good Ideas Come From*, he writes:

Good ideas are . . . constrained by the parts and skills that surround them. We have a natural tendency to romanticize breakthrough innovations, imagining momentous ideas transcending their surroundings, a gifted mind somehow seeing over the detritus of old ideas and ossified tradition. But ideas are works of bricolage; they're built out of that detritus. We take the ideas we've inherited or that we've stumbled across, and we jigger them together into some new shape.

The printing press is the classic example, an invention whose parts—ink, paper, movable type, and press (for extracting olive oil and grape juice to make wine) all previously existed. Johannes Guttenberg simply combined these elements in a new way—in this sense, he didn't invent the printing press out of thin air. Inventors inevitably borrow ideas from the world around them, though this shouldn't diminish at all the value of fresh combinations and insights produced by creative thinking and tinkering. Engineers and designers get inspired by the things people have already made, even flipping through magazines just to see what other people have come up with. In Guttenberg's case, this approach was enough to come up with a new technology that revolutionized and modernized humankind. In other cases, however, engineers working this way can get stuck, essentially repeating what has come before and offering nothing new.

Johnson's point is precisely why looking to the natural world for engineering inspiration has been and continues to be so fruitful for humankind. The natural world vastly expands the range of ideas that can inspire us. When we consider not just what the human mind can come up with but include what 4 billion years of evolution in tens of millions of other species can invent, the "detritus" we have to work with is immeasurably enhanced. When you really think about it, what are the creative forces on this planet? The human mind and the rest of the natural world are the two major creative forces on this planet. For the former to ignore the latter would be like a firefighter fighting a fire with a Y-shaped hose with one of the taps turned off, unnecessarily limiting the available resources. That's why so many of the most creative and significant engineers throughout time have been those open to inspiration from the natural world. Inventors that aren't open to ideas from Nature either haven't been introduced to the idea or assume that what Nature has invented has little relevance to what humans need.

Engineers who draw inspiration from Nature tend instead to assume the opposite: that in the natural world we can find solutions to many of the challenges humans face. After all, all of Life shares the same planet. We've all had to figure out how to survive and thrive under similar conditions. These engineers study the vein patterns of leaves because they realize a leaf, transporting nutrients to every one of its cells, performs the same essential function as a city's road systems, distributing people and goods. These engineers study bones because they realize a skeleton is an optimized structure for safely supporting loads using minimized weight. They study human lungs because they see not just an organ for breathing but a device that can capture and remove carbon dioxide from flowing fluids, just as we might want to remove it from the air rising through coal-fired flue stacks. And they see Nature's systems that transform materials, energy, and information to create thriving and enduring benefits potentially full of lessons for humankind to create a more sustainable human-built world. When an engineer perceives the analogies between human technological challenges and biological phenomena, the possibilities for innovation, for "jiggering" things together in new ways, magnify explosively.

ALL OF LIFE SHARES THE SAME PLANET, and thus many of the same challenges, so Nature's solutions often have relevance for humankind's challenges.

DEFINING *NATURE-INSPIRED* ENGINEERING

Just as with the concept *engineering*, you've got the challenge of conveying to your students what *Nature-inspired engineering* means. Though it makes perfect sense to look to Nature for engineering inspiration, both logically and historically, your students still won't know what you mean if you just utter the words "Nature-inspired engineering" or any of its many derivatives (such as innovation inspired by Nature, bio-inspired design, or biomimicry). It's too many different concepts all at once, like a quiche, and your students, who perhaps have had only scrambled eggs, won't yet be accustomed to processing all of these concepts together simultaneously.

> **ACTIVITY:** **Experiencing Nature-Inspired Engineering Design**
> Nature-inspired engineering and its synonyms are inherently confus-
> ing terms to the uninitiated. To provide an experiential definition that
> you can use with your students at this point, let's return to the marsh-
> mallow tower activity. The goal is to create the tallest self-standing
> tower possible, but engineers often have to meet more complex crite-
> ria. For instance, skyscrapers need to be tall, but they also must safely
> withstand earthquakes. To make your point, have students now test
> their towers against an "earthquake."

You can simulate these using an earthquake simulation table—there
are lots of designs for these of varying complexity, and they can be a lot of
fun for students to build. A simple one requires nothing more than masking tape and a metronome, either real or digital. Have students build their
marshmallow towers on a small piece of cardboard, so they can be moved
easily. Now place two pieces of masking tape a few inches apart, and with
your hand move the cardboard foundation under each tower back and forth
between these pieces of tape at a regular speed. You want the motion to be
rigorous enough that at least some, if not all, of the towers fail. Standardize
the frequency of the shaking using the metronome. It's that simple.

Let students know at this point that they'll have an opportunity to
redesign, rebuild, and retest their towers. This time, the tallest tower that
can withstand the earthquake test will be the winner (i.e., two criteria for
success). Before they get to redesigning, ask students to describe what the
design challenge now is, in their own words. What do they want their
tower to be able to do? (Be tall and stable despite movement.) Have them
write down a list of ideas for how to do this. When they run out of ideas,
ask them where they might get other ideas for how to design the structure.
Where could they maybe find ideas people might not think of on their
own? How does Nature make tall but stable structures?

Show students images of Nature's solutions to this problem, and let
them make their own observations. Among the many examples, mangrove
trees grow in the shifting mudflats along the shorelines of many tropical
rivers and oceans, a perfect analog to the students' spaghetti tower challenge. Mangroves have a variety of growth forms, such as stilt roots with

LEARNING FROM NATURE. Roots of Australian mangrove plants have broadened bases and distinctive triangular shapes that help stabilize the plant in shifting mudflats (left). After redesigning their marshmallow towers following similar strategies used in Nature for stabilizing structures, preservice teachers at the University of Louisiana test them using a simple shake table (right).

triangular structures, and broadened bases that help them manage instability. Strangler fig trees use their unique aerial roots, which grow down from their branches and lock into the earth like guy-wires, stabilizing themselves with tension. African termite mounds sport buttresses to stabilize their walls, just like European gothic cathedrals.

Once students have seen lots of examples of analogs from Nature and their implicit strategies for being tall but stable, let them redesign their towers and retest them under earthquake conditions again. How do the towers perform now? Why? You've now given students a first-hand example of what Nature-inspired engineering is, and they're well on their way to "getting it," experientially instead of only abstractly.

Remember, the term *Nature-inspired engineering* won't mean anything to your students at first. It's similar to explaining the word *irony*. The dictionary defines *irony* as "a state of affairs or an event that seems deliberately contrary to what one expects and is often amusing as a result." That definition does next to nothing to convey what *irony* actually is! But if I tell you that Charlie Chaplin once participated in a Charlie

Chaplin look-alike contest and came in twentieth, or that the founder of the highly successful dating site Match.com lost his girlfriend to a man she met through Match.com, you gather exactly what irony is, no further definitions necessary. Same thing with saying that Nature-inspired engineering is "learning from Nature how to create a thriving and more sustainable human-built world," or, in the words of Janine Benyus, that Nature-inspired innovation is "the conscious emulation of Life's genius." This is a beautiful definition, but no one will know what Nature-inspired innovation actually is from these words. You need to provide your students with examples.

> **ACTIVITY: Stories about Nature-Inspired Engineering**
> An experiential approach to defining things is great, but it's just a data point. You also want students to grasp something of the power and scope of Nature-inspired engineering, to inspire them early on, but you don't have the time at the very beginning to compress all of the experiences it requires to really grasp this. Fortunately, humans have a great method for conveying a large amount of experience to one another in a small amount of time: stories. You'll want to share brief stories of what others have done through Nature-inspired engineering, to expand students' conception of what this is all about relatively quickly. Providing examples of Nature-inspired engineering, experientially as above and by describing what others have done, right on the heels of any kind of definition, is crucial.

Fortunately, there are hundreds of examples of Nature-inspired engineering you can use to familiarize your students with the concept, inspire them, and start to broaden their understanding of its relevance to innovation. I've mentioned several already, such as the phone, the computer, and airplanes, and I'll mention many more examples throughout the rest of the book. You can choose examples that illustrate what Nature-inspired engineering is as clearly and as engagingly as possible. You can choose examples that relate to students' interests. And you can choose examples that establish the power and scope of the approach. Three of my favorites for first introducing the concept to students are the cat-inspired thumbtack, gecko-inspired dry adhesives, and bio-inspired coloration.

Cat-Inspired Thumbtack. In college, designer Toshi Fukaya became interested in a common problem many of the rest of us have simply come to accept: the villainy of thumbtacks. "As an industrial design student in college," Toshi explained, "we often presented our idea sketches on the wall using thumbtacks. To hang many papers on the wall, we would grab a handful of thumbtacks in our hands . . ." and inevitably, Toshi would get pricked by the tacks' sinister ends, a sticky problem that bothered him a lot.

> *Then one day when I was playing with my kitty, Goofy, I saw him scratching the carpet with his sharp nails which reminded me of the sharpness of the thumbtack . . . when I touch his hands, it is always very soft and fluffy and fun to play with his paw pads. That moment, the paw and the thumbtack idea linked in my mind and I started playing with my cat's paws and observed how the nails come out and back in. As I pushed his fingers, the nails came out.*

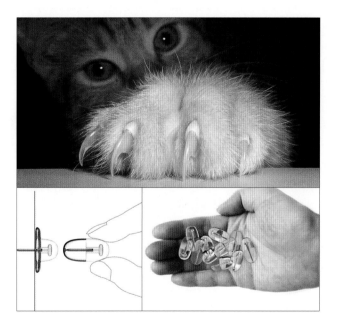

Toshi went on to invent a thumbtack encased in a compressible silicone capsule, a retractable thumbtack. Push it in the wall, and it works just like a thumbtack; pull it out, and the capsule resumes its elliptical shape, encasing the tack's metal pin so that it can't accidentally poke someone.

Gecko-Inspired Dry Adhesives. There are probably more engineers studying geckos today than biologists. The feature of geckos that grabs engineers' attention is their ability to stick to virtually any surface. This attachment is very strong: the four relatively small feet of a gecko can theoretically support 133 kilograms (nearly 300 pounds). A person with this ability could hang upside down from the ceiling using just their hands and feet, with a space shuttle strapped to their back!

How do geckos achieve this enormous adhesive strength? It's not through glue—their feet actually aren't sticky at all; they are completely dry. Instead, geckos use interatomic forces (which forces, exactly, is disputed). These are weak physical forces such as electrostatic charge and van der Waals forces. In essence, geckos can stick to walls because the atoms of their feet literally combine with the atoms of whatever surface they're climbing on.

This is pretty neat, until you consider the fact that a strong adhesive force like that would be a death sentence. If geckos couldn't also *detach* their feet just as readily (gruesome image up ahead), we'd have dead geckos hanging all over the ceilings and walls. Fortunately for geckos, these wizardy lizards can do this with ease, running up walls attaching and detaching their feet as many as twenty times per second. How do these little creatures, with their enormously strong, adhesive feet, just as easily detach them?

To answer this we have to peer very closely at a gecko's foot—at over a thousand times magnification, in fact. It isn't the smooth, lizardy foot most people see from a distance—up close it becomes evident that geckos' feet are covered by hairs, lots of them. With over 14,000 hairs per square millimeter, gecko feet are harrier than the feet of hobbits. Not only that, but the end of each of these hairs is frayed into hundreds of yet smaller structures.

If you measure the adhesive interatomic force exerted by just one of these incredibly miniscule spatula-shaped structures, at the end of just one microscopic gecko foot hair, it actually exerts a very weak adhesive force. And therein lies the gecko's manifold brilliance: the strength of a gecko's attachment comes from *multiplying* this weak force times the enormous surface area created by the thousands of frayed hairs on their feet. It's like a room full of whispering people: if enough people are packed into the room, you won't be able to hear anything over the accumulated din, even though each person is only whispering. Because each individual attachment exerted by a frayed foot hair is weak, all a gecko needs to do to detach its foot is peel back a single toe, snapping the weak adhesive forces one hair at a time, which is exactly what geckos do when they want to run up a tree or across a wall.

A strong but reversible adhesive is something humans have never been able to make, and never even *thought* of making until we started studying how geckos climb things. Now gecko-inspired materials that work using the same interatomic

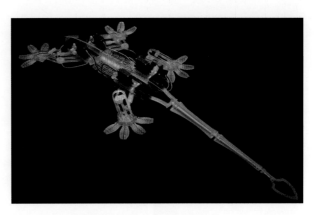

THE STICKYBOT, a wall-climbing robot created at Stanford University using gecko-inspired materials for foot pads.

forces that geckos use are a reality. These materials have nearly infinite potential uses, such as making wall-climbing robots, creating reversible medical bandages, and replacing the plebian picture hook. A cell phone or car assembled using gecko-inspired adhesives would be much easier to disassemble and recycle. A lab in the mechanical engineering department at Stanford University recently succeeded in making gecko-inspired materials that enable a person to scale a sheer glass skyscraper, à la Spiderman.

Bio-inspired Coloration. One day in July 2013, dead fish started floating up in Manukau Harbor near Auckland, New Zealand. The banks of the Oruarangi River, which flows into the harbor, turned a bright shade of violet. By the time the source of the problem was determined, a thousand liters of industrial dye had leaked into the waterway. The purple dye is used as a colorant to enliven plastic trays used in the agriculture industry. "Our kids come down here and they play," said Te Werena Taua, a spokesman for indigenous Maori that live in the area. "They fish every day and we don't know if the fish are going to be edible and how the discharge is going to affect the whole place."

A similar event happened in Fort Myers, Florida, where in 2017 a dye discharged accidentally from a hospital turned the Caloosahatchee River red. And the community of Toms River, New Jersey, has disproportionately high cancer rates from forty years of drinking textile dyes that had found their way into the community's drinking water. Dyes for coloring human-made products find their way into places where we don't want them on a routine basis.

THE WORLD OF A SIMPLE BUTTERFLY WING: scanning electron micrographs with increasing magnification. The repeating spaces with the diameter of blue wavelengths of light (465 nm) are easily seen in the profile view (bottom right).

Industrial pigments and dyes are used to color everything. Just look around: how many of the human-made things that you see are black and white? We color everything: pens, tennis shoes, soccer balls, bed sheets, plastics, hair, makeup, cars, paint, jeans, you name it. Unfortunately, the events at Manukau Harbor and Fort Myers and the situation at Toms River are not rare. Twenty percent of all industrial water pollution comes from coloring textiles alone. In China, seventy-two toxic chemicals are known to come from the textile industry. They are found in 90 percent of China's groundwater today.

The starter materials for making these pigments and dyes might surprise you. One of the first industrial dyes was discovered in the 1800s. It was extracted from coal tar, a waste product from burning coal. It's still used extensively in cosmetics and hair dye today. How about food dyes? Most, like Red No. 40 and Yellow No. 5 (found at the end of the ingredients label on nearly every processed food, including farmed salmon, hot dogs, yogurt, syrup, pickles, chips, and candy), are also derivatives of fossil fuels. Other pigments and dyes, such as many used in textiles and plastics, include heavy metals mined from the earth, primarily lead, cadmium, chromium, and copper.

Our use of pigments and dyes is problematic, to say the least, but it turns out that using pigments and dyes of questionable safety is not the only way to make things colorful. Reflect a moment on the green June beetle (*Cotinis nitida*) of summer, the common blue butterfly (*Polyommatus icarus*) or its dramatic cousin the tropical blue morpho (*Morpho* spp.), or the iridescent flash of a common pigeon's or hummingbird's throat feathers. These are all examples of a different approach to creating color, common in the rest of Nature, called *structural color.* Pigments and dyes generate color because their specific chemical makeup absorbs certain wavelengths of light (through the excitation of electrons) while reflecting others. In contrast to chemical color, structural color doesn't rely on specific chemicals to create color. Rather, color is produced by physical structures, whose geometry reflects and amplifies some wavelengths of ambient sunlight more than others. For example, in the case of butterflies like the blue morpho, repeating structures on the wing scales all have the diameter of blue wavelengths of light (465 nanometers). This amplifies the color blue to the viewer's eye, while the rest of the color spectrum is simply scattered. It's hard to believe, but there are no blue pigments or dyes in this stunningly blue butterfly's wings at all—it's a trick of light. Like an equalizer emphasizing certain base tones over the treble, the physical geometry of the structures on the butterfly's wing acts as a selective prism and mirror, amplifying the color desired out of the ambient white beams of sunlight.

You can demonstrate this to yourself if you are fortunate enough to find a green or blue feather. Greens and blues in Nature are frequently the result of structural color. Hit the feather with a hammer and observe the result: the green or blue color has vanished. That's because the physical structures that reflect these wavelengths have been demolished, and the colors are no longer produced. A dye or pigment-based color would be unaffected.

Nature-inspired color has a wide variety of applications to human tech-

LIP SERVICE. Cosmetic hues produced by bio-inspired structural color are potentially much safer than chemical-based colorants.

nologies. L'Oréal has produced cosmetics based on structural color, for instance, a promising idea. The chemicals used to make cosmetics can be a health concern, particularly because they're applied right on skin. A Japanese company has produced stunningly iridescent textiles by layering nylon together, no pigments or dyes necessary. Both of these approaches are potential game changers.

One of the cleverest applications of structural color may be in electronic screens. Because the color made by structural color is based on geometry, this geometry can be changed, dynamically. That means colors don't need to be static but can be tuned in real time. Electrical and optical engineers have applied this idea to generating color in the pixels of electronic screens: passing small amounts of electrical current through a display changes the spacing between the optical units, which in turn changes what colors the display reflects.

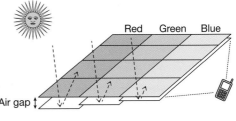

NATURE-INSPIRED STRUCTURAL COLOR APPLIED TO ELECTRONIC SCREENS. Varying the distance between optical elements in the subpixels can produce any color on the screen. Because the colors are produced by selective reflection of ambient sunlight, the screens get brighter in the sun, adding usability and reducing battery consumption.

Since this approach to creating color on electronic displays relies on ambient sunlight, you can actually see these screens easily outdoors; in fact, in bright sunlight they just get brighter (no more trying to squint outside at your dark cell phone screen, trying to see who's calling). And because these screens don't need to use backlighting to show up, they use just a fraction of the battery power to run. Dynamic color changing means that, in theory, you could create a car that's one color in the summer (say, white) and a completely different color in the winter (e.g., black). Want to change the color of your kitchen walls? Just turn a dial on the wall.

Another widespread application of Nature-inspired color is in anti-counterfeiting technology on currency. Look at the numbers in the corner of any U.S. bank note $10 or larger; as you tilt the bill, the numbers will change color, another example of dynamism afforded by making colors structurally. These optically variable inks are difficult for criminals to reproduce but easy for cashiers to assess—another example of Nature-inspired engineering right in our pockets.

Finding Examples of Nature-Inspired Engineering. These are just a few of hundreds of possible examples of Nature-inspired engineering, but they are great for kicking things off. Inspired by his cat, Toshi Fukaya's retractable thumbtack is a clear example of Nature-inspired engineering to which any school child can relate, especially those in primary school. The example of materials inspired by geckos illustrates the sheer power of Nature-inspired engineering—it can literally give humankind the powers of superheroes! And structural color has so many useful and clever applications, with the potential to improve human and environmental health. Plus, you can see a real-world example of it just by opening up your wallet.

In selecting your own examples of Nature-inspired engineering to share, key considerations are the age of your students and their interests. Your guiding principle should be to connect and inspire. For younger students, that means finding really neat examples; for older students, finding examples that give them hope is also important, hope that we can improve the world through technology and find ways for technology and the natural environment to coexist.

To find your own examples, just go to the Internet. All you need are the right search terms. These include *biologically inspired* or *bio-inspired* (sometimes written as one word, *bioinspired*), which is the term typically used in American academia. If you're searching for original research about Nature-inspired engineering (e.g., on Google Scholar), you'll especially want to use these terms. The equivalent term in European academia is *biomimetics* (though in German *bionik* is preferred). *Biomimicry* is also a useful term: this tends to focus primarily on Nature-inspired engineering related to environmental challenges. (For more information, see the Additional Resources section at the end of this chapter.)

There are so many examples of Nature-inspired engineering, you can narrow your search to topics of potential interest to your students simply by combining terms, such as "bioinspired" + "space travel." While enjoyable enough, you don't have to do this research alone. You can have the students do their own research to find examples of Nature-inspired engineering, which they can then share with the rest of the class, write up in executive summaries or reports, and so forth. Setting alerts (e.g., on Gmail) using these terms is also a really helpful way to let Google do the searching for you and have current examples of Nature-inspired engineering sent right to your inbox.

> **C**hildren want the same things we want. To laugh, to be challenged, to be entertained, and delighted.
>
> –Dr. Seuss

It's also useful, especially for older students, for you to find examples that illustrate the *scope* of Nature-inspired engineering. Engineers and designers today use Nature-inspired approaches in virtually every design-related endeavor you can think of: architecture, automotive engineering, medicine, economics, software programming, traffic planning, national security, sports, and much, much more. There are so many examples of Nature-inspired engineering, in fact, that there is no single answer to how to illustrate the approach's scope. The best advice is to cover the range of subjects you feel are important and of interest, and to avoid picking too many examples of the same type. For instance, if all of your examples have to do with the design of vehicles (e.g., trains, cars, and airplanes), you probably should diversify.

THE SCOPE AND POWER OF NATURE-INSPIRED ENGINEERING

One particularly helpful conceptual framework regarding the scope of Nature-inspired engineering has to do with the types of natural phenomena we can learn from and emulate in our technologies and designs. You can think of there being three conceptual levels to the kinds of natural phenomena we can make use of:

- *Biological forms, behaviors, and interactions.* These include things like the shapes of leaves, the texture of shark skin, the way spider webs reflect ultraviolet light, and quorum sensing in microbes.
- *Biological processes.* This includes physiological processes like photosynthesis and the Krebs cycle.

- *Ecological systems.* This includes multiple components, often over larger spatial scales, that interact with and affect one another, such as nutrient cycling (e.g., in the Amazon basin).

This is a helpful conceptual framework because it maps fairly cleanly onto key types of technological aspects of human engineering activity:

- Biological forms, behaviors, and interactions correspond to **what we make**, like tennis shoes and door hinges.
- Biological processes correspond to **how we make it**, like the manufacturing processes involved in making cement or plastics.
- And ecological systems correspond to **how what we make, and how we make it, fits into the larger systems of which it's part**. This includes the whole economic/environmental context of making stuff, from the extraction of natural resources to the disposal of products.

Examples of emulating biological forms, behaviors, and interactions are generally all you need to think about for younger students. The texture of gecko feet (form), the production of color from a butterfly's wing (behavior), or the way bees communicate to find nectar (interaction) provide a range of possible biological phenomena that younger students can readily understand and observe. You can include these kinds of examples when working with older students too.

But with older students (middle and high school), you'll also want to include examples where engineers address sustainability challenges by emulating biological processes and ecological systems. Since these correspond with manufacturing and a product's entire life cycle, from extracting materials to disposing of products, these kinds of examples feature centrally in discussions about sustainability and help demonstrate the broad scope of human activities that engineering inspired by Nature can address.

Coral-Inspired Concrete
It's no secret that we could use help learning how to manufacture human-made things in more environmentally sustainable ways. Looking to Nature makes sense for this, when you consider the fact that the rest of Nature has good reasons to make things using readily available materials, processed with minimal energy or toxins. An exciting example of this kind is coral-

inspired concrete—a Nature-inspired technology that touches on all three aspects of the conceptual framework described above.

Humans use concrete to make a huge range of products, from skate parks to skyscrapers (*things we make*). We currently manufacture concrete by mining billions of tons of limestone out of Earth's crust each year, transporting it long distances by truck or rail, and cooking it at whopping temperatures of 1500°C to make cement, which is then added to sand and gravel to make concrete (*how we make it*). The cooking part is necessary to change cement's reactivity with water, so you can go down to the hardware store, buy a bag of the stuff, simply mix it with water, and presto!, make something out of concrete. But that convenience comes at a cost. Both the mining and cooking involved in manufacturing cement are highly detrimental to the environment, creating some 7 percent of all carbon dioxide humans emit in a year, from just this one industry (*how it fits into the larger system*).

While in graduate school, Stanford biologist Brent Constantz was studying how organisms like coral produce their hard exoskeletons out of the atoms floating around in seawater, when a momentous thought floated through his mind. Corals produce the exact same material that we use to make cement (calcium carbonate, a.k.a. limestone or $CaCO_3$), but they do it at ambient ocean temperatures (~17°C), not at 1500°C. Moreover, to precipitate the calcium carbonate molecule out of seawater, corals pull carbon dioxide out of the environment, fixing it within the $CaCO_3$ molecule. For coral, carbon dioxide is an industrial feedstock, not an effluent.

Brent began wondering if we could look to corals to learn how to make cement in a more environmentally benign way. The manufacturing process he subsequently developed creates the limestone starter material for cement by redirecting carbon dioxide from a coal-fired power plant. Instead of flowing through flue stacks into the atmosphere, the greenhouse gas flows into Brent's concrete. By borrowing corals' chemical recipe for making their exoskeletons, Brent has been able to create cement that doesn't require mining anything from Earth's crust at all. Moreover, the process of making it actually cleans the atmosphere, just as corals do when they make their exoskeletons—this coral-inspired concrete is carbon negative. (More about this amazing instance of Nature-inspired engineering in Chapter 6, including an activity where students make their own cement out of car exhaust!)

A CONCRETE EXAMPLE: Humans manufacture more concrete than any other material. The manufacturing process for this single industry requires mining billions of tons of limestone from Earth's crust each year and produces about 7 percent of humankind's greenhouse gases annually. Stony corals (order Scleractinia) manufacture the same substance, but they do it by pulling CO_2 out of the environment instead of releasing it. Learning from Nature's physiological processes can be a source of dramatic innovation in humankind's manufacturing methods.

Examples like Brent's coral-inspired concrete manufacturing process are the reason that these kinds of examples of Nature-inspired engineering are so important to make your students aware of, especially older students. The natural world's general approach to manufacturing—minimal material, minimal energy, minimal pollution, minimal waste—contains loads of ideas for a species trying to make its own way of life sustainable.

This conceptual framework for categorizing examples of Nature-inspired engineering is especially important to keep in mind when exploring Nature-inspired engineering with older students. The framework covers the entire scope of biology that Nature-inspired engineering can draw inspiration from, across all spatial scales. The framework sketches for us a comprehensive picture of what Nature-inspired engineering can do for humankind, helping improve what we make (by emulating biological forms, behaviors, and interactions), how we make it (by emulating physiological processes), and how the things we make fit into the larger environmental systems of which they're part (by emulating ecological systems, a subject treated in depth in Chapter 6).

An abstract way to visualize the relationship among these three conceptual types of Nature-inspired engineering is as nested, interacting categories. The categories are nested, or interconnected, because generally *how*

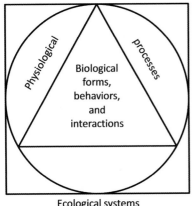

Ecological systems

we make things (analogous to physiological processes) mediates between what we make (inspired by biological forms, behaviors, and interactions) and the larger systems we inhabit. In other words, how we produce something seemingly discrete, like cement or a tennis shoe, has implications for the entire world.

With older students, examples that address manufacturing processes, and the complexities that arise when the human-built world collides with the natural environment, are important aspects to explore as part of a quality engineering education. With younger students, however, most of your examples are likely to be those inspired by biological forms, behaviors, and interactions. In fact, personally, I steer clear of sustainability and environmental issues when talking with younger students (e.g., elementary school). Children need to fall in love with Nature before they become concerned about it. Instead, I choose examples of Nature-inspired engineering mostly based on the "cool" factor (e.g., gecko-inspired adhesives) and mention sustainability-related issues only if students bring them up. For older students, however, exploring the connection between engineering and creating a healthier, more sustainable world is essential. Fortunately, Nature-inspired engineering is a terrific approach for both sets of young people.

Biomorphism Versus Nature-Inspired Engineering
It should go without saying that Nature-inspired engineering has nothing to do with making something merely *look* like something in Nature, but this is an important distinction to clarify with students, especially younger ones. Visual appearance of a product or process is rarely part of what we mimic in Nature-inspired engineering—very often, a Nature-inspired technology ends up looking little or nothing like the biological model that inspired it (the cat-inspired thumbtack is a good example of this).

Rather, Nature's genius is *abstracted* and applied to human technology. If a car is painted to look like a cheetah but doesn't perform any better because of this appearance, it's not an example of Nature-inspired engineering (that's merely biomorphism). Nature-inspired engineering is about improving the *functional* performance of what we make, however that's measured, by drawing inspiration from excellence in the natural world. Guiding students in discovering how drawing inspiration from Nature can indeed improve our technologies and designs is the subject of the next several chapters.

TEACHER ENGAGEMENT EQUALS STUDENT EXCITEMENT

The most important part of introducing the subject of Nature-inspired engineering to your students is *you*. If you are enthusiastic about the subject, your students will greet the subject with interest. So, before you put yourself in front of your students, give yourself time to learn about the approach and some of the amazing work that's happening to improve the human-built world through engineering inspired by the living world around us. Check out the Additional Resources section at the end of this chapter. Give yourself time to just explore the topic in an open-ended way. Research shows that teacher enthusiasm is a big determinant of student interest and success, but you can't fake that sort of thing. Fortunately, with Nature-inspire engineering, you won't have to.

And you don't need to become an expert on the topic, either, before you get started in the classroom. Nobody is really is an expert on the topic: it's too big and dynamic for anyone to ever stop learning. But in short order you can become knowledgeable and energized by what you learn about this exciting and optimistic approach to reimagining and recreating the human-built world through engineering. By bringing this way of thinking and learning to your students, you are doing the most important job of all: fostering the appreciation, skills, and aspirations of the next generation to shape the future of humankind.

Additional Resources

Sources of Nature-inspired engineering examples

The Center for Learning with Nature: https://www.learningwithnature .org/—see the first lesson within any of the *Engineering Inspired by Nature* curricula; choose the curriculum relevant to your students' ages.

Google Scholar (https://scholar.google.com/), or any Internet search engine—search using such terms as *biologically inspired*, *bio-inspired*, *bioinspired*, *biomimetic*, *bionic*, and *biomimicry*.

In-depth examples in magazine format at *Zygote Quarterly*: https:// zqjournal.org/

Examples of bio-inspired innovation from the Biomimicry Institute: https://biomimicry.org/biomimicry-examples/

AskNature.org—click "Inspired Ideas" on the top navigation bar. This is a great website for teachers to explore, but I strongly recommend *not* sharing it with students new to Nature-inspired engineering. AskNature .org is designed to suggest bio-inspired models to address design challenges. It thus automates the very cognitive skills you want your students to develop for themselves. Students exposed too early to AskNature.org are easily tempted to plagiarize from the content there and tend to have the development of their own engineering cognitive skills stifled.

Marshmallow challenge

The Center for Learning with Nature: https://www.learningwithnature .org/—see the first lesson within any of the *Engineering Inspired by Nature* curricula; choose the curriculum relevant to your students' ages.

Stanford Design School: https://dschool.stanford.edu/resources/spaghetti -marshmallow-challenge

To make the simplest earthquake simulation table possible, simply place two pieces of masking tape on a table, place between them the cardboard base on which students have built their towers, and shake the cardboard back and forth between the tape. Standardize the motion further by using a regular, vigorous rate of shaking (e.g., set by a metronome or various online programs).

3

SHAPE AND STRENGTH: LEARNING STRUCTURAL ENGINEERING FROM SCHOOLYARD TREES

What kind of engineering topics to explore first? There are so many different subfields within the larger fields of engineering and design—it's like being confronted right off the bat with a hallway of a hundred doors. When I wrote my first Nature-inspired engineering curriculum back in 2014, I was immediately confronted with this same question. There are nuclear engineers, who manipulate atoms and their particles for practical ends (such as energy); chemical engineers, who design and fabricate molecules; material engineers, who make materials; and the list goes on: structural engineers, mechanical engineers, product designers, architects, civil engineers, urban planners. . . . Engineers and designers are involved in everything humans make, at every spatial scale, from the architecture of molecules to the design of megacities. Where in this vast spectrum of engineering activity should K-12 teachers focus first?

Around this time I read the book *The Science of Structures and Materials*, by material scientist James E. Gordon (1913–1998). Gordon is considered one of the founders of the field of material science and, interestingly, also one of the forefathers of Nature-inspired engineering. Gordon is both of these because, while he was pioneering explorations of material science, he was doing it through investigating the structure and behavior of natural materials, such as wood and bone.

Gordon was a strong proponent of the value of examining everyday phenomena and physical things to generate understanding and insight. He had lived through a time when engineers were uninterested in material science, particularly in natural materials, and largely ignored structural engineering, despite the fact that materials and structures comprise the day-to-day world humans inhabit. I don't know about you, but most of us don't consciously experience atoms or intergalactic dynamics while walking down the street. Right now I'm sitting on a chair, typing on a computer, which rests on a desk, inside a house. I can hear the chair creak when I shift my weight. These are not remote phenomena. And for Gordon, these phenomena were fascinating causes for curiosity.

Gordon's down-to-earth views helped me determine where, along that vast spectrum of spatial scales across which engineers work, and all the various types of engineering and design that exist, to begin exploring the topic of engineering with K-12 students. Materials and structures are easy for students to relate to because that is the world they interact with every day. It's also fundamental to all engineering: every engineer builds things out of materials. (Even software engineers depend on a world of silicon and electrical circuits.) You can touch materials, and you can explore how a material's shape affects its behavior. Moreover, materials and structures are vitally important in everyday life. What could be more important than if a skyscraper or bridge stays up? When materials and structures fail, people perish. Materials and structures, I realized, were the logical place to begin.

COMPRESSION AND TENSION

Of all the concepts important in materials and structural engineering, none is more central than the idea of *mechanical force* (sometimes known as physical force). These are forces that occur through obvious physical mediums (such as a block of wood), distinct from the so-called natural forces (such as gravity, or the forces that occur within and between atoms). And of the mechanical forces, none are more fundamental than the two opposite forces of compression and tension. *Compression*, of course, is a force that pushes things together, as in the force my chair is experiencing right now under my weight. *Tension*, in contrast, is a force that pulls things apart. Skyscrapers and trees are under obvious compression; suspension bridges and spiderwebs are under tension.

Compression and tension are such important ideas in structural engineering because, of all the many things natural and human-made things must do and functions they must perform, none is more essential than *not breaking*. Things must be strong enough to hold themselves together, and the most elemental forces they must hold themselves together against are compression and tension.

You can have a surprising amount of fun exploring compression and tension with students while imparting something of fundamental importance in engineering. And you can explore these topics and their impact not only to the things engineers make, such as airplanes and bridges, but also within the context of how Nature cleverly manages the compressive and tensile forces ubiquitous in the living world. Along the way, you may find yourself doing some pretty unorthodox things with eggs, finding sidewalks suddenly fascinating, and never being able to see the trees in the schoolyard quite the same way again—but that's all part of the fun.

Of all the things abstraction is useful for, introducing unfamiliar ideas to students for the first time probably isn't one of them. Fortunately, it's extremely easy to viscerally understand mechanical forces such as compression and tension—if your back has ever gone out on you, you know these are not abstract ideas! We can literally *feel* these forces as they pass through our own bodies, which is more than one can say about most educational concepts. So let your students experience it. It's as simple as having them stand up and grab the hands of a partner. By leaning in, palm to palm, they'll be able to feel compressive forces flow into their bodies.

MAKE IT INTUITIVE. Leaning in and out, with a partner, is a simple, highly effective way to intuitively convey the meaning of compressive and tensile forces.

By leaning out while holding hands, they'll feel the same tensile forces as a guitar string stretched across a guitar.

This is one of the more unusual and interesting things about forces: they *flow* through materials and structures. You can't see them when you look at the Eiffel Tower, but thanks to gravity, compressive forces are streaming down the structure at all times, as surely as if the structure were made of straws and someone at the top were pouring water through them. (We'll explore this consequential fact in a whole new way a little later on.) Structural engineers have this understanding and intuitive sense of forces coursing through materials and structures, even while everyone else sees only a static table, chair, building, or bridge. Knowledge of mechanical forces has a way of bringing the inanimate world to life.

Once you have an understanding about compression and tension, a number of things about certain common structures start to become clear. Before we're done, for instance, you'll understand why dandelion stems are hollow, and why I-beams are shaped like the capital letter I.

BEAMS AND LOAD

Let's consider the effect of compression and tension on a beam. A *beam*, of course, is simply a structural element that resists forces applied to its side. There are several supporting the floor you're standing on right now, for example, or if you're outside, every tree you see is a vertical beam, which must resist the lateral force of the wind. When a mechanical force such as compression or tension is applied to an element such as a beam, structural engineers call it a *load*. A load is just an applied force. What happens to a beam when a compressive load is applied to it? An elephant sitting on a tree branch is a good example of this. If it doesn't break, good ol' Horton will certainly cause the tree branch to bend down. That means the top side of the branch, right underneath Horton, will have to stretch, actually getting longer. Meanwhile, the underside of the branch will squeeze together—it actually gets shorter.

ACTIVITY: The Sponge Beam

We can use a mildly stretchy material to observe this tension and compression in bending, and a kitchen sponge works perfectly. With a black marker, outline the top, bottom, and middle of the side of the sponge, draw a few evenly spaced perpendicular lines to create segments, and then bend the sponge. Now you can actually see the effect that a compressive load has on a beam. Here the beam is more like a hammock, held at both ends (unlike a tree branch), but the principles are the same. When loaded, the top side of the sponge compresses: see how the line segments on the top side of the sponge shorten? And look at the line segments on the underside of the sponge: see how they elongate? Nothing strange here. But that line running lengthwise through the very middle of the sponge is telling. Is the line compressed or elongated? Relative to the line on the top side of the sponge, it's elongated; relative to the line on the underside of the sponge, it's compressed. But one thing's for sure: it's the least changed of any of the three lines. Why?

When a beam gets bent, by elephants or otherwise, it deforms under the compressive load. One side of the beam compresses, just as expected. A consequence of this is that the other side of the beam spreads out, as we've just seen; the opposite side of the beam is hence under tension. That's kind of interesting. It's a little unexpected, but it makes sense once you give it some thought. Beams are two sides of the same coin. Whatever happens to one side of the coin causes the opposite to happen to the other. Compression and tension are opposite forces, the cats and dogs of the structural engineering world.

But here's the kicker: as the compressive force on one side of the beam passes across the beam, it becomes the *opposite* force of tension on the other side of the beam. How does that work? And what happens, then, in the very middle of the beam? Let's think about it this way: if we assign a value of +1 to the compressive force on the one side of the beam, and −1 to the tensile force on the other side of the beam, the force travels from a value of +1 to −1 as it crosses laterally through the middle of the beam. What's the value of the force in the middle?

Yep: zero. But that would mean . . . yes, it's kind of strange: when the beam gets loaded with a force such as compression or tension, the very middle of the beam experiences essentially no force at all. It's a logically necessary zone, where one force transitions to be its opposite—the eye of the storm, if you will. Structural engineers call this part of a beam the *neutral axis*. Conversely, as forces move from the middle of a beam toward its edges, the load increases. In fact, it's the very outer edge of a beam that carries most of a load.

A lot of things start to become clear once the neutral axis idea and importance of a beam's outer edges are understood. For example, why are bamboo and dandelion stems hollow? See if you can think it out. . . . When the wind blows, it's their outer edges that manage the forces of compression and tension; the middle is irrelevant. Why spend effort to create material you're not actually going to use? Figuratively and literally, that's just not natural. What about human-made beams? A cylindrical or square beam may be the easiest shape to use for a beam made from, say, a tree trunk. But if you're making a beam from scratch, say, by pouring steel in a mold, it would be more useful to minimize the material in the middle of the beam (which carries little load) and put most of it toward the edges, where the load is actually carried. Indeed, that's exactly why an I-beam is shaped like a capital I: less material in the middle, more at the edges. It's a form of material efficiency.

The implications apply as much to an entire building as to an individual beam. The development of supertall skyscrapers, such as the 2,717-foot

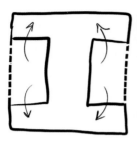

PUTTING STRENGTH WHERE IT'S NEEDED: An I-beam is a square beam in which material from the middle has been displaced toward its edges, which do most of the work resisting loads. For the same reason, dandelions don't bother growing material in the centers of their stems, where they don't need it.

Burj Khalifa in Dubai, has only recently become possible because of this understanding. For decades, skyscrapers were built using grids of steel beams running more or less evenly throughout the building, from one end to the other, across the interior. This worked fine for buildings up to a moderate height. But beyond that, it's difficult to make a building rigid enough to withstand the forces of winds common at higher altitudes, not to mention earthquakes.

A structural engineer named Fazlur Khan changed all that. Khan boldly concentrated most of the substructure of a skyscraper at the outside of the building, like a kind of exoskeleton. Since this is actually where most of the loads on a building travel when buffeted by winds or shaken by earthquakes, Khan was able to make buildings more secure by doing this. As if this weren't beneficial enough, Khan was able to achieve greater stability using *less* material. Khan's skyscrapers could extend to thousands of feet, using half the steel. Engineers are used to dealing in trade-offs, but this was a win-win, as close to a free lunch as you can get—all by changing a building's structural design, applying what can be learned from looking at any dandelion.

THE NATURE OF THE WORLD'S TALLEST BUILDINGS: The John Hancock building (left), one of structural engineer Fazlur Khan's most famous works. Like the strangler fig tree (right), common in Southeast Asia where Khan grew up, the Hancock building is held up by steel trusses surrounding the outside of the structure. Moving a building's substructure to the perimeter makes it stiffer against horizontal forces, reducing construction costs and materials, and enables building far taller skyscrapers than before.

SHAPES AND MATERIALS

I-beams, skyscraper substructures, dandelion stems, and strangler fig trees: the physical world is one full of shapes. Shapes are everywhere, and in Nature they are full of meaning. You're able to understand what I'm saying right now only because these lines on the page all have distinct shapes. The interplay of the shape of something, and how it manages mechanical forces such as compression and tension, is fundamental to structural engineering. Yet we often overlook the role of shape, instead emphasizing the importance of materials alone. Entire periods of human history are known, for example, by the materials characteristic of them: Stone Age, Iron Age, Bronze Age.

How do we decide what materials to use for a certain job? Naturally we consider the material's behavior. Materials behave in certain ways. Some materials are strong, such as concrete and steel. Some materials are flexible, such as leaves and rubber. The way materials behave is important: you wouldn't make a boat out of toilet paper, would you? Or a hammer out of Jell-O? These are simply poor choices of material for the jobs you want them to perform.

ACTIVITY: Balance This Book on a Sheet of Paper

To explore materials further, and the overlooked role of shape in a material's behavior, try using a piece of paper to hold up this book you're reading. Simply cut a piece of cardstock paper in half lengthwise (4.25 inches by 11 inches). Now, try to balance this book on the edge you just cut. As you attempt this futile feat, the paper will wiggle and twist under the weight of the book like a fish held by its tail. Impossible, right? The paper isn't strong enough to hold up the book. It's the wrong material to use.

Or is it? If I give you an inch-long piece of masking tape and challenge you to hold this book up with the piece of paper now, I'll bet you'll be able to do it. . . .

Have your students try this at their desks. Just about everyone will bend the paper into a cylinder, fasten it with the tape, and use it as a column, with the book now resting effortlessly on top. What happened? One moment ago the paper was wiggly and flimsy; the next, stiff and strong.

This seems to defy something we often implicitly believe: that materials are more or less immutable—steel is steel, paper is paper. And yet, we can completely change how a material behaves, it appears, just by altering its *shape*. The material hasn't changed—it's still just a piece of paper—but its behavior couldn't be more different. Indeed, playing with shape reveals the true Dr. Jekyll and Mr. Hyde behavior of materials. By changing its shape, we have converted a piece of paper into something that acts very differently.

There is something almost magical about such a transformation, though we hardly slow down enough to appreciate how odd it truly is. It's also of great practical importance, because materials are expensive, whether we buy or grow them. That's why in Nature we rarely if ever see materials cast as an undifferentiated bulk: they are always *shaped* to perform a function with a minimal amount of material needed. It's very useful for humans, too, if we can simply manipulate the shape of materials to use less of them and make our structures less expensive while at the same time work better.

We're all accustomed to the idea of using columns to hold things up. The idea must have occurred to our ancestors quite naturally, from the ubiquitous tree trunks holding up their expansive canopies. In fact, some of the earliest columns we know about were literally made of trees, whole trunks chopped off at the top and bottom used to support the Minoan temple at Knossos, for instance, built around 2,000 B.C. on the island of Crete, in modern-day Greece. Given the plant-based origin of this common architectural element, it's no wonder that early stone columns often were decorated with visual references to plants. Early Egyptian columns were fluted, reminiscent of the Nile reeds ancient Egyptians bound together to make boats. And classic Corinthian columns of Greek and Roman architecture sprouted canopies of carved leaf-like patterns, in case there was any doubt about the origin of their inspiration. Trees' impact on architecture through originating the idea of the column is enormously consequential. (The two-by-four studs holding the walls of my house up are all examples of minicolumns.) What else might Nature show us about strengthening material through shape alone?

ACTIVITY: Exploring Material Shapes
Now that your students know what Nature-inspired engineering is, a logical question is this: could Nature give us other ideas for transforming the shape of paper, so that it could support a book? Let's explore other shapes in Nature.

Nothing helps students perceive the shape of something more than temporarily removing their ability to see at all. Especially for objects we have encountered many times before—a pencil, a roll of tape, a bird's feather—our eyes and brains shut off all fresh exploration in an instant, as we categorize these "known" objects automatically and instantaneously. To avoid this, and to make familiar objects unfamiliar again, simply have older students close their eyes, or use a blindfold, and put the object of interest in their hands. For younger students more prone to peeking, place the object at the end of a long athletic sock (clean, of course!). The thought of peeking now won't even enter their minds. Instead, students reach deep inside with the thrill of anticipation and, with their sense of touch and not their eyes, discover a common object as though experiencing it for the very first time.

REAWAKENING THE SENSES: Using blindfolds or placing objects at the end of a sock can be a simple, effective way to help students rediscover familiar objects and appreciate their shape and texture as though for the first time.

Next, with the challenge of making their half-sheet of paper hold up a book fresh in mind, have your students explore a scallop shell without their eyes but with the part of their brain connected solely to their fingertips. Then see what they do to their paper. When they transfer the idea of corrugation from the scallop shell to their piece of a paper, they will again see that changing the paper's shape completely changes its behavior. Once floppy, the paper once more becomes almost magically solid. It's

A SCALLOP SHELL suggests a simple way to strengthen materials. Applying the idea to paper transforms the material's behavior.

cool, but something even more important has just happened: you have just held your students' hands through the process of transferring a functional idea from Nature to an innovative application in human engineering—the crux of Nature-inspired engineering practice. And with this simple activity using a physical model of corrugation to investigate materials, shape, and strength, you've also simultaneously covered a slew of engineering design components involving shape and function in the Next Generation Science Standards.

STIFFENING AND STRENGTHENING

If for millions of years seabirds had gnawed on you with their beaks and dropped you from the skies onto the shore below, while otters banged rocks on you in the sea, you'd likely have evolved corrugation just like scallops have. Their shells of calcium carbonate are effectively made of stone (albeit biologically produced), but nonetheless the demands placed on their shells are extreme. The corrugation provides additional strength to their armor through the unique gifts of its structure. To begin with, the thicker a material, the better it tends to handle compression. That's why your paper has no problem now holding up a book: the compressive load of the book is countered by the increased crosswise thickness of the paper, effected by the corrugation, reducing the tendency of paper to buckle.

Corrugation, moreover, is triangular in profile, a generally strong geometry by virtue of splitting a load in half down two separate, well-positioned members. That's why corrugation is added to cardboard, highway guard rails, and the tops and sides of canned food tins. Hand a person a heavy log to put on the fire, and they will spread out their legs and lock their knees to receive it, changing the shape of the lower half of their body to be more triangular. This strengthening strategy is built into the design of our very bodies. You might say people can corrugate, too (albeit with a single corrugation).

Structural engineers need to ensure the structures they design are strong enough to handle the jobs desired, and to do so, they frequently stiffen them. Strength, after all, is a measure of how much force a material can take before it deforms. But as materials become increasingly rigid, they can acquire a different problem: they can crack, suddenly and cataclysmically.

Many of the worst engineering accidents in history have been the result of the chillingly termed *catastrophic structural failure*, often the result of materials suddenly cracking. In 1943, for example, during the height of World War II, the 523-foot *SS Schenectady* floated calmly in port off the city of Portland, just prior to deployment to the European theater, when the tanker suddenly snapped straight through the middle and sank—just like that. In the early 1950s, three commercial jet planes made by the de Havilland Aircraft Company crashed, killing everyone on board, each the result of cracks propagating through the hull midflight. And in 2007, the I-35W Mississippi River bridge, carrying an eight-lane piece of the interstate through downtown Minneapolis, collapsed in the blink of an eye, killing 13 people and injuring 145. A crack had propagated through the rivet holes in its supporting structure, tumbling the bridge down like it were made of children's blocks. Even as I write, news of a massive bridge collapsing suddenly in Genoa, Italy, is hitting the headlines. According to the American Society of Civil Engineers, nearly 10 percent of the 600,000+ bridges in the United States alone are considered "structurally deficient." This isn't a problem that's going away anytime soon.

Cracking is such an important problem in structural engineering that material scientists have christened a new term for how well a material resists cracking: *toughness*. Toughness is related to strength. Whereas strength measures how much force a material can take before it deforms, toughness measures how much force a material can take before its deformations cause it to break. The concept of toughness is thus a combination of strength and flexibility. (Material scientists refer to a material's flexibility as *ductility*.) The concept implicitly involves resilience—the strong man at the circus is *strong*; the strong man who lost his job at the circus and went back to night school to get his nursing degree to support his wife and family is *tough*.

THE I-35W MISSISSIPPI RIVER BRIDGE through downtown Minneapolis after its sudden collapse in 2007. Cracks had propagated through the supporting structure.

ACTIVITY: Break an Egg?

As you might suspect, just as the shape of material can influence its strength, so can shape influence its toughness. Egg shells are an excellent example of this. Made of calcium carbonate, like the scallop's shell, egg shell is a highly stiff material, but thin and notoriously brittle. Simply snap a piece of chalk and you'll see how brittle calcium carbonate really is. This might seem like a shortcoming of general bird strategy, until you think of the baby bird inside, folded up like a pretzel and with less space than sardines in a tin can, whose muscles have never had the effort of work pumped into them, which must successfully peck through the egg to see its first day. And yet, eggs must also be strong enough that they don't break when squeezed through the birth canal or when mom sits on them for incubation. Strong enough to be sat upon by full-grown adult birds, weak enough for a child to break, eggs are the mother of all paradoxes.

Nature solves this Godzilla of design challenges using our go-to friend shape. Yes, the curved shape of an egg is useful for other reasons (getting through the birth canal, for instance) but the real virtues of an egg's shape become apparent when considering its superlative toughness. Nothing can convey this fact more viscerally than trying to break one with your own hands. The key here is to try to break the egg by squeezing it in your palm. Make sure no rings or fingernails are involved. Have students lean

over a sink, garbage can, or plastic (just in case), and then place an egg in their hands and have them give it a death squeeze. (It's advisable to trade out the egg after a few students have tried this, just in case hairline fractures form.) Remarkably, this object made of chalk less than a third of a millimeter thick is very unlikely to give way.

You've had so much fun already, why stop now? Try having students stand on them: set two cartons of eggs with the lids off next to one another, and have students remove their shoes and stand on them, gently placing one foot on each dozen. You may also choose to close the lids of the cartons or use an intervening piece of cardboard to create a more even surface. The key here is to have students place their feet gently on the eggs, rather than try to press down and break them. Also have students put their hands on something (e.g., a desk, a classmate's shoulder) and put their weight on that support as they place their first foot on the eggs, so all their weight isn't on one foot before they get both feet on the eggs. Again, the eggs shouldn't break, but do the activity outside or with plastic underneath, just in case.

SPREADING FORCES

Why do we have to make sure not to use fingernails or have any rings on our fingers when squeezing the egg? Alternatively, why, when we *want* to crack an egg, do we rap it against the edge of a frying pan? Likewise, why is an unborn baby chick's beak pointed? In all of these cases, the entire force of compression becomes concentrated on a relatively small area of the egg, and the outcome is completely different than when we squeeze an egg in our entire hand. The impact of a force, the pressure it actually exerts, is divided by the area the force acts upon: the larger the area, the lower the pressure. Mathematically, we can write this relationship as

$$P = F/A$$

where *P* is the pressure, *F* is the force, and *A* is the area. If you ever find yourself on a bed of nails, this equation can keep you from oozing blood, because it means that, by spreading out your body, you might not get punctured. Conversely, if you fall out of an airplane over the ocean, spreading out your body on impact might be the ruin of you, but going in lengthwise and pointing your toes or hands should reduce the impact of the ocean—hard as a brick wall when falling from high places—against your body.

> **ACTIVITY: Exploring Shape and Force**
> Have your students hold a hose with water coming out of it, and ask them how they might increase the water pressure. You can either turn up the faucet (the total amount of water), or you can put your thumb over part of the hole—now you've made the hole smaller, but the same amount of water has to get through it. With the same amount of water now coming through a smaller area, the pressure increases, even though you didn't add any more water from the faucet. All you did is change the area of the hole the water is hitting. Pressure is directly related to force, scaled up or down by the amount of area it acts upon.

NOTCHES AND FORCE FLOW

All of this is fine and good, but it doesn't really tell us *why* the shape of an egg is so effective against compressive forces. Not being the chickens that have to lay them, many an engineer might be tempted to argue eggs should be made square rather than roundish. After all, don't we have to pack them inside nice flat, rectangular boxes just to stack and transport them around? Why not just make them square in the first place?

It seems like a good argument, and it deserves some further investigation. In fact, much of what humankind makes sports corners, what structural engineers call a 90-degree *material notch*. Notches of various angles are everywhere. Whenever a material changes direction, it's a notch. A window opening has four of them, in each place where the drywall changes direction. Your hand has notches where one finger joins with another at the base. Notches aren't bad—they're a reality of life. Basically, if you aren't a straight, one-dimensional line, you've got notches. Everything people make has notches. A screw has notches running along between the threads and the central shaft. A single car has a nearly uncountable number of notches.

How mechanical forces interact with notches is the key to understanding the toughness of materials and structures—why things such as bridges and airplanes break apart or not. Remember, the chair you're sitting on or table you're leaning on might not seem like it has forces flowing through it, but it does, at all times. These are flowing rivers of forces, shaped like chairs and tables. If you want your students to be able to see the world this way—the way structural engineers see the world—it would be useful to have a nonabstract way of demonstrating this. It would be amazing if students could observe these flowing forces directly themselves. It would be incredible if students could somehow put on a pair of magic goggles and actually *have* the X-ray vision structural engineers have, just for a little bit, watching forces flow through materials and structures in real time. Wouldn't that be great?

ACTIVITY: Analyzing Stress With the Photoelastic Effect
One of the most wonderful educational blessings is that there *is* a way to watch forces flow through materials, in real time. Moreover, the setup is cheap. All you need are some pieces of plastic and two polarizing filters, like sunglasses and a computer screen. With these tools, students can literally see mechanical forces flowing through materials in real time and examine the interaction of these forces and different shapes in the material, such as notches and various kinds of curves.

To try it out yourself, and then have your students try it in class: go to your recycle bin, garbage, or refrigerator and find yourself a piece of the right plastic. You're looking for PETE or PET plastic (polyethylene terephthalate), also denoted by the number 1 in the recycling triangle on the bottoms of most plastic containers. It's the kind of plastic generally used for plastic clamshell containers used for packaging things like strawberries at the grocery store and for to-go boxes at restaurants. Get a few flat, clear swatches of this plastic (about 4 inches square)—three swatches if you can.

Then you need two polarizing filters. The easiest ones to use, generally, are a computer or cell phone and a pair of polarized sunglasses. The

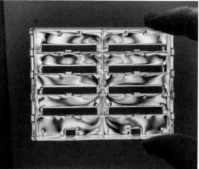

TO SEE MECHANICAL FORCES FLOWING THROUGH MATERIALS IN REAL TIME, simply hold a piece of no. 1 PETE plastic between two polarized filters (left). The colors are the direct result of mechanical forces flowing through the material (right).

screens of electronic devices tend to be polarized—simply open up a white screen (e.g., a blank Word doc, or the Google home page). To tell if your sunglasses are polarized, look at the white screen through your sunglasses and then tilt your head to one side. If the screen changes brightness, your sunglasses are polarized. (An alternative to using a computer or cell phone for the other polarizing filter is to buy a polarizing filter and tape it to a window so it is backlit.)

Now, hold up your swatch of plastic in front of the screen, and look at it through your polarized sunglasses. You should suddenly be seeing colors in the plastic, where before there were none. Next, manipulate your plastic swatch: bend it, twist it, pull it. What do you see? What do you notice happens to the colors?

When you push and pull on your plastic, you are making minute changes to its thickness, as molecules of plastic bunch up in some places and stretch out in others. The varying thicknesses result in light being bent at various degrees, so it doesn't leave the plastic the same way it came in. Instead, the light gets separated into its component colors, just like a prism. That means the colors you see in the plastic are the direct result of forces applied to it.

These color patterns thus show us compressive and tensile loads in real time, where these forces go in the material, how they flow, and even, by the color pattern, their magnitude. Physicists call this phenomenon the *photoelastic effect*, which just means "stretchy light effect," and engineers often use it for doing structural analyses. (The polarized filters don't contribute in any way to the production of color; they just do what filters are meant to do: remove stuff, in this case the glare of light bouncing around the plastic. The filters help us see the color patterns more clearly.)

ACTIVITY: Analyzing Notch Stress Concentration

We now have a way to examine, for ourselves, how material notches perform under mechanical loads. Perhaps we can use this to better understand why eggs are so strong and why they are curved rather than square.

First, ask students to make a 90-degree notch in their plastic. This is as easy as using a pair of scissors to cut out the shape of a blocky L from the plastic. Try to make the interior corner come together neatly. Now, have students hold the sample between two polarized filters and apply some tension to it, simply by grabbing the "legs" of the L shape and pulling them away from each other. Ask them what they notice about the colors: where do they appear? Do the colors form a different pattern than they did when they manipulated the uncut sample?

The colors will concentrate rather dramatically at the corner of the notch. The tension introduced by pulling on the sample doesn't flow smoothly through the plastic; it gets "stuck" at the corner, piling up there. Engineers call this a *notch stress concentration*, and they like few things less. If stress tends to concentrate at notches, where do you think cracks in a material are most likely to form?

MODELING THE EFFECT OF TENSILE LOADING on a 90-degree notch in plastic (left) and using photoelasticity to examine the result (middle). Notches create stress concentration. This understanding can transform how we see and understand the human-built world around us, such as the cracks in sidewalks (right).

ACTIVITY: Observing Nature's Notches

Once students have seen how mechanical forces tend to concentrate in notches, a simple walk home from school becomes a journey of discovery. Students start to notice cracks in the sidewalk and can begin thinking about how they were formed. Many of the cracks they observe will emanate from corners, the result of notch stress concentration. You may want to have students take pictures of examples they discover and have them discuss how they think the cracks formed and why. Nothing validates classroom learning better than being able to see it in action in the real world immediately after class.

CURVED NOTCHES AND STRESS CONCENTRATION

In turns out that notch stress concentration plays a major role in the accidents that sometimes occur with the things engineers build. The crack that unexpectedly broke apart the *SS Schenectady* in 1943 started in the corner of a deck hatch. Similar cracks appeared in hundreds of boats the U.S. Navy built during this time, all starting in the exact same locations. Resolving this problem was vital to defeating the Nazis in World War II.

The de Havilland airplane crashes of the 1950s were caused by cracks propagating window to window through the hulls. Most people don't know that airplane windows used to be rectangular, like the windows you'd see in a house. It was because of the de Havilland disasters that airplanes windows today are rounded.

ACTIVITY: Improving on the 90-Degree Notch

Let students try to improve on the 90-degree notch. Give them new swatches of plastic, a pair of scissors, and let them go to town. To test their solutions, students can load their swatches in tension and compare the color patterns between notches of different shapes they create.

And how are notches managed in the natural world? We have already seen the example of an egg, but is this approach to managing notches characteristic in Nature, or an anomaly? This is a good question with which

A DE HAVILLAND COMMERCIAL JET, CIRCA 1949:
Note the squared windows, like you'd see in a house.
Crashes of jets like these are why today's airplanes have
rounded windows.

to let students loose upon the schoolyard, preferably with hand lenses, pen, and paper. Even a schoolyard of asphalt or mowed grass will hide many examples of Nature's notches. The leaves of a weed growing in a crack in the pavement are flat, like our samples of plastic; what shape are these leaves? What shape are any indentations in the leaves? Each leaf meets at a notch with the weed's stem; how is this corner handled? A flower, a tree, a passing ant—a world of notches.

Have students draw what they observe and share the results—they more deeply absorb the patterns and shapes they perceive when they translate them into a choreography of hand and arm motions to draw them. The natural world is full of notches, but what matters is the students' own discovery of this ubiquitous pattern and discerning its meaning.

To show students in a more structured way the relative advantage of a curved rather than 90-degree notch, cut out a L shape from your plastic, almost as before, but this time create a rounded inside corner instead of a sharp one. To do this to near perfection, simply place a small curved object (such as a nickel) in the notch, trace a quarter-circle for the interior corner, and cut along this line instead of making a 90-degree turn. This will produce a "quarter-circle notch fillet"—*fillet* is a term for the material used to round the notch (conveniently pronounced "fill it"). Now for the moment of truth: have students apply tension to the sample as before, and examine the photoelastic effect. What do they see? What is the pattern of colors now? How is it similar or different to the L-shaped plastic sample with a 90-degree corner?

Students should see a very different picture. Where before the colors concentrated in the corner of the notch, now they spread out along the curve. Is the area covered by the colors greater or smaller in the curved versus the cornered notch? What is the pattern of color on a quarter-circle notch telling us, compared to the color pattern for a 90-degree notch? In which situation do students think a crack is more likely? Recall the relationship of force and area, $P = F/A$: the greater the area A upon which the force F is spread, the less pressure P there is in any one spot.

Now, despite the stubborn difficulty in packaging and transporting them, we can finally understand why eggs are not square! But we also have the basis for understanding much more. We can grasp why Nature so rarely

MAKING A CURVED NOTCH with a quarter-circle fillet is easy to do (left). Load it with some tension and examine it using the photoelastic effect (right). How does the concentration of force compare with a 90-degree notch?

designs with 90-degree corners, and why humans should do so only with caution. In the end, these investigations also highlight one of the major benefits of Nature-inspired engineering: it transforms not only how one sees the natural world but also how one understands the human-built one too.

THE WISDOM OF TREE CURVES

Our journey so far into the world of materials and structural engineering has covered activities and concepts for students across the K-12 spectrum. The next projects work well for older students in that spectrum, in middle and high school.

Let's take a more critical look at our model of a quarter-circle notch. Yes, the tensile load is better distributed around the curve than in the case of a 90-degree corner, no question, but there is nonetheless some concentration of force at the site of the notch. Should we be concerned? Well, in the case of the crack that propagated through the substructure of the I-35W Mississippi River bridge, its course ran right along the rivet holes of the bridge's undercarriage. When you think about it, rivet holes are essentially four quarter-circle fillets, joined like pieces of pie to form complete circles, punched straight through the steel. Moreover, the windows of the de Havilland airplanes, upon closer examination, were actually not quite square: their corners were each softened by quarter-circle fillets. These and many other related catastrophic failures remind us that, even though quarter-circle fillets reduce stress concentration, they are not foolproof solutions.

In the 1980s, a terrible car accident left two people dead and German engineer Claus Mattheck with a shattered leg. The pins and screws used to squeeze bone back together in such situations can be imperfect, to say the least, resulting in pain, impaired motion, and frequent follow-up surgeries. Claus traces his interest in more structurally sound solutions to this experience. But it wasn't until he found himself gazing at a tree a few years later while on vacation that he started wondering whether trees might have the answers he was looking for.

A decade later, Claus found a most curious thing about trees: they curve all their various corners (such as branch to trunk and trunk to roots), but they don't use quarter-circle fillets to do it the way human engineers do. Trees don't use a constant-radius curve to smooth out their notches. Trees use some other kind of curve. Understanding how fundamental notches are to all structures, Claus began wondering what kind of curve trees were using and why. Why didn't trees use the curve human engineers use to deal with notch stresses?

In Nature, the base of a tree just might be the mother of all notches. From the trunk, the tree makes a 90-degree turn as it transitions to its roots. And this notch takes a beating: every time the wind blows, the extensive canopy of sun-seeking leaves catches an immense load of air. Add up the surface area of all the leaves on a mature broadleaf tree, such as an oak, and you get an area equivalent to one entire side of a professional basketball court. If you have ever tried to hang up a mere bed sheet on a clothesline during a gusty day, you have an inkling of the kind of force trees deal with upon every breeze, much less a stormy gale.

What hits the canopy, moreover, is the least of it: a tree is a force funneler. All the force caused by the wind and caught by a tree's leaves and branches is funneled down to the tree's closest fixed spot—the base. When the wind blows, the canopy catches the wind, and the tree bends: the far side of the tree's base

> Almost invariably, living things are so successful in solving . . . structural problems that we do not notice how they do it. For nothing attracts less curiosity than total success.
>
> –James E. Gordon

experiences monumental compression, while the windward side experiences colossal tension. It's a somewhat subtle thing to realize—roots are underground, after all—but Claus looked at trees the way a Swiss watchmaker examines the parts of a watch. He realized the base of a tree was a material notch extraordinaire. And, for some unfathomable reason, trees weren't managing the notch stress concentration there with a quarter-circle fillet.

ACTIVITY: Capturing Tree Curves

To see what Claus saw, have your students find a tree in the schoolyard where the curve between the trunk and roots is easy to view. It's usually easier to see the tree curve on older trees than on younger trees. Trees build these characteristic curves over time, in response to wind loading, so the older the tree is, the more force it has experienced and the more time it has had to lay down additional wood in the notch between its trunk and roots. It's also generally easier to see this curve on broadleaf trees than on conifers. With their needle-shaped leaves, conifers experience far less wind loading than broadleaf trees. Also, sometimes the tree curve is completely or partially buried in the dirt; the closer the roots of the tree are to the surface, the easier it is to see the entire curve between the trunk and roots. (If you can't find a tree nearby showing a good example of a tree curve, you can always use images of trees with your students.)

If we make a model of a tree curve, we can take it with us into the classroom and start to examine and explore it in various ways. An easy way to make a 1:1 scale model of a tree curve is to use bendable wire, pressing it along the length of a tree curve to take an impression of its shape. This is a great way to extract just the shape and remove everything else, making it easier to concentrate on the element of interest.

Take the full-scale model of a tree curve back to the classroom and lay it flat on the floor. Superimpose a right angle next to the wire model to more easily examine the tree curve as a notch fillet, and begin asking your students questions:

How would you describe the tree curve? Is it a quarter of a circle? That is, does it have a constant radius?

No? Okay, so the radius of the shape changes as you progress along the curve, unlike a circle. Is the curve symmetrical? Which side flattens out more?

The part along the trunk? Okay, so the curve extends farther along the trunk than along the roots. Why?

Which side of a tree probably moves more in a breeze, the trunk or the roots? Could that have something to do with the asymmetrical shape of the curve?

If the roots of a tree moved as much as the trunk, would the curve be symmetrical?

These Socratic questions about the tree curve's geometry help students think through why the tree curves the way it does. Over its lifetime, trees add woody material where they experience stress, in order to manage these loads. A tree curve is built over time, breeze by breeze, and its shape tells us where stress gets concentrated.

TREE FILLETS: Where the trunk of a tree meets its roots is a material notch, subjected to an enormous amount of mechanical force. The characteristic curve found here, a tree fillet, differs from the quarter-circle fillets characteristically used by human engineers.

ACTIVITY: Analyzing Tree Curves

Perhaps you are already thinking of examining the tree curve shape using photoelasticity? That is a superb idea. Using the photoelastic effect, we can actually model how the tree curve shape responds to force and compare this response to the quarter-circle fillet, the standard shape used by engineers to manage notch stress in a 90-degree corner. To trace and cut out a tree curve from a small swatch of plastic, you'll need to scale your tree curve down to fit. One way for students to do this is to take a photograph of the wire model, scale the image to any size they want on a computer, print it out, and trace it on their plastic—pretty easy.

Another way to scale the tree curve to any size desired is to use a method developed by Claus Mattheck, which he called the "method of tensile triangles." This approach uses a series of triangles to approximate the tree curve shape geometrically. All your students will need is a protractor and ruler. Here are step-by-step instructions on how to do it:

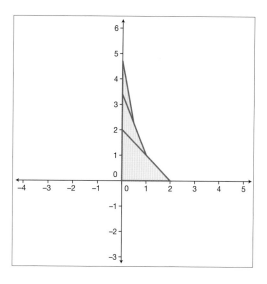

1. Draw a 45-degree equilateral triangle in the notch, large enough to work with.
2. From the midpoint of the first triangle's diagonal, make another equilateral triangle, by making a diagonal to the vertical line, at an angle of 22.5 degrees (half of 45 degrees).
3. From the midpoint of the second triangle's diagonal, make a final equilateral triangle by making another diagonal to the vertical, at an angle of 11.25 degrees (half again).

Students then make a template to trace this onto their plastic sample, or draw it directly on the swatch, and cut it out, smoothing the curve at the vertices as much as possible. The advantage of using the tensile triangle method is that students can recreate a decent approximation of the tree curve to any scale they want. You can provide your students with the method outright, or try to have them derive the tensile triangle method themselves—maybe they'll discover a different way of recreating a tree curve!

Once students have their tree curve modeled in plastic, ask them to load it with tension just as they did in the other samples, and look at the results between the polarizing filters. What do they see? How does it compare with the model of a quarter-circle fillet? The stress distributes itself over the curve, if you can see much strain at all. Colors are distinctly less apparent in the tree curve sample than on the quarter-circle fillet, indicating far less buildup of stress. The tensile forces, in other words, flow relatively smoothly through the tree curve, despite there being a notch in the material.

Is this a fair test? Nah. After all, it's very possible the amount of tension students place on each sample is not the same in each case. But we can easily make it a fair test. All you'll need is a hole punch and inexpensive spring scale, or a fishing weight. Put a hole in the bottom of each plastic sample. Then, use the spring scale to load each plastic sample in tension to the same degree. Or hang the same fishing weight (or any small weight) from each curve, thus applying the same amount of force each time. Now your comparisons are fair.

From the perspective of meeting the performance expectations of the Next Generation Science Standards, this simple series of activities surrounding material notches covers an enormous amount of ground. Students have identified a major design challenge: ensuring the safety of structures. They have iteratively modeled different solutions to notch stress concentration (a 90-degree notch, a quarter-circle notch, and a tree curve notch). And they've tested these models to generate conclusions. Along the way, they've learned fundamental concepts in material science and structural engineering, at play in everything from the desks students sit at to the skyscrapers that inhabit the horizons of modern life.

As important, your students have seen for themselves a concrete example of how engineering solutions inspired by Nature really do work. Tests done by Mattheck showed that using a tree-curve fillet in notches reduces stress concentrations over quarter-circle fillets by a whopping 57 percent! Trees really know what they're doing. The implications of such a dramatic

CLAUS MATTHECK'S TENSILE TRIANGLES closely approximate the tree curve fillet. Modeled in plastic, you can see how little force concentrates as it flows along this curvature invented by trees.

improvement in a material's performance, just from changing the shape of its notches, are profound. By finding this solution right in their own schoolyard, students have taken a step toward transforming how they understand human design challenges, how they seek engineering solutions, and how they perceive and appreciate the abilities of the natural world around us.

Additional Resources

Curricula on Nature-oriented approaches to structural engineering
"Cool Curves" (elementary) and "Fracture Mechanics" and "Tutelage of Trees" (middle/high school), in the *Engineering Inspired by Nature* curricula available at The Center for Learning with Nature: www .LearningWithNature.org.

Excellent, accessible books on structural engineering
Gordon, J. E. 1988. *The science of structures and materials.* Scientific American Library.

Gordon, J. E. 2009. *Structures: Or why things don't fall down.* Da Capo Press.

Agrawal, R. 2018. *Built: The hidden stories behind our structures.* Bloomsbury.

More on the structural mechanics of trees and plants
Mattheck, C., Kappel, R., and Sauer, A. 2007. Shape optimization the easy way: The "method of tensile triangles." *International Journal of Design and Nature and Ecodynamics, 2*(4), 301–309. https://www.witpress.com/Secure/ejournals/papers/JDN0204001f.pdf

Niklas, K. J. 1992. *Plant biomechanics: An engineering approach to plant form and function.* University of Chicago Press.

Math connections

High school
TeachEngineering. Stress, Strain and Hooke's Law: https://www.teach engineering.org/lessons/view/van_cancer_lesson2

TeachEngineering. Mechanics of Elastic Solids: https://www.teach engineering.org/lessons/view/cub_surg_lesson02

Middle school
TeachEngineering. Stressed and Strained: https://www.teachengineering .org/lessons/view/cub_mechanics_lesson07

Physics background on the photoelastic effect
http://en.wikipedia.org/wiki/Photoelasticity

A free, online program for drawing triangles
http://www.math10.com/en/geometry/geogebra/geogebra.html

Great books about other aspects of trees and plants

Wohlleben, P. 2016. *The hidden life of trees: What they feel, how they communicate—Discoveries from a secret world*. Greystone Books.

Chamovitz, D. 2012. *What a plant knows: A field guide to the senses*. Scientific American/Farrar, Straus and Giroux.

Great fiction book featuring trees

Calvino, I. 2017. *The baron in the trees*. Houghton Mifflin Harcourt.

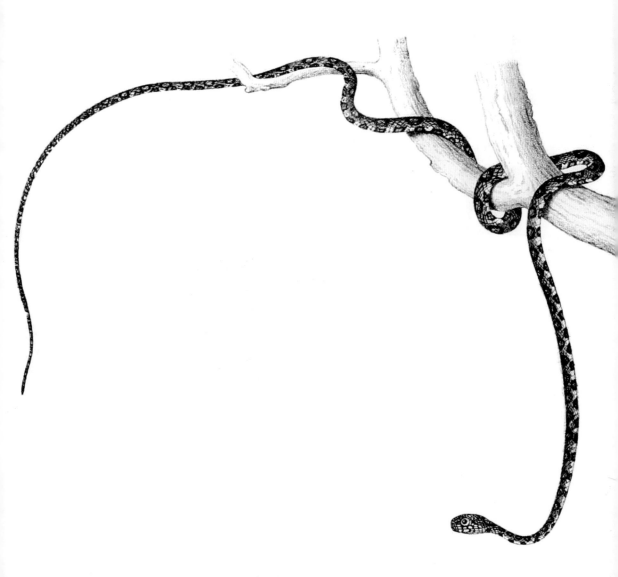

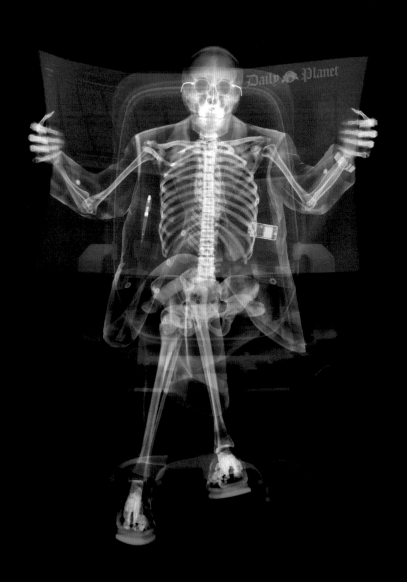

ENLIGHTENED BY BONES

It seems that perfection is finally attained not when there is no longer anything to add, but when there is no longer anything to take away.

–Antoine de Saint-Exupéry

Trees are extraordinary structures, and wood is an amazing material, with a great deal to teach us, such as how exactly to add material to our structures to make them tougher and safer. The other side of this same coin is how to *remove* material from our structures, to make them lighter and more materially efficient. No better model for this vital objective exists than another superstar of Nature's inventions: bone.

THE STRUCTURE OF BONE

Notwithstanding what amoebas might tell you, bones are vital and fascinating parts of our bodies. Because we see them only as skeletons long after their residence in the body, we forget that bones are actually alive, as alive as your heart tissue or brain. Your bones not only mechanically hold you up but also serve many other functions, including physically protecting vital body parts, protecting you from foreign microbes (by producing your immune system's white blood cells), protecting you from cuts (by producing sticky platelets that plug holes in your skin), and making the red blood cells that carry oxygen throughout your body, so that your cells don't suffocate—pretty important stuff. Bones also store and regulate the presence of certain minerals in your body (such as calcium). Without bones, not only wouldn't you be able to get out of bed in the morning, but you'd have difficulty eating (teeth are part of our skeletons), and you wouldn't be able to hear the songs of birds either (the hammer, anvil, and stirrup in our ears are bones, too). Bones are important, make no bones about it.

It's a little ironic, because bones are one of the heaviest things in our bodies, but probably the most important lesson engineers have learned from bones has to do with making stuff *lighter*. Why should engineers care about this? Why is it important that the things we make be as light as possible?

The need for *lightweighting* something like airplanes is obvious, but for anything we make, efficiency in our use of material is actually paramount: the more material we use, the more natural resources we must extract and process, and the more energy and labor we must employ. Thus, any material we use exacts economic and environmental costs in direct proportion to the amount of material required to make the products we desire. More than ever, a species of billions needs ways to reduce these costs in order to continue living well and living long.

As you will see, the thing that's holding you up is the perfect model for keeping these costs down. Recall the classic engineering joke: three people are staring at the same partially filled glass of water. The optimist says, "The glass is half full." The pessimist says, "The glass is half empty." The engineer shakes his head at the other two and says, "The glass is twice as big as it needs to be!" Bone has proven the perfect model in the engineer's quest for material efficiency.

Like trees, our skeletons not only have the capacity to add material precisely where needed, but they also *remove* material where it is not. Over evolutionary time, this lightweighting of natural tissues is essential: a gazelle with more bone than needed can't outrun a cheetah; a cheetah with more bone than needed starves. And anything that uses more material than necessary beggars for the increased energy and time it takes to make it.

But skeletons don't develop based on hard-wired genetic programming alone; they also continually reshape themselves during their lifetime, based on the loads placed on them during actual use. That's one reason exercise is vital as we age, and why astronauts, whose skeletons no longer must resist gravity, suffer bone loss in space. Our bones shape themselves by feeling our muscles strain against them. Without this strain, specialized cells called osteoclasts work to actively remove bone tissue, like an eraser wiping chalk from a chalkboard.

Though researchers still aren't exactly certain how bones rewrite themselves, it's a brilliant arrangement, even in skeletal outline. The balanced system of bone development in response to muscle strain and the removal of unloaded bone by osteoclasts ensures that our bone structures are continuously optimized for the work they must actually perform and no more. Imagine the energy efficiency of a car that reshapes its steel frame continually, based on how it is driven, the road conditions, and the passengers and cargo it needs to carry, making sure it is only ever as heavy as necessary to get from point A to B. Or how about a bridge that alters the density of its supports as heavy traffic use puts more load on its structure? Real-time optimization is the gold standard of good design, a process we are beginning to see analogs for in human activities, such as on-demand printing of books and 3D printing.

LISTENING TO BONES. The author's son demonstrates some readily available magic: actually hearing your own bones developing in real time.

Don't just take it from me—you can actually *hear* this biological process happening for yourself. To hear the signals your skeleton responds to when adding bone tissue, simply place the palms of your hands over your ears and press inward (like you're trying to squash your own head). With enough pressure, you'll start to hear a low rumble. That rumbling is the sound of your arm muscles contracting up to 70 times per second, a signal your bone cells respond to by reproducing. A windy day cues trees to add wood to their trunks and branches; going for a jog does the same thing for your bones. Every movement, every stance, every piano lifted up a flight of stairs, every long day spent sitting in a chair is recorded in the ledger of your skeleton. Though less expressive than living tissue, which is green, soft, or animated, wood and bone are living tissues too, ever listening to the world around them for how best to design themselves for service.

People began appreciating the structural design of bone as early as 1866, when an engineer named Carl Culmann witnessed a dissection of bones by biologist Georg von Meyer at a meeting in Zurich. Cross sections of these bones revealed that, far from being solid, bones were instead composed of networks of boney material, interpenetrated by lots and lots of space (in living bone, these spaces are filled with flexible collagen protein). Bone are hard, in other words, but they aren't solid. It was Culmann, a structural engineer, who pointed out that the particular pattern of this boney network appeared designed as a response to the typical loads of compression the bone experienced during use. In essence, the various parts of the boney network, called *trabeculae* (from the Latin *trab*, meaning beam), acted as struts, keeping the bone intact when compressed, while using bone material only where most needed. In other words, bones aren't just solid in the right places; they're *empty* in the right places too. As von Meyer put it, "I find that the trabecular arrangement suggests its purpose: such an arrangement of the bony mass allows a larger outer circumference without a large weight."

This meshwork approach to creating larger structures is the same approach engineers take in aligning metal struts, evident, for example, in the construction of truss bridges or in the iconic metal latticework of the Eiffel Tower. In fact, it was a student of Culmann's, Maurice Koechlin, that drew the basic design of this famous tower while working for Gustave Eiffel. The savvy of using a meshwork of material (rather than a solid mass) to create a structurally functional shape is well illustrated by the Eiffel Tower. The tower is at once impressive and a masterpiece of material minimization. The total volume of iron used in the Eiffel Tower is miniscule compared to the amount of space the tower actually occupies. In fact, if you drew the smallest cylinder possible around the tower, the *air* inside that cylinder would weigh more than all the iron used to create the tower itself!

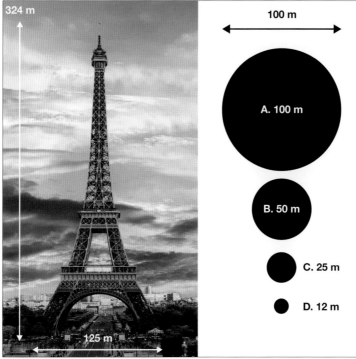

BONE ISN'T SOLID—IT'S A MESHWORK. Scanning electron micrograph of bone showing its trabecular structure (top left). This enables structures to have the strength and size they need while minimizing the material necessary to achieve it. The amount of air inside a cylinder drawn around the Eiffel Tower weighs more than the tower itself (top right). If you melted down all the metal used in the Eiffel Tower (bottom), do you think it would form a ball 100 meters across (A), 50 meters across (B), 25 meters across (C), or 12 meters across (D)? (The answer is D.)

MATERIAL EFFICIENCY

Material efficiency, which essentially means creating the same result with less raw material, is the norm in natural structures. With raw materials in perpetually limited supply, and the victors in Life those fastest to develop and reproduce, Nature has been strongly encouraged in every instance to design materially efficient ways to accomplish whatever it needs to do—whether growing toward the sun, chasing gazelles, leaping from a lily pad to ingest a passing fly, or rolling balls of dung across a hot desert. "In her inventions," Leonardo da Vinci said of Nature, "nothing is lacking, and nothing is superfluous." Nature lightweights to survive and thrive.

Nature is economical when using material to resist not just compression but tension, too. In an instant, a window cracked by a wayward baseball illustrates where the weaknesses of glass lie to resisting fracture. Now compare this pattern of cracked glass to that of a spiderweb. A spider uses the material of its silk only in these *same lines of weakness*, and no place else. Why waste time and effort putting silk where it experiences little force? It's as though a solid sheet of silk were dissolved by evolutionary time into the precise minimum necessary to stop a ballistic projectile. A speeding fly hits a spiderweb like a baseball hits glass, and a spider knows just what's necessary to resist the impact, investing nothing more than needed into the structure to secure a meal. Why use more effort to acquire dinner than the dinner itself provides?

Lightweighting structures is something not only structural engineers but also industrial designers and product designers must contend with. Nearly every human-made object you can see in your home, classroom, or office was designed by a product designer, whose choices of design and material have far-reaching implications for both the performance of the object and its impact on the world when produced in quantity. The average car, for instance, contains about 4,000 pounds of processed materials (steel, plastic, etc.); last year, the world produced 97 million of them, for a total of 388 billion pounds of material, mined from the earth and processed (or recycled) with chemicals and fossil fuels into their final form. A small tweak to any part of a car's design can impact millions of pounds of material—how it gets used and whether it gets manufactured in the first place. Whatever can be safely removed, in other words, is multiplied by the magnitude of production, which in the case of humankind is immense, whether for cars, carpets, or cardboard.

One of the neatest and most significant applications of bone-inspired lightweighting is employed through a computer-assisted design or CAD program. These software programs are used by nearly all engineers and designers today to help them model their work. What if the way bones assess the forces at play on them, adding material in loaded areas and removing it from unloaded areas, could somehow be programmed into these CAD tools? That's exactly what has been done by Altair Engineering, Inc., a CAD program maker founded in Michigan. Its popular Opti-Struct program translates principles of bone growth and lightweighting directly into the objects that designers model, so they obtain their final structure as though a lifetime of use had "grown" them. Loaded areas are strengthened, and unloaded areas are lightweighted, until an optimized structure emerges.

Who uses these bone-inspired CAD programs today to design things? Such companies as Boeing, Airbus, Ford, GM, Toyota, Volkswagen, the U.S. Department of Defense, Lockheed Martin, Caterpillar, John Deere, Harley Davidson, Procter & Gamble, Nokia, Adidas, Kohler, and Fisher Price—and that's a short list. Boeing alone used Altair's software to redesign 150 separate components of its 787 Dreamliner. With Altair's software, Airbus was able to drop the weight of its A380 by an astonishing 1,100 pounds. Add it up, and Altair estimates its software saves 1.3 *billion* pounds of material annually and prevents nearly 1.8 *billion* pounds of carbon dioxide a year from entering the atmosphere. As if saving money, saving material, and protecting the planet weren't enough, bone-inspired design also saves individual lives. Using Altair's software, the

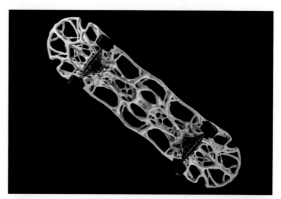

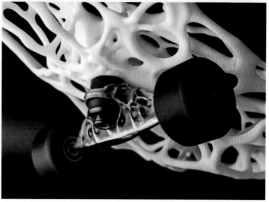

A 3D-PRINTED SKATEBOARD reimagined and redesigned through the wisdom of bones. Many solid objects humans manufacture could be similarly lightweighted without sacrificing performance, greatly reducing the economic and environmental impact of industry.

medical device company Medtronic redesigned heart stents, whose not infrequent failure is commonly lethal. The optimizing software allowed Medtronic to reduce the buildup of mechanical stress in stents by a spectacular 71 percent.

> **ACTIVITY: Redesigning an Everyday Object**
> You don't have to have a fancy CAD program to explore what bones can teach us about product design. All you need is the same setup from Chapter 3 to explore material notches using photoelasticity, plus some graph paper.

After introducing your students to the wonderful capacity of bones to remove unneeded material, and how they've inspired engineers to rethink how we design everything, ask them how they might use this approach to redesign a common object, say, a clear plastic ruler, to be as light as possible. If you can, give your students a day or two to chew on this question. They have all the information they need to figure it out, but it takes some figuring all the same.

To begin with, students need to select a plastic object they will redesign using a bone-inspired approach. As long as the plastic is clear and made of polyethylene terephthalate (PET or PETE no. 1 plastic), polystyrene (no. 6 plastic), or polycarbonate (no. 7 plastic), the activity will work. Many things are made of these materials, such as tape dispensers, protractors, CD cases, containers of various kinds, plastic utensils, and coat hangers.

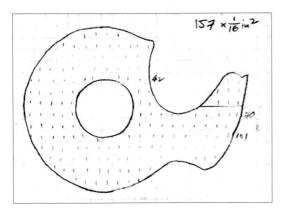

Next, instruct your students to measure their object's surface area. (If this object is more three-dimensional than a flat ruler, such as a tape dispenser, have them measure just one of its surfaces.) To measure the object's surface area, simply draw an outline of the object on graph paper and count up the squares. For squares that are bisected by the object's outline, estimate the fraction of the square within the outline (one-half, one-fourth, etc.). Then, multiply the number of squares by the size of each square to get the total surface area of your object.

Now we want to analyze the loads placed on these objects to see where the material of the object is structurally necessary and where it isn't. We can do this using photoelasticity, just like in the exercises in Chapter 3 analyzing notch stress. By determining parts of the object that are not under stress when loaded with force, we can identify parts of the object that are candidates for removal.

Note that these areas are merely *candidates* for removal. That's because there are a couple things to keep in mind before selecting an area for removal. When we simply place an object between two polarizing filters, we are seeing what engineers call its *static loading*, that is, the load it's experiencing from the weight of its own structure. For a bridge, this would include compressive forces from gravity. (Sometimes plastic exhibits stress that isn't actually important to its structural integrity; for instance, parts that got stretched or squeezed during fabrication, and thus show colors between the filters, but which may still be viable candidates for removal.)

A bridge experiences different loads when it's actually used, however, so it's vital that, before we start identifying areas for removal, we analyze the loads on the bridge during actual use. Engineers refer to this as an object's *dynamic loading*. For a bridge, this would definitely include the loads it experiences during traffic (and, in reality, other occurrences such as earthquakes and wind). So students should try as much as possible to analyze the object during its regular use, so they don't get a misleading idea of what material is actually vital or not to the object's functioning. For our purposes, students can do this very easily, simply by loading their objects with some compression and tension as they do their analyses.

Another thing to keep in mind when identifying areas for removal from an object is what the object is used for. A plastic cup, for example, might have lots of areas that are structurally unnecessary, but removing them might result in a design that doesn't hold water.

Once students have used photoelasticity to identify the areas they plan to remove from their objects, have them draw the outline of the redesigned object on their graph paper again and, just as before, count up the squares to determine its new surface area. Then students can compute the percentage of material they saved by redesigning the object to remove its unneces-

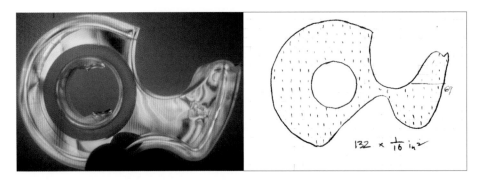

LIGHTWEIGHTING A COMMON OBJECT: Using the photoelastic effect on a tape dispenser (left) reveals areas of the object that may be structurally unnecessary and thus can be removed. The subsequently redesigned dispenser (right) uses 16 percent less material to get the same job done.

sary parts. Doing this process with a tape dispenser reduced the amount of plastic necessary by a hefty 16 percent.

Students may notice that redesigning these objects introduces a whole bunch of notches in the object that weren't there before. Is this a problem? Your students know quite a bit about the risks of material notches by now. What can they do to minimize these risks? As a final iteration, you can have your students redraw their bone-inspired redesign, this time shaping any notches using tree-inspired curvatures as appropriate. If you have the capacity to 3D print these redesigns onto clear plastic, or draw them onto plastic swatches and cut them out, students can then analyze the redesigned shapes using photoelasticity. Regardless, you'll have walked your students through cutting-edge Nature-inspired product design, with little more than plastic, graph paper, and insight into some of the natural world's most broadly applicable engineering and design lessons.

Want to bone up on this topic further? Check out the following resources.

Additional Resources

Curricula on bone-inspired approaches to structural engineering and product design

"Enlightened by Bones" in the middle/high school *Engineering Inspired by Nature* curriculum, available at The Center for Learning with Nature: www.LearningWithNature.org.

More about how bones remodel themselves

Wolff's Law: https://en.wikipedia.org/wiki/Wolff%27s_law

More about the Eiffel Tower

See the terrific article by Aatish Bhatia: https://www.wired.com/2015/03/empzeal-eiffel-tower/

Bone-inspired CAD software

For more about the super-cool skateboard and other work by designer Seth Astle, see his website: sethastle.com.

More about Altair, the company that pioneered bone-inspired CAD

Altair's web page on leadership in optimization describes several applications: https://www.altair.com/optimization/

More about this history of the concept Altair pursued: https://www.forbes.com/sites/amitchowdhry/2013/07/22/altairs-software-enhances-the-design-of-transportation/#6191fa75624d

Additional information about Altair: https://www.popularmechanics.com/cars/a9164/carmakers-copy-human-bones-to-build-lighter-autos-15677023/

5

FUN WITH FLUIDS

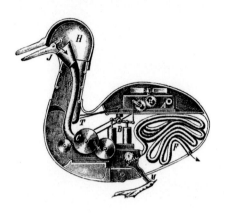

So far, we have explored two of the most important forces engineers contend with, compression and tension, and done so by looking at materials and structures that are solid. But engineers think about other physical forces as well, and other forms of matter that, well, matter. For a planet whose surface is mostly liquid, it would be slipshod of us not to explore the engineering of fluids, especially when so many remarkable examples exist in the living world to inspire innovation. Just consider the powerfully nutritious honey of honeybees, the blinding venom of spitting cobras, or the improbable disappearing ink released by fleeing octopuses. Life does wonders with solid materials, but it's also a virtuoso with fluids.

Our own bodily liquids show dizzying variety, displaying an extraordinary number of abilities: self-patching blood, sweat that springs from internal sprinklers to cool us down, tears that convey our inner emotional state to our tribe, saliva that starts digesting food on contact, and nose mucus that traps would-be invading microbes in a death goo. Many examples also exist of the unique ways Nature, instead of fashioning its own extraordinary liquids, uses common liquids around it to extraordinary effect. These include a leaf's routine surgical splitting of water molecules to abscond with sticky hydrogen atoms for building complex sugars and starches, a puffball's ingenious use of raindrops to propel its offspring into the air, and an archerfish's deadly insect-dislodging spitballs.

In short, Nature's liquid talents are nothing to sneeze at, and exploring them opens up for students a whole new window into the amazing natural world around us, as well as a world of fresh technological possibilities for humankind. This chapter explores just a few fantastic ways to engage students in the wetter side of engineering. By the end, no one will ever be able to accuse you of teaching a dry subject!

If we *Homo sapiens* thought we were in charge of the planet, here was clear evidence to the contrary. The humble snail and its clan have a far older, and stickier, foothold on the earth than we more recent creatures. It was clear to me that gastropods should make front-page headlines in the *New York Times*, and mammals, particularly the human sort, should be relegated to the back sections. But then, with its many-toothed radula, cellulose-digesting enzyme, and lack of vision, my snail was more likely to eat the *Times* than read it.

Elisabeth Tova Bailey,
The Sound of a Wild Snail Eating

MAGICAL MUCUS

From an engineering perspective, one of the most interesting fluids out there is mucus, especially that invented by our most unhurried of planet-mates, the snails. Snails and slugs are members of a large group of species known to biologists as gastropods, *gastro* derived from an ancient Greek word meaning "stomach," and *pod* from the Greek word for "foot." Gastropods, thus, are "stomach feet," referring to the fact that these unusual characters slide around on their bellies—I think we can all agree not the most common mode for travel.

MAKING TRAILS: Uniquely among species, both humans and snails alike construct a substrate over which to travel.

How can an animal with only one "foot" even get around at all? Moreover, how can an animal with just one foot make any progress *on sticky glue*? From an educational perspective, snail mucus, and how snails use it, provides an engaging context for students to explore various STEM topics, while at the same time deepening their fondness for the ingeniousness of snails and the natural world more broadly. Snail mucus is kind of gross (to some), which has its advantages from an engagement perspective. It's also just a plain strange behavior: who produces goo to get around? Humans are perhaps the only other species besides snails and slugs to make a substrate over which to travel, as our own road-building activities attest.

While snail mucus is used in locomotion (one of the main subjects of this chapter), it simultaneously serves additional purposes. Like a Swiss Army knife, snail mucus is multifunctional. Snail trails also provide information, not unlike the ticker tape of old. For instance, snails can tell if a snail trail they encounter was produced by an individual of the same species or of a different species. They can tell if that individual is capable of having offspring or is sterile. And, they can determine the condition of the individual's nutritional state, all key questions in the game of Life. In short, snail trails are useful for both finding and attracting potential mates—a dating profile, if you like, which snails post far and wide.

Unfortunately, predatory snails (snails that eat other snails) also can use these trails, but for the more sinister purpose of locating potential prey. Fortunately, snails can also use their trails to alert other snails of danger. For example, when harassed, gastropods use chemical warnings placed in the material of their trails to let other snails know peril may lie ahead, deterring others from following. This communal spirit among snails is more than a little heartening. Charles Darwin, in his 1871 book, *The Descent of Man*, recounted this provocative story:

> *Mr. Lonsdale informs me that he placed a pair of land-snails . . . one of which was weakly, into a small and ill-provided garden. After a short time the strong and healthy individual disappeared, and was traced by its track of slime over a wall into an adjoining well-stocked garden. Mr. Lonsdale concluded that it had deserted its sickly mate; but, after an absence of twenty-four hours, it returned, and apparently communicated the result of its successful exploration, for both then started along the same track and disappeared over the wall.*

While trails can facilitate snails' search for food and camaraderie, snail mucus can also be used as a source of food itself. Trails of snails may be used (or reused) to minimize the amount of new mucus required for locomotion, for instance. Snail trails can also trap or grow other types of food (e.g., algae), which is subsequently eaten—a clever form of agriculture.

The Nature of Fluids

To explore our central question about how a creature with one foot can travel over this rather wondrous substance, students first need to have some key background concepts under their belt. For instance, what is a *fluid*? In physics and engineering, anything that flows is a fluid, including gases. Fluids like snail mucus, or water, air, and so on, can be described by their *viscosity*, or thickness, a measure of their resistance to flowing, or the degree to which these materials resist a force of pressure. Run your hand through a bathtub of water and you can feel water's viscosity. Air, obviously, is less viscous, and honey more so.

We tend to think of viscosity as a fixed quality of a fluid material. Water and air, for example, are common examples of materials whose viscosity doesn't generally change with force. The more pressure you place on these materials, the more they deform, just as one might expect. These fluids are known as "normal" or Newtonian fluids, after English physicist Isaac Newton (1643–1727), of the famous "for every action there is an equal and opposite reaction" idea. A *Newtonian fluid* is not, as it sounds, rare bottled phlegm from Isaac Newton himself but, rather, any fluid in which the relationship between stress and strain is positive and linear; that is, the more force you load on it (stress), the more it deforms (strain). Newton and especially his colleague Robert Hooke (1635–1703) first described these kinds of relationships in material in the 1600s. However, there is no rule that this is how fluids *must* behave, and indeed, other fluids can act in astonishingly nonstandard ways, as we will see.

The viscosity of some fluids is not positive and linear but, rather, changes with force. Oobleck—named after a material dreamed up by Dr. Seuss in the 1949 book *Bartholomew and the Oobleck*—is a great example of this. The material behaves like a normal fluid at low pressures (e.g., running your hand slowly through it) but at greater pressure, or especially with sudden pressure, the liquid's viscosity increases dramatically. If you haven't played with oobleck before, I hope you'll pause reading right now and go make some. After all, you don't need Royal Magicians to make oobleck the way Dr. Seuss did. All you need is a little cornstarch and water (approximately 2 parts cornstarch to 1 part water). Oobleck feels like thick goo, roughly like hummus dip. Drop a bowling ball on it, however, and the heavy ball will literally *bounce* on the surface of the oobleck before sinking—not your standard goo!

Oobleck is famous for its ability to captivate students' attention, of course, but rarely if ever is it used to elucidate ideas in engineering or natural history. (There will be no such missed opportunities here!) Such marvelous liquids are known as *shear-thickening* fluids, which introduces another mechanical force, slightly more complicated than compression or tension. *Shear* is the force that a material experiences when it undergoes pressure in opposing directions at the same time. Scissors, or "shears," work

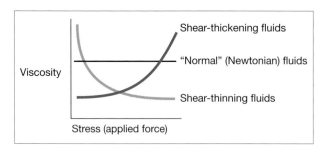

PUTTING IT ALL TOGETHER: How viscosity changes with force in shear-thickening, shear-thinning, and "normal" fluids.

this way. When you twist open a screw-top lid, or nibble off the top of a cheese stick with your incisors, you are using shear forces to do it. Move or shear your hand slowly into a bowl of oobleck and the liquid deforms easily around it, like a normal fluid, but shear it through quickly (causing some oobleck to travel rapidly against the oobleck further from your hand) and the substance "locks up," behaving more like a solid.

Other fluids, known as *shear-thinning* fluids, behave in just the opposite way: they have a lower viscosity under shear force, flowing more easily rather than less easily under pressure. There are many real-world examples of shear-thinning fluids, too, no more exotic than on the wall in front of you. Paint is a shear-thinning fluid: it sticks to a paintbrush, but when you press it across a surface, it flows off the brush and onto the wall. Once on the painted surface, it once more regains viscosity, which helps reduce dripping. Blood is also a shear-thinning fluid: inside your body, flowing against your veins, blood becomes thinner. In some places, earthquakes are extremely damaging because the soil effectively thins on shaking (called *liquefaction*), acting like a shear-thinning fluid.

LINES OF THOUGHT: Students can write their observations and reflections about snails in the shape of a snail.

Fluids that change viscosity or thickness with pressure or shear are interesting for having such unexpected qualities, but they are also important technologically. Shear-thickening fluids are used in certain four-wheel-drive vehicles, for example (much more on technological applications later on). They are also the key to understanding how a creature with one foot can travel over glue.

ACTIVITY: Icky, Sticky Goo

To engage your students with the question of how a snail can travel over glue using just one foot, begin by asking them what they know about snails and slugs. What are some interesting and unique things about them? Give students some time to list things; for example, snails carry their homes on their backs, they can retract their eyes inside their bodies, and they can see around corners. Feel free to add a few things students may not know, such as that slugs are basically snails without shells; that snails are relatively closely related to octopuses and clams; that snails are found nearly everywhere on Earth, from the deepest parts of the ocean to the highest mountains and driest deserts; that the smallest land snail could crawl through the eye of a needle; and that snails are generally hermaphroditic (having both male and female reproductive organs).

After someone mentions the fact that snails make mucus, zero in on this by asking students why snails make mucus. What do snails use mucus for? Once students point out that snails make mucus to get around, ask your students whether they like snail mucus. When at least some students express disgust at the question, ask them what they don't like about it. Have fun with the discussion! For example:

"I don't like snail mucus because it's gross!"
"Why do you think it's gross?"
"It oozes out of their body!"
"Doesn't liquid ooze out of your body?"
"No!"
"Really? What about sweat?"
"But theirs is sticky!"

Make a dramatic pause here.

"Wait a second, how can snail mucus be sticky? Don't snails use their mucus to get around?"
"Yeah . . ."

"Well how can snail mucus be both sticky *and* slippery? Aren't sticky and slippery opposites? That doesn't make sense!"

Finally, ask your students the million-dollar question:

"How can an animal with only one foot walk . . . on glue?"

SNAILS COME IN ALL SIZES: The largest is as big as a person's foot. The smallest could crawl through the eye of a needle.

Feel free at this point to let your students know they will not only learn the secret to how snails can make a fluid that is simultaneously both a lubricant and an adhesive, and the secret to how snails can somehow manage to travel over sticky mucus, but also learn what all of this has to do with how quicksand works and with inventing things like armor strong enough to stop bullets yet flexible enough for doing ballet.

Oobleck. It's best to have your students discover the ideas of normal and non-Newtonian fluids themselves, first by observing what happens to water when they move their hands through it, and then what happens when they try this with oobleck. What do students notice? What does the water do? Have them push their hand through the water again, this time quickly. What does the water do now?

The key thing for students to notice is that water moves out of the way as their hand passes through it; if their hand moves slowly, the water moves out of the way slowly; if their hand moves quickly, the water moves out of the way quickly. The water does just what you expect a liquid to do.

Now, have them try this with oobleck. What's different about this liquid's behavior compared to water? Have students describe it. You want students to notice that, while the thickness (or viscosity) of water doesn't change with pressure, the thickness of oobleck does. Oobleck gets thicker with pressure: the faster you press into it, the firmer it becomes. In contrast, the water doesn't change as you press on it, except to move out of the way faster or slower depending on how fast you move your hand, just like you would expect. Some liquids behave the way you expect them to; others don't at all!

(While the reason oobleck behaves this way isn't the focus of the lesson, your students may wish to know: moving your hand slowly through the oobleck gives the particles of cornstarch time to flow, but moving your hand quickly doesn't, and the particles bump into each other, creating friction and forming a temporary solid.)

An optional activity that is a lot of fun is to make oobleck in a rectangular tray, approximately 9 inches by 13 inches and 4 inches deep (the size of a lasagna pan or larger), with plastic underneath. Have students take off their shoes and socks and run barefoot toward the pan, stepping once in the pan as they go by. (You can cover the oobleck with plastic if needed, to keep toes and floors dry.)

SILLY PUTTY (shown dripping over a bottle) is a shear-thickening fluid.

Ketchup and Shear Forces. Ask your students, if some liquids get thicker when you push on them, can you think of anything else a liquid might do when you push on it? After they come up with some ideas, that's when you reveal to your students a half-filled bottle of ketchup. Ketchup is a pretty thick liquid, which can make it challenging to get it out of a bottle. To get the last bits out of the bottle, what do you do? Demonstrate by first turning the open end of the bottle upside down over an empty bowl, so that no ketchup comes out. Then, shake the ketchup bottle once, abruptly halting the movement, repeating until the ketchup comes out. That's one way to do it. Now stick a knife into the ketchup until it flows out. That's another way to do it. What you're doing, without really thinking about it, is introducing a shear force into a shear-thinning liquid.

With some ketchup now in the bowl, use a stir stick and, stirring in circles, stir the ketchup around in the bowl. What do students observe? For comparison, put a couple cups of water in a bowl, and use a stir stick to stir the water. Notice how all the water eventually turns in the direction the stir stick is stirring? What about the ketchup? The ketchup next to the stir stick will turn with the stick, but the rest of the ketchup in the bowl won't move. Students should observe that the ketchup around the moving stir stick gets thinner and runnier, even though it's normally a thick liquid. Ask students to describe what's happening. Is it the same as oobleck, or different? How so? Ketchup is a liquid that gets thinner and runnier under pressure, the exact opposite of oobleck.

ACTIVITY: Watch That Snail!

How might liquids that change thickness with shear pressure help us understand how a snail travels over sticky mucus? The only way for students to grasp what's coming is to show them a snail in motion. You can either do this using videos (see Additional Resources at the end of the chapter) or simply collect a snail and show students its underside as it travels over a pane of glass. What your students will observe are curious lines or linear regions on the snail's underside that seem to move starting from the snail's back, traveling to the front. The bottom of a snail is muscle. Snails contract this muscle in a flowing sequence, starting from the rear and moving forward, like Popeye flexing his bicep in the fashion of a conveyor belt. But how does this help snails move smoothly over adhesive mucus?

MAKING WAVES: By pressing down on its mucus (the wave region), a snail turns its normally sticky secretions into a lubricant so it can advance, while pushing against the adhesive mucus in between (interwave region).

For snails, shear thinning turns out to be the key to their magical mucus. Snail mucus is generally viscous and sticky, which helps snails move over thin branches or up vertical surfaces. Adhesives are very useful in these situations, but not if you can't somehow simultaneously travel over them without sticking yourself! The situation seems hopeless, until one considers the possibility of a fluid that can *change behavior*. And that's pre-cisely what snail mucus does.

Here's how it works. As the snail travels, muscle contractions flow across the snail's foot. Where the snail's muscle contracts, it bulges, just like when you flex your bicep. When pressed by a passing muscle contrac-tion, the snail's mucus switches from being a viscous adhesive to becom-ing a flowing lubricant—a perfect example of a shear-thinning fluid. The snail mucus remains sticky, however, between these waves (the "interwave" regions). This allows the snail to push off the sticky parts while continu-ously advancing wherever the mucus has become slippery. The result is a smooth, elegant mode of travel, which works whether advancing over flat ground, where a lubricant is most helpful, or up vertical walls, where the opposite adhesive is needed.

You can demonstrate this to your students by using a simple glue stick and paper. Press the glue stick straight down onto the paper, and lift the glue stick up so that the paper comes along with it, stuck to the glue. Remember, snail mucus is normally sticky. Now, pressing down-ward, move the glue stick smoothly over the paper: just like snail mucus, under pressure the glue temporarily changes to thin and runny. It becomes a lubricant, just while it's under pressure, before switching back again to being sticky (touch the line of glue on the paper and lift up, demonstrating that it's sticky again).

In theory, snails could reverse this order. Snails could make mucus normally slippery, and only sticky with pressure. Why do you think snails make mucus that's normally sticky? What if they did the opposite? Which of these two kinds of mucus would you use to climb a wall, and why? Let your students think this through.

The answer is that, if snail mucus were sticky only when pressed, then snails would have to constantly press down while climbing vertical surfaces. It takes much more energy to climb a wall than move over the ground. By having mucus that is an adhesive by default, snails can hang onto vertical surfaces effortlessly, yet move smoothly along as needed.

Oh, the Technological Possibilities!

Snails have certainly found a way to make their magical mucus useful. What about us? In what situations might a liquid that changes its viscos-ity with force be useful to humans? Have your students think of where

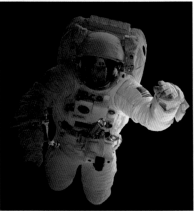

WHAT TECHNOLOGICAL IDEAS MIGHT SNAILS GIVE US? Shear-changing liquids have been used, for instance, to quickly fix potholes and as speed bumps. Hardening on impact, potholes disappear. Meanwhile speeders get a physical reminder to slow down, while law-abiding drivers never feel a thing.

they might apply this idea to improve something humans make or do. Now that students know about the possibility of shear-thinning and shear-thickening liquids, new technological possibilities might emerge when they brainstorm.

For instance, let's suppose you are designing body armor for police, or protective clothes for mountain bikers. What are some challenges in designing armor for people who need to move around? You're looking for students to recognize that, because traditional armor is thick and rigid, it can't be worn over parts of the body that need to flex. Could a liquid that changes thickness with pressure help in this situation? Liquid armor that is shear-thinning like snail mucus might work great. Over knees and elbows, such a substance would get thinner during movement, allowing greater mobility, yet thicken when stopped, providing protection.

Such armor in fact now exists, as well as kneepads that floor installers use, puncture-resistant surgical gloves for doctors, tear-resistant spacesuits for astronauts, and more, all based on the same shear-changing liquid principle. The gains in performance and efficiency in these innovations can be dramatic. For instance, a bulletproof vest soaked in a shear-thickening fluid dissipates just as much ballistic energy as plain Kevlar but requires one-third less thickness. Not only is such a vest much more flexible, but it's lighter too.

Once you're aware of shear-changing liquids, a whole new world of engineering innovation becomes possible, and a lot of things become clearer. You're not likely to look at a snail moving through the garden or across the sidewalk the same way again.

This kind of knowledge can even save your life. Quicksand is a shear-thinning fluid, for instance. Knowing this, what should you do (and not do) if you get stuck in it? Well, what you *shouldn't* do is panic or agitate the quicksand—this just liquefies it further. Instead, moving slowly is vital (other tips include backtracking toward solid ground, throwing off any extra weight, and, if necessary, laying on your back to spread out your weight to avoid sinking further).

As you can see, snails have a lot to teach us . . . and we're just skimming the surface. You can have lots of educational fun exploring shear-changing liquids further, and even have students invent and build things with it. To explore more, see the Additional Resources section at the end of this chapter.

INDOMITABLE DROPS

Sometimes it's not the amazing fluids Nature makes but the amazing ways Nature manipulates plain old liquids that deserves our inquiry. Consider, for a moment, the grass and plants of the schoolyard or a backyard ravine. How does this vegetation stay so sparkling clean? It's not as though janitors tiptoe into the forest at night while we're sleeping and scrub down all the plants. And yet, every morning these places look green and good as new, no janitors required. Even the plants along a dirt road or in a muddy swamp often look as hygienic as if

Always the beautiful answer who asks a more beautiful question.

–E. E. Cummings

they'd been dusted by a feather duster. What gives? Give kids ten minutes horsing around outdoors, and it looks like the elements positively aimed and threw up on them. How do plants manage to look so immaculate?

ACTIVITY: Droplet Magic

To begin exploring the mystery of how plants keep themselves so tidy, place students in groups and drop a pinch of ground black pepper on a clean surface in front of them. Challenge students to use a piece of tape to pick up one or two specks of pepper. Once they have successfully done this, provide them with a container of water and an eyedropper, and challenge them to do the same thing, but this time with water. Your students will discover that, by squeezing the eyedropper so that a drop of water bulges out the end, they can also pick up the pepper flakes with water, just like they did with tape. This should successfully make your point: water is sticky.

Of course we know this about water already, though we really don't think about it much. If water didn't stick to things, you wouldn't need windshield wipers on your car. Getting your toothbrush wet at night would be a futile exercise. And you'd have a terrible time trying to wash your dog. Fortunately, however, water *is* sticky. Pepper flakes sticking to a water droplet is an example of *adhesion*, that is, two dissimilar substances sticking together. Water is adhesive. Water isn't only adhesive towards other substances, however, it's so sticky that it even sticks to itself, a phenomenon sufficiently unique that physicists give this kind of stickiness its own term: *cohesion*. Have students push a drop of water to the outside of their eyedropper again and look at it. What shape is it? Why? Why isn't it square? Or shaped like a hot dog bun? Or some other shape?

Instruct students to hold their eyedroppers about one inch above a swatch of wax paper on the table surface and place two equal-sized drops of water a centimeter apart on it. Then, slowly lift up one edge of the wax paper so that one ball of water cautiously approaches the other. When the two drops of water bump into one another, what happens?

The two drops join into one bigger ball of water, yes, but what's instructive is *how* they join together. They don't just glom together ho-hum like two people bumping into each other on the sidewalk. No, water droplets positively *snap* together, like magnets, like a puppy greets its owner. Water

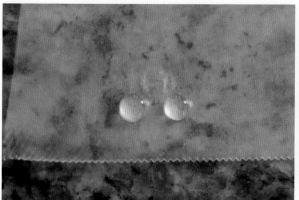

COHESION: With nothing else to stick to, water sticks to itself, forming a characteristic droplet, on wax paper (left) and in space, about to be eaten by astronaut Sunita Williams (right).

droplets *love* each other! Water, this little activity demonstrates, is enthusiastically attracted to itself.

Given water's attraction to itself, it's no wonder the drop of water at the end of an eyedropper is round and not square. If it were square, there would be parts of the water drop (the corners) farther from the center of the water drop than absolutely necessary, which something in love with itself would never do. (This isn't a strictly scientific-sounding explanation, I realize. A physicist might say, a bit less colorfully, that a round shape has the smallest surface area, which requires the least energy to maintain.) There are wonderful videos of astronauts playing with water in space that are well worth viewing with your students at this point (see the Additional Resources section at the end of the chapter).

For contrast, have your students put a drop of water on a glass slide. What shape is the water now? Why is the shape of this drop different than the shape of water at the tip of an eyedropper? Is this an example of adhesion or cohesion?

The interim take-away message is this: water is sticky, and it can stick to things, or, if it has nothing else to stick to, it will stick to itself. In other words, the shape of a water drop can *change*, depending on what it's touching. If it's something to which water sticks, the droplet kind of spreads out; if it's something water doesn't stick to, the droplet sticks to itself, becoming more of a ball. Keep this behavior of water in mind.

ACTIVITY: Be the Droplet

Especially with younger kids, it's great to have students *become* the water drops at this point, to really drive the ideas home. If you have a nice grassy place outdoors for students to lay down on, tell them to pretend they are each water drops. First, have them pretend they are a water drop that sticks to the ground (kids should spread out over the ground). Now ask them to pretend they are a water drop that doesn't stick to the ground at all. What happens? (Kids should ball up.)

Now pretend the ground is shaking; there's an earthquake! (Kids should roll around). You bump into another water drop . . . what happens to you? A great kinetic option, as I say, for younger kids, to help students really imbibe the ideas.

ACTIVITY: Water on Leaves

So, the shape of water drops can change depending on what they're touching. Then what is the shape of water when it's on plants? Have students explore this open-ended question with their eyedroppers in the schoolyard, or with potted plants in the classroom, going around placing single drops of water on different plants and observing the result. What shape does the drop have once it's touching the plant's leaf? How does the water drop behave when the leaf is tilted verti-

cally? What shape does the drop have once it's touching other parts of the plant (stem, flower petal, etc.)? Try this on several plants and plant parts and then discuss what the students observed. You'd be surprised how captivating students find what seems like surgical gardening, delicately placing little balls of water on plants.

If you want something a little more structured, you can have students keep track of their results using a table whose first column includes a plant identifier (e.g., species name, or "plant by the basketball hoop"), a second column for the part of the plant tested (e.g., leaf, flower, petal), a third column to describe the droplet and its behavior (e.g., flattened, roundish, rolls), and a drawing of the droplet's shape.

Some plants, known as *superhydrophobic* (literally, "very scared of water"), have what seems like a magical force field against water droplets. This is sometimes referred to as the *lotus effect*, because texture-based water repellency was discovered first in studies of the lotus plant. To explore this, you'll need some fresh kale, from any grocery store, the fresher the better. Have students place a water drop carefully on a leaf and observe the results. The backside of the leaf is often best. (If you happen to be near any fresh kale while you're reading this, take a moment to go get a leaf and try this out for yourself.) What shape does the drop have on the leaf? What happens to the water drop when the leaf is tilted?

Have students play with a water drop on the kale, try to roll the drop around just inside the outline of the leaf, without letting the drop roll off the leaf. Students can pass water drops from one  leaf to another; see if the whole class can pass a water drop around from leaf to leaf, without letting it fall. You can even use a hole punch on a leaf and try to roll a water drop around the leaf without having it fall through any of the holes (like those wooden maze games that use those shiny metal balls).

Leaf Wash. Let's review a bit what students have observed at this point. Does water behave the same way on all plant leaves? No. How does the behavior of water drops differ between different plants? Why do you think plants might want to prevent water from sticking to them?

Let's recall for a moment what leaves do for a plant. We know that leaves do at least two major things: they absorb gases out of the air (they use carbon dioxide for construction supplies) and they use sunlight as energy (to power their construction activities). The solar panels on a Mars rover use sunlight to create energy too. What happens after a dust storm on Mars? How well do you think the solar panels work then? How about on a leaf? Do you think leaves work well if they're covered with dust and debris?

Could water drops *help* a leaf? Instruct students to put some pepper flakes on the kale leaf. Place a drop of water nearby, and turn the leaf so that the water drop rolls over the pepper flakes. What happens to the flakes? (The ball of water picks up the pepper flakes and removes them as it rolls by.) Now, imagine the pepper were dirt. What do you think happens to the leaf, water drop, and dirt when the wind blows? How might a ball of rain rolling over a leaf be useful for a plant?

Water drops can help leaves by cleaning dirt off them. On certain plants, at least, water balls up (because of cohesion). Dirt sticks to the water as the drops roll by (because of adhesion). Water drops thus carry away dirt from the leaf's surface, cleaning leaves as they go, just like tiny rolling brooms. Why do you think plants figured out how to use water drops to

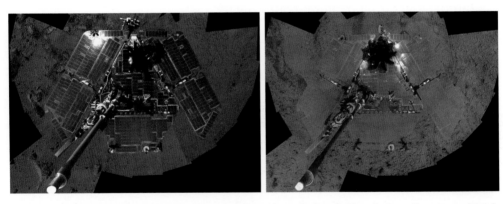

SOLAR PANELS ON A MARS ROVER, from above, before (left) and after a dust storm (right). Just like a solar panel, leaves don't work if they're covered in grime.

keep themselves clean? When you think about it, plants don't have moving arms or towels to clean themselves with (or any janitorial staff). Water is available, and its shape and behavior can be controlled by the leaf, so that plants can use rain to keep the their leaves clean. Pretty clever! Whoever guessed plants could be so smart?

Modeling a Wet Leaf. But wait a second . . . exactly *how* do plants like kale cause water to ball up? How do they prevent water from sticking to them? To help students explain this phenomenon, let's go over what we know so far:

FACT #1: Water is sticky.

FACT #2: If water is surrounded by air or space and doesn't have anything to stick to, it sticks to itself and forms a ball.

FACT #3: Water forms a sphere on certain kinds of leaves (kale, for instance), even though it seems like the water in this case *does* have something to stick to (the leaf surface).

Our facts don't quite all line up nicely, do they? Solicit students' ideas about what causes the water to ball up on kale, remaining noncommittal. If needed, you can nudge the students toward a hypothesis using a little inference: from Fact #2 we know that if water doesn't have anything to stick to, it sticks to itself, forming a ball. And we know from Fact #3 that water forms a ball on certain kinds of leaves (like kale). Therefore, one possibility is that, even though it appears otherwise, *maybe the water is not actually touching the kale leaf.*

How could this be? Again, solicit the students' ideas. What if there is something very small that we cannot see, a microscopic texture of some kind, trapping a layer of air between the leaf and the water? In theory, that might keep the water from really touching the leaf and cause it instead to stick to itself, forming the ball that we see.

How might one test such an idea? Let's make a model of a smooth versus a textured leaf surface, and test these competing models using water to see what happens. To make your two contrasting leaf surface models, all you need is the materials you've already used, and a piece of sandpaper. You want coarse-grained sandpaper (60-grit or less), and dark-colored sandpaper is better than tan, because you can see the water drops better. (Dark sandpapers are usually made of silicon carbide or emery and are sometimes called "emery cloth" at the hardware store.)

Have your students place their swatch of sandpaper next to a microscope slide. Explain that the microscope slide is made of glass, while the sandpaper is made of many individual mineral particles attached to paper. Thus, the surface of the microscope slide has a smooth texture, while the sandpaper has a very rough texture. What do students think will happen to water placed on these two different surfaces?

Ask students to use their eyedropper to place an equal-sized drop of water on each surface and observe the result. What do they notice? Is each drop the same shape? How are they different? Look at how round each drop is by looking at the drops from the side (profile view). Look at how wide each drop is by looking at the drops from above (top view). Optionally, have students measure the height and diameter of each drop using a ruler—making sure not to touch the drops!

To get more technical, have older students measure the contact angle of each drop. Contact angles are how physicists quantify the relative roundness of a water drop on a surface, which also serves as a measure of how "wettable" a surface is (i.e., how well water sticks to it). It's an angle described by the horizontal surface, and a line from that surface tangential to the water drop. You can see that if the water drop is spread out (i.e., a wettable surface), this angle will be small. If the water drop is rounder (i.e., a less wettable surface), this angle will be larger. It's hard to use a protractor with a water drop without the water drop getting the worst of it, so try taking photographs of the drops in profile instead, and have students do their measurements with these.

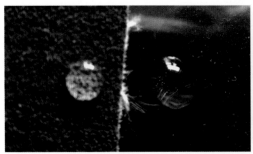 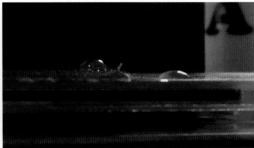

A GREAT SIMPLE LEAF SURFACE MODEL: Side-by-side water drops of equal volume on coarse sandpaper (left side) and smooth glass (right side). Notice the difference in drop diameter and height on each material. The increase in particle roughness (i.e., edges) and space between particles traps air and makes the coarse sandpaper more hydrophobic, while the smooth glass gives the drop more surface upon which to adhere.

See if students can now explain what's happening. Ask them a series of questions: Why might the shape of the drops be different between the two surfaces? Think about what we know about water drops and what determines their shape. Remember the pepper? Water is sticky. If it has something to stick to, it will stick to it. But remember the wax paper? (Water is also attracted to itself. If it has nothing to stick to, it will stick to itself, forming a ball.) Now, think about the different textures of these two surfaces, glass and sandpaper. How does the texture of the two surfaces differ in terms of things for water to stick to? (The microscope slide has a very smooth surface. The water drop has a continuously smooth surface to adhere to. The sandpaper, in contrast, has a rough texture, with many mineral particles on its surface. The particles themselves have sharp edges, and the spaces between them are filled with air.) Any idea now about why the shape of the water drops is different on the different surfaces?

With all of its particles, the coarse sandpaper presents an extremely rough surface to the water drop—not much to adhere to. And there is space between the particles, filled with air, to which water doesn't stick. The result is a water drop that sticks more to itself and is rounder. In contrast, the glass slide is smooth, so there is little or no space to trap air and more of a surface for water to stick to. The result is a water drop that is flatter. The balance between adhesive and cohesive forces, driven by the different surface textures, determines the outcome.

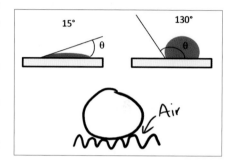

It's a decent theory anyway. If it's true, what do you suppose we'd see if we looked at each drop through a hand lens? Try it. Trapped at the bottom of the water drop on the sandpaper, you should be able to see small bubbles of air. The air around the mineral particles of the sandpaper is normally invisible, but trapped underneath a water drop, they show up. At the bottom of the water drop on the glass slide no such air bubbles will be apparent.

Testing the Theory. Ask your students: Now that you've seen how the texture of the sandpaper influences the shape of water drops, do you have any guesses about how kale works? Could kale have a microscopic texture, too small to see, full of edges and lots of space, like the coarse sandpaper?

How might we test this theory to see if it's true? Your students may already have an idea. If it's true that microscopic textures on certain leaves makes water ball up on them, then when we *remove* that texture from the leaves, water shouldn't ball up on them. Can we test this with the materials we have? Sure!

Have students take their kale leaf and rub a part of the leaf with their finger (If you have a rubber glove, that is even better, so oil from your hand isn't a factor.) You want them to rub the leaf vigorously, but not so much that it tears. Now, have them put a water drop on the spot they rubbed. For contrast, ask them to put a droplet next to it, on an unrubbed portion of the leaf. Are the drops the same shape? Different? How so? What appears to have happened to the leaf when we rubbed it?

So, it seems that certain plants, like kale, do indeed appear to use texture to control the shape and behavior of water on them. That's curious—why do you think kale would go to the trouble of doing this? What does making water behave like a ball do for the plant?

If need be, remind students of what leaves do for plants, steering them toward understanding that water sitting on a leaf can create problems by blocking sunlight and encouraging the growth of other creatures (e.g., mold, bacteria). But also, by making water ball up, the slightest breeze rolls the ball of water over the leaf, mopping up dirt as it goes. Leaves can thus manipulate the shape of water to clean themselves with it. Remember, plants don't have hands. They don't have bath towels. They can't scrub themselves. But they don't need them, either. All some plants need to stay clean is certain microscopic texture, rain, and a little breeze. That's it! That's how many of the plants in the schoolyard stay perfectly clean, without a janitor sweeping them off every day.

THE MICROSCOPIC SURFACE OF A LEAF, showing balled-up water droplets. Notice the dirt picked up from the leaf surface by the rolling balls of water.

ACTIVITY: Water-Repellant Cloth

The way some plants repel water can certainly help them. Some plants, like kale, have a clever way to use water to keep themselves clean. Ask your students: Do you think their clever idea could help people, too? How so? (See what students come up with.) What kinds of things do people need to keep clean? How could the way some plants repel water using microscopic texture give inventors and engineers ideas for how to keep the things we make clean?

Fabric stains are a common human challenge, one parents have made kids well aware of. To see an example in action, you'll need the water and eyedroppers you already have, plus some food coloring (for drama), two swatches of white cotton fabric, and a spray-on cloth coating now commonly available. A number of commercial spray-on coatings now exist that have bor-

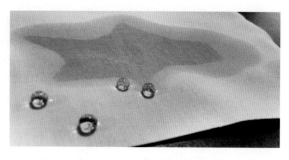

COTTON FABRIC treated with microscopic spray-on particles, inspired by hydrophobic leaves (foreground), and untreated cotton (background).

rowed this leaf-inspired approach to creating hydrophobic surfaces using microscopic texture (for a list, see the Additional Resources section at the end of the chapter). To explore how leaves might help us solve this problem, leave one cotton swatch untreated, and treat the other with the coating—and let your students know it. Now simply have students place a drop of colored water on each swatch and observe the difference. The untreated fabric stains as the water droplet sinks in. But on the treated fabric, the colored water drop just stays on the fabric surface. To clean it, all you have to do is roll the water droplet off the fabric. Cool!

There's actually a human and environmental health aspect to this story, too, though it isn't necessary to bring it up for the lesson to work. For younger students, its highly recommended you don't distract them with it. But for older students, there is greater meaning still in leaf-inspired approaches to self-cleaning materials.

Plant-inspired approaches to self-cleaning surfaces typically use silicon dioxide to create the microscopic texture that conveys hydrophobicity to a material. Since small amounts of silicon dioxide are already naturally in the environment, these materials are generally considered safe. However, hydrophobicity is achieved in many human-made materials using chemical methods, and here the story is different. This use of rather exotic, human-made compounds raises a number of health concerns. To begin with, these chemicals, known as *perfluorinated compounds*, are bound to fluorine, an atom not typically used in organic materials and bonded with such strong chemical attachments that decomposers, even if they found them palatable, generally cannot break them apart. The result is that these hydrophobic chemical coatings find their way into the environment and our bodies after being sprayed onto clothes and carpets and coated onto pots and pans, and there they stay, building up in the environment and inside of us. Perfluorinated compounds have been found in drinking water across the United States and elsewhere. Studies have found correlations between per-fluorinated compounds and a variety of health issues, including ADHD in children, hormone disruptions, increased cholesterol levels, birth defects, heart disease, and cancer. Naturally, plants had to develop a feasible way of repelling water that was safe for living tissues, thus their texture-based approach, using microscopic structures made of benign materials. Chapter 6 describes how Nature-inspired approaches to engineering can help us address many other health and sustainability challenges.

GALLIVANTING GLIDERS

Gases, from a hydrodynamics standpoint, behave much like liquids, so these two classes of matter are grouped together as types of fluids. This series of lessons is very simple and straightforward. It begins by looking at examples of gliding in the natural world and then has students build and test their own gliding devices. Gliders are fun and easy to make, enjoyable to watch, and easy to test, making for a perfect activity to explore engineering and Nature at the same time. Along the way, students learn about some fundamental physical principles having to do with fluids, especially with engineering devices that glide or fly, not to mention address a number of aspects of the Next Generation Science Standards. Moreover, this activity, like most of the others, can be done pretty much across the K-12 spectrum.

To introduce the activity to students, pick some situations

The Wright brothers flew right through the smoke screen of impossibility.

–Charles Kettering

We could hardly wait to get up in the morning.

–Wilbur Wright

ENGINEERING EPIPHANIES: How might Nature help us think of new approaches for helping people trapped in a building to escape?

where gliding devices are useful. Humans use gliding or floating devices whenever a motor is unnecessary or impractical. These situations might include making supply drops to people in need (e.g., after a flood), landing a space capsule onto a planet, or floating a pilot ejected from an aircraft safely back down to Earth.

For older students, you might elect to describe a dramatic scenario in which people are trapped in a building during an earthquake or a fire. The elevators don't work or aren't safe to use. There's no time to use the stairs, and they're blocked anyway. What could an engineer do to anticipate and address such a possibility?

Some people say the mechanics of having an epiphany are altogether too mysterious to understand, but if you want to catalyze your students' looking to Nature for ideas at this point, simply show them an image of a building during such a calamity, and next to this image, place an image of a dandelion, releasing its seeds into the air. Then ask your students: is there anything in Nature that might suggest a solution to such a terrible situation? Sure, it's leading a horse to water (and probably even making it drink), but that's one of the objectives these activities. After all, we're helping students build the cognitive machinery for exactly these kind of epiphanies, because that's how Nature-inspired engineers think. By repeatedly show-ing students how to find these solutions, and how useful they can be, you can finally let them try out Nature-inspired engineering all on their own (a focus of Chapter 8).

Gliding Principles

Before you let your students design and build their own gliders, let's first spend some time looking at how the natural world approaches this mode of travel, and see what we can learn. People who study this will tell you that things moving through the air are acted on by four main forces: weight, lift, drag, and thrust. *Weight* is the mass of an object times grav-ity; as long as a glider is heavier than air, its weight will tend to cause it to descend. *Lift* is a force that keeps airborne objects up in the air; it works in direct opposition to the weight of an airborne object. *Drag*, caused by air friction or partial vacuums, is generally shown as opposing thrust, although drag can oppose any forward motion (which can actually be useful, as we'll see). *Thrust*, the force generally shown opposing drag, is provided by the engine in an airplane. In gliders, thrust is provided by anything Nature can get its hands on, particularly air movement (e.g., wind) and gravity.

Everything that glides in Nature manages these forces to stay in the air for an adequate amount of time to get the job done. For a seed, that means staying in the air long enough to put distance between itself and the mother plant. A seed that doesn't disperse will fall next to the mother plant and be forced to compete with it. In the case of dandelions, a com-mon occupant of schoolyards or cracks in concrete everywhere, that means employing several strategies. You can use the example of the dandelion to show students how they can use these forces to make their own gliders:

- *Weight.* The seed of a dandelion (the part below the fluffy white para-chute, or *pappus*) is very light, around 0.6 milligrams (0.00002 ounces). All of the gliders your students will make in the activity that follows will have the same amount of weight to carry (a paperclip), so we won't be able to reduce the weight of the cargo, or "seed." But the weight of the nonseed part of a glider *is* something we can address through design. The heavier our glider is overall, the harder it has to work to stay airborne. So there is generally an advantage to using the lightest structures possible to remain airborne. The fluffy pappus of a dandelion seed is exceptionally light, especially for how effectively it helps keep the seed aloft.

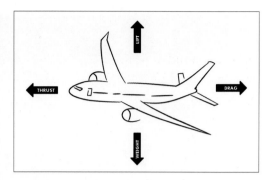

- *Drag.* The dandelion pappus works by creating air resistance, using a light, high-surface-area structure. Generally, the greater an object's surface area, the more air resistance, or drag, it experiences. This effectively slows the seed's descent and increases the amount of time in the air, so that a gust or breeze might arise to carry the seed farther away. What if the day isn't windy? As any kid knows, dandelion seeds remain pretty firmly attached to the rest of the plant unless a fairly strong puff of air comes by. (When you think about it, this is a very smart dispersal system: dandelion seeds couple their mechanism of detachment with their mechanism of dispersal, which helps ensure they release from their mother plant only on a day that is good for gliding.) A simple way to illustrate the relationship between air resistance and (cross-sectional) area is to have students wave a half sheet of cardstock through the air and compare this to how it feels to wave a full sheet of cardstock through the air.
- *Thrust.* Dandelion seeds may not have an engine to create thrust, but they don't need to: they can use a passing wind for thrust, simply by delaying their fall. This is actually a very clever use of drag. Drag is usually considered counterproductive to flight. A dandelion seed's entire design is premised on the idea of using wind for thrust, which suddenly turns increasing drag (to delay descent) into a design *goal*, rather than something to try to eliminate. This radically upends the assumptions of an engine-propelled airplane. A dandelion seed gets to where it needs to go without using a drop of gasoline.

Lifting Forces

Creating a lot of air resistance, or drag, is one strategy to slow a gliding device's descent. Another strategy is to create lift to counteract a gliding device's weight. Any design that reduces relative air pressure above the gliding device creates lift. This is loosely referenced as Bernoulli's prin-

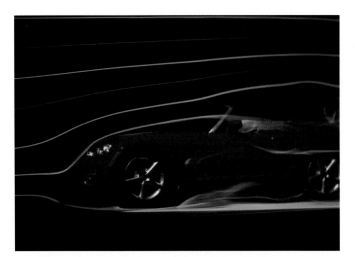

A STREAMLINED OBJECT passing through a volume of air: notice how the air going over the top of the car gets compressed between the car below and air above.

ciple, after the Swiss physicist Daniel Bernoulli (1700–1782), who wrote in 1738 about the inverse relationship between the speed of a fluid and a fluid's pressure: a fluid's pressure goes down when its speed goes up. I used to own a powder blue 1970 Oldsmobile Cutlass Supreme, an absolute classic convertible, and always found it curious that when I drove it down the highway the canvas top would bow upward. This gave my car the equivalent of a potbelly, in a very unclassy way. What was happening? Imagine a rectangle of air moving toward a car, slightly larger than the car itself. The air in that space doesn't just get freely displaced (pushed away) as the car passes through it, because the air outside that space somewhat constrains (puts pressure on) that block of air from the outside. Thus, that block of air has to *deform* in order to get around the car. The air that flows over the top of the car actually gets squeezed, between the car below it and the ambient air above. As it gets compressed, the air accelerates (just like narrowing the opening of a garden hose with your thumb to increase water pressure). As the air over the top of the car accelerates, its pressure drops (à la Bernoulli). Since the air pressure inside the cabin of my car didn't change, up went the canvas top of the convertible.

The same thing happens with the wing of an airplane. An airplane wing isn't just a flat piece of material like a pizza box. English inventor George Cayley (mentioned in Chapter 2), who greatly influenced the Wright brothers, observed that a bird's wing has a very specific shape that enables it to fly. Wings (a.k.a. *airfoils*) are shaped, subtly, with a curve or *camber* running crosswise (front to back). A wing is curved downward on its leading edge. This "ramps" the flowing air upward, constricting it so that it speeds over the wing more quickly than the air flowing unimpeded beneath the wing. Thus, there is greater air pressure below than above the wing, and up the wing lifts, just like the top of my classic convertible. (An airplane propeller works using lift in the same way. With a cambered leading edge on each blade, a spinning propeller causes air pressure to drop in front of the plane. Higher air pressure behind the propeller pushes the plane forward. The Wright brothers were the ones who figured out that a propeller works best when it's designed to create lift the way birds' wings do.)

You can demonstrate lift very easily by holding a well-used dollar bill to your bottom lip and blowing. Up comes the dollar bill—it seems magical: nothing at all appears to be lifting the dollar bill, and yet up it rises. Air pressure differential is an extremely powerful tool; birds use it to migrate thousands of miles every year. We're too accustomed to seeing airplanes weighing tens of thousands of pounds suspended in completely insubstantial air—we should be doing double-takes with our jaws dropping and pointing speechlessly every time an airplane goes by, for how odd yet tremendously effective this behavior of air truly is.

Nature's Gliding Strategies

The dandelion seed, with its parachuting pappus, is one example of seed dispersal by gliding, but Nature uses other techniques. A seed that resembles a wing a great deal, rather than a parachute, and uses lift to disperse is that of the Javan cucumber (*Alsomitra macrocarpa*), a tropical climbing vine found in the Malay Archipelago. The seed is surrounded by a papery material having a specific winged shape and launches out from its gourd-like fruit over the forest canopy to find a new place to grow, sailing for hundreds of meters or making wide loops toward the ground. The seed is positioned within the papery airfoil in such a way that its center of gravity tilts the leading edge downward, a prerequisite for generating lift.

What's striking is how perfectly balanced and stable the seed is as it glides. Its downward angle (i.e., angle of attack) is 12 percent, an optimum amount to cause the seed to descend the minimum necessary to create lift over its wing, and no more. As a result of this very shallow angle of attack, the seed descends as little as 0.3 meters per second. Meanwhile, the swept-back shape of the wings improves the stability of the seed, including *yaw* (the nose moving right or left) and *pitch* (i.e., front-to-back stability)—the swept-back wings effectively make more of the glider covered by horizontal wings, nose to tail, which stabilizes the glider against pitch. Pitch control is particularly important for aircraft that lack a tail wing; in fact, the Javan cucumber seed has served as an inspiration both for human-made gliders and tailless airplanes (a.k.a. flying wings). The seed's wingtips are also slightly bent upward (*dihedral*), which helps stabilize the craft in *roll* (banking) and yaw.

Another fascinating adaptation of the seed for flight control is its flexible, almost crumbly edges; these appear weak and poorly made until one grasps their function. For instance, the default position of the seed's trailing edge is bent slightly upward, which pushes the back end of the wing downward (like the spoiler of a race car) and helps keep the wing's leading edge up. However, if the wing stalls and starts to dive, the trailing edge flattens from the air pressure, removing the spoiler effect and helping correct the error. The same self-correcting behavior occurs if the wing banks (roll), bending with the increased pressure to help regain a more horizontal posture.

Another approach to seed gliding, a spinning seed (i.e., "helicopter seed," sometimes called a samara), also glides by creating lift to forestall descent, yet in a very different way than an airfoil like the Javan cucumber seed. Unlike an airfoil, in which air flows horizontally over its edge, a descending helicopter seed has air flowing vertically, upward from below, over the wider face of the blade. As a result, an eddy forms on the leeward (sky-facing) side of the blade. The same thing happens when you stick the flat of your palm in a stream and an eddy forms on the backside of your hand. The water cannot reseal around your hand perfectly on the backside, so a partial vacuum forms there. Water from downstream actually flows backward, going upstream temporarily, in order to fill the space. Every trout angler knows this a good place to deliver or dead drift a fly, because the backflow is an energy-free space in which trout like to rest against the predominant current. Since it is a vacuum, this eddy sucks from all directions, however, pulling whatever is upstream also backward, which is why this is actually a form of drag (*pressure drag*). Immediately at the back of a motored boat, where the wake begins, you can see the water is below water level, sucked in by the partial vacuum left by the moving boat. Our friend George Cayley was the first person to identify pressure drag. An astute observer of the natural world, Cayley solved the problem at the same time, noting that the tapered shape of trout and ducks helped reduce the vacuum's formation. Modern aircraft taper in just this fashion as a result.

Pressure drag is a drag unless you are a clever little helicopter seed. The genius of a helicopter seed is to *use* pressure drag to suck itself upward, against gravity, and thus delay descent. To maintain this drag as it falls, the seed is designed to autorotate with phenomenal stability, helping keep a constant eddy of negative pressure on top of the blade the whole time. The use of pressure drag is extremely effective, extending a helicopter seed's time in the air by a monumental 36 percent over seeds relying solely on air resistance to slow their descent.

Seeds are great for exploring gliding, but animals glide too. There are gliding mammals (such as flying squirrels and Asian colugos), gliding lizards, gliding frogs, and even gliding snakes and gliding ants! Showing examples of these can spice things up, though it's hard to beat seeds for their diversity of gliding strategies and familiarity to students.

ACTIVITY: Making a Glider

Once you've shown your students some of the strategies used in the natural world for gliding (or had them research these on their own and describe them to the rest of the class), provide them with materials to build their own gliders: cotton balls, paper of different thicknesses, tape, and so forth. To equalize the challenge among students, explain that every glider will have to transport the same cargo (a paperclip) and every glider will receive the same amount of thrusting power, provided by a floor fan. (This activity is fun to do outside too, on a windy day. Although this may increase the variability of thrust each glider receives, increasing the number of trials can address this somewhat.)

Have students passively drop their device into the wind stream (not push it, as one would do with a paper airplane); this eliminates a variable (pushing) that has nothing to do with glider design. To measure the performance of each glider, have students simply use a long tape measure to quantify the distance each glider travels from its drop. After the first set of trials, let students use what they've observed and redesign, rebuild, and retest their gliders. If you choose, you can have students first build gliders, and then learn about gliding strategies in Nature; they can then redesign, rebuild, and retest their gliders once, twice, or more, using what they learned from Nature's strategies.

Keep track of the performance of each student's glider with respect to its design. There are lots of opportunities for student discussion and explanation here. Students can explain the connection between their design and gliding strategies in Nature, the basis for their redesign, and any patterns they observe in the data. With a sensitive enough scale, you can record the weight of each glider and compare this to distance traveled. Another interesting thing to measure is the time each glider stays aloft: is it true that time aloft and distance traveled are correlated?

Tumbleweed Gliders. There's one more form of glider too fun to pass up, which I call tumbleweed gliders (a.k.a. walk-along gliders). Tumbleweeds don't seem like gliders, but they are pushed by the wind in their unique seed dispersal system. Tumbleweed gliders, invented by John Collins, a noted innovator in the world of paper airplanes, glide through the air by tumbling (hence the reference), and students actively keep them aloft by walking behind them holding large, flat pieces of cardboard to create a constant updraft. The result is this suspended, moving, constantly spinning glider.

The only materials you need for tumbleweed gliders are phone book paper and cardboard. To learn the process for making and flying them, check out the Additional Resource section at the end of this chapter. To add yet more fun, make a target out of cardboard (with holes large enough to fit a glider) and challenge students to fly their tumbleweed gliders into the target for points.

Once students have flown their tumbleweed gliders, you can have them compare the different flight principles of tumbleweeds versus "regular" gliders, and how these compare with different gliding strategies in nature.

You can explore Nature-inspired engineering using this sort of activity with respect to making almost anything. We've used gliders here, but you could do it with toy boats, paper airplanes, towers (as in Chapter 2), anything that students can readily design, test, and then redesign and retest based on design lessons learned from related strategies Nature uses to accomplish similar ends.

You can also address a large number of elements in the Next Generation Science Standards through this kind of activity, in life science, physics, and of course engineering. After all, you've identified and addressed a design challenge (creating gliding devices), as well as generated, modeled, tested, and optimized these designs. To wrap the chapter up, I'll leave

it to John Collins, speaking of paper airplanes, who explains perfectly the potential value of doing these sorts of activities:

The idea that you can teach science to someone and get them interested in science is an amazing idea to me. To my way of thinking we have a number of serious and real global issues that are only going to be solved with technological answers. There are global energy shortages, water shortages, this little thing called global warming and we need the best and brightest working on that stuff. Paper airplanes are a really simple way into science. The whole scientific method is right there in a paper airplane. You take a guess about what an adjustment will do, you do the adjustment— that's the experiment—you throw it, generate results, analyze what went wrong and repeat. . . . And whether kids realize it or not, they're doing science just by folding and flying a paper airplane and experimenting with it. So I try to parlay that into an interest in science. . . . We have no spare brains anywhere on the planet. We need everybody working together to solve this stuff.

Additional Resources

Curricula on fluid dynamics and engineering
The Center for Learning with Nature: https://www.learningwithnature .org/—see "Magical Mucus," "Indomitable Drops," "Gallivanting Gliders," and "Beetle Boats" in the upper elementary version of the *Engineering Inspired by Nature* curriculum.

More technical treatments of fluid dynamics in biology
Denny, M. W. 1993. *Air and water: The biology and physics of life's media.* Princeton University Press.

Vogel, S. 2013. *Comparative biomechanics: Life's physical world.* Princeton University Press.

Magical Mucus

Videos demonstrating how snails travel
Hatsopoulos Microfluid Lab. Non-Newtonian Fluid Dynamics Group: https://nnf.mit.edu/home/billboard/topic-3

Also see *Cornu aspersum.* Wikipedia. https://en.wikipedia.org/wiki/ Cornu_aspersum

Math connections
See, e.g., EdInformatics. Science of Fluids. http://www.edinformatics .com/math_science/science_of_fluids.htm

More about liquid body armor
D3o. Wikipedia. https://en.wikipedia.org/wiki/D3o

TrialByFireMMA review of D30 jacket. YouTube. https://www.youtube .com/watch?v=zbTkl7iH7F4

Mashable Deals about D30. YouTube. https://www.youtube.com/ watch?v=NVSA7TMYYhI

How Stuff Works. How Liquid Body Armor Works: https://science.how stuffworks.com/liquid-body-armor1.htm

University of Delaware. Liquid Armor. YouTube. https://www.youtube .com/watch?v=k6VzzvA7frI&index=32&list=PLjtW_T3jHfIoISlhXCRW27 epy4Wo1coJ7

Language arts connections
Check out Elisabeth Tova Bailey's wonderful book: Bailey, E. T. 2011. *The sound of a wild snail eating.* Text Publishing.

Also see the educational resources on her website: http://www.elisa bethtovabailey.net/for-educators/

Indomitable Drops

Math connections (contact angles)

See, e.g., Good, R. J. 1992. Contact angle, wetting, and adhesion: A critical review. *Journal of Adhesion Science and Technology, 6*(12), 1269–1302.

Water in zero gravity

Astronaut washing hair: https://www.youtube.com/watch?v=uljNfZbUYu8

Astronaut playing Ping-Pong with water: https://theverge.tumblr.com/post/137819053492/astronaut-scott-kelly-celebrated-300-straight-days

Water-repellant plants

More on the "lotus effect": https://en.wikipedia.org/wiki/Lotus_effect

More on superhydrophobicity: https://en.wikipedia.org/wiki/Ultrahydrophobicity

Environmental and human health connections

More on perfluorinated compounds: https://en.wikipedia.org/wiki/Perfluorinated_compound

Leaf-inspired spray-on hydrophobic coatings

> There are many such coatings on the market, but it is important for this lesson to use a texture-based coating, because this is the mechanism primarily used by hydrophobic leaves. Fluorine-based sprays (e.g., Teflon) work using chemical principles, rather than texture, and are not inspired by leaves. (Some texture-based coatings also include fluorine chemistry, which are fine for the purposes of this lesson.) Hydrophobic fabric sprays that are texture based include Waterbeader, LiquidOff, Liquiproof, UHC-Tex, and Gyeon. Fabrics that come already coated include those using GreenShield and Nano-Tex.

Video showing leaf-inspired coatings on fabric: https://www.youtube.com/watch?v=BvTkefJHfC0&t=200s

Videos of shear-thinning liquids

Peanut butter: https://www.youtube.com/watch?v=9puevzYv3dY

Ketchup: https://www.youtube.com/watch?v=djwahGRi5iE

Gallivanting Gliders

Math connections

See, e.g., materials from the U.S. Federal Aviation Administration: https://www.faa.gov/regulations_policies/handbooks_manuals/aircraft/glider_handbook/media/gfh_ch03.pdf

Making tumbleweed gliders

Using phone book paper: http://www.instructables.com/id/Walkalong -Glider-Made-from-Phone-Book-Paper/

Seed dispersal videos

Overview of seed dispersal: http://www.cornell.edu/video/naturalist -outreach-seed-dispersal---the-great-escape

Javan cucumber in flight: https://imgur.com/gallery/ARGnn

Great overview for younger kids: https://vimeo.com/218127343

Language arts connections

Wright, O., and Wright, W. 2018. *Early history of the airplane.* Seltzer Books via PublishDrive.

McFarland, M. W., ed. 1953. *The papers of Wilbur and Orville Wright, including the Chanute-Wright papers.* McGraw-Hill.

Also see: Letters from Wilbur Wright: https://www.commonlit.org/texts/ letters-from-wilbur-wright

More activities on engineering and aerodynamics

NASA STEM Engagement:https://www.nasa.gov/offices/education/about /index.html

Fun with Bernoulli. eGFI: http://teachers.egfi-k12.org/tag/aerodynamics/

6
TEACHING SUSTAINABILITY THROUGH ENGINEERING

Sustainability is a vague, emergent property of often wicked complexity.

—Moeller et al., 2013

Look out your window or take a walk outside, and you will see a world astonishingly different from the one humans are busy creating. True, you will see a world that, with its colossal trees, fields of grasses, buzzing insects, and cryptic animals, is surprisingly productive, like ours. But you will also see a world that is beautiful, that provides for all of its inhabitants, that somehow begets more abundance the more it makes, leaving behind yet more productive capacity rather than wasted land, stifling pollution, and unsightly garbage. How does Nature do this? How does Nature follow productivity with yet greater productivity? That's the world *we* want, too— but with all the things in it we want, like movie theaters and restaurants and gadgets, *plus* the colossal trees and butterflies.

NATURE'S SECRETS TO SUCCESS

Just for fun, pick out any human-made object near you right now. Then, on a piece of paper, list everything about that object that works. Next to this, make a list of everything about the object that doesn't work. Go ahead, I'll wait . . .

I'm being vague about what I mean by *works*, I know—that's intentional. What we mean when we say something "works" is something we'll explore in this chapter.

The Six-Month Building

Imagine intentionally designing a skyscraper that lasted for only six months. Because of the materials you selected, and the way you designed everything to be held together, the building was destined to fall apart after just half a year. Just as everyone gets themselves moved into the building and set up in their offices and apartments, the building begins to crumble, piece by piece. Soon, the structure is just a giant pile of rubble on Earth's surface.

How would you feel about making a building like that? If you designed buildings this way, how long do you think your career as an architect would last? And yet, like the architect in this scenario, we don't expect our engineers and designers to design a world that lasts. What do I mean by this?

For starters, humans make things by extracting limited natural resources from the environment in any desired quantity, no matter how destructive the means. That can't last. We then manufacture these raw materials into finished products using forms of energy and chemicals that routinely pollute air, water, and land. That can't last. And, without any constraint whatsoever, the finished products we create come off assembly lines into the world every year, despite having no ready way of breaking back down again into natural components or usable resources. Our fabrications are destined to pile up in the world, functionally forever. That can't last.

Let's put some specific figures on this. There are roughly 13,000 active mines around the globe, from which humans currently extract about 68 billion tons of material out of Earth's crust every year. If that sounds like a lot of raw material, it's because it is—ten cubic *miles* of material, every year. A cubic mile is a very, very big box: in ten of these boxes, you could pack one happy pharaoh 16,000 Great Pyramids of Giza. Manufacturing all of this material into the things humans make (automobiles, carpet, beach balls, martini glasses, etc.) releases some 9.5 billion tons of carbon dioxide into the atmosphere yearly, plus 10 million tons of toxic chemical effluent, dumped into the air we breathe, the water we drink, and the soil we grow food in.

Naturally this has an impact on human and nonhuman well-being. Cancer rates are expected to more than double in the next couple of decades, and half of the species on Earth are projected to go extinct by the end of this century. Most of the products we manufacture will eventually end up in landfills or elsewhere after they're used, where they will never turn back into useful resources. We add 300 million tons of plastic trash, for instance, to the planet each year. Less than 10 percent of it gets recycled. By 2050, there will literally be more plastic in the ocean than fish. The fish we eat today already contain plastic bits and fibers, a reality that is going to get much worse.

PRODUCT LIFE CYCLE: A bucket wheel excavator surface-mines the earth for raw industrial materials (top left), which a factory manufactures into finished products (top right). These products are sold and used by people (bottom left) and then disposed of in pit landfills when no longer wanted (bottom right).

Logic tells us that this way of making things cannot and should not go on forever. A production system premised on unlimited raw materials, which assumes an infinite planet in which to dump pollution and waste, cannot persist indefinitely on an obviously limited planet. And yet we keep doing it. Engineers that design these processes and products rarely if ever have classes about biological sustainability or environmental science in their college curricula. They are rarely encouraged to think about how the things they make fit in with the larger systems of which they are part, and really, neither are the rest of us. (Did you have anything written down on your piece of paper in the "doesn't work" column?) Implicitly, then, we are actually encouraging our engineers to design a human-built world that *can't* last, to design processes and products that *don't* work, at least in the long run. And the long run matters—certainly our children will think so. From an educational standpoint, this epic omission makes no sense at all.

It's a weird, uncomfortable situation, and a lot to unpack. The standard mode of our production system is so problematic, so thorny, yet so important, that most of the time it doesn't even get addressed or, if it is, gets addressed in a murky or unsatisfying way, even though it is *essential* to address it—for engineering education in the immediate term, and for the future of humankind in the long run. So, this chapter unpacks it, offering a clear, practical, solution-oriented way to address these issues in a manner that works for students. We'll use a Nature-inspired approach to both understand humankind's unsustainable way of life, and discover how we can find solutions to address it.

Why use a Nature-inspired approach for this, you might ask? For one very good reason: the living world is the only empirical example of sustainability we have. As such, it's our best model, and one we're tremendously fortunate to have at all. It means we don't have to make this up completely on our own; rather, we have an extraordinarily rich and interesting resource to learn from. And it means we can be confident that *a sustainable way of life is possible*, which should give us great hope and motivation. A Nature-inspired approach to learning about sustainability is an optimistic approach to a subject too long defined by doom and gloom. Indeed, as you'll see, by learning from Nature's example of sustainability, people have already been making brightly promising and deeply heartening progress toward the realization of a sustainable modern way of life.

Curriculum note. This chapter is aimed at teachers of middle and high school students. It's great for primary school teachers to be aware of these issues, and there may be places in an engineering curriculum to touch on sustainability issues in primary school, but it should be a light touch, at best. Remember, kids need to fall in love with Nature before they start to worry about it! But by middle and certainly high school, covering sustainability is imperative.

Lifting the Heavy Piano

Sustainability is one of those concepts that can seem so complicated, so overwhelming, that we might prefer to just ignore it and wish it would go away. We regard sustainability as one might a large piano a neighbor has asked us to help lift up a flight of narrow, rickety stairs. We could opt not to lift the piano and ignore the neighbor, but socially this just doesn't feel right. How to proceed? It sure would help if we could separate the piano into a few smaller pieces for carrying. Upon closer examination, it turns out the hulking thing can be detached into a small number of more manageable segments.

The tool for doing so is called a product *life cycle analysis*, or *LCA* for short. LCA is a tool people use to assess the environmental impact of a human-made object. The environmental impact of making almost anything today is extremely involved, but an LCA is the analytical tool that can help us wrap our minds around it. Without it, it's like trying to do surgery with a dull rock. But with an LCA as an analytical framework, we can make real progress through the fog of sustainability.

Where did product LCAs come from? The framework of an LCA was developed by analogy to another conceptual tool, the life cycle, used by biologists to describe the lives of organisms. The life of an organism can be described as having distinct phases: they are born, they develop, they live their adult lives, and then they die. Similarly, a product life cycle of, say, a tennis shoe involves the raw materials used in the shoe (its "birth"), how the materials are processed into a shoe (its "development"), the use of the shoe by people (its "adult life"), and what happens to the shoe upon disposal (its "death"). When biologists think about the living world, they regard organisms as part of a process. Similarly, when thinking about the sustainability of a human-made object, we need to see beyond the seemingly static tennis shoe in front of us and consider the *process* by which the tennis shoe came about and where it's headed, and that's where the LCA comes in. It identifies the story behind any human-made object, usually a pretty lengthy, interesting one.

It's fun and instructive to ask students to do a basic product LCA of a human-made object. LCAs can get pretty detailed and technical, but even a basic analysis of a simple human-made object is eye opening. Let's take a look at one example.

The Anatomy of a Pencil

Consider the workaday yellow pencil. A pencil is made of a small number of parts, which you can see at a glance: the lead, the wood casing, the eraser, the metal connector, and the paint. That's pretty much it. Pencil lead is a misnomer, of course. Roman styluses were made of lead, and when graphite was discovered in England in the mid-1500s, it was assumed to be a form of lead—it's not; it's a unique form of coal. (Once it was discovered that graphite was useful, to improve the process of making cannonball molds, for example, the graphite mines became so valuable that the Queen of England essentially nationalized them. To protect the graphite, miners were searched before going home each day, and when the mines weren't being worked, they were literally flooded with water to deter thieves.) Pencil leads today are made by mining graphite, adding clay, and hardening the mixture in ovens at 980°C (1796°F).

The leads are sandwiched between two slabs of wood before being cut into individual pencils; if you look at the exposed wood around a pencil lead, you can see the seams where the two wood slabs are glued. Trees like red cedar (*Juniperus virginiana*) were preferred for pencil wood until about the 1920s, when overharvesting of old growth reduced the large-diameter trees available. In England during World War II, wood for pencils became so scarce that owning a rotary pencil sharpener was actually made illegal, in an attempt to reduce waste. Today, wood for pencils comes from trees like incense cedar (*Calocedrus decurrens*), found in the Sierra Nevada foothills and mountains of California. Attempts to certify the sustainable management of forests for pencil wood production exist, but they are imperfect, with some operations still clearing old-growth forests, applying toxic herbicides in plantations, and so on. (And the sustainable management of these forests is further challenged by the increasing number of wildfires, exacerbated by climate change, that are incinerating them.)

It wasn't until 1858, some three hundred years after the pencil was invented, that someone first attached an eraser to a pencil. Before people realized they could use the dried latex of the Brazilian rubber tree (*Hevea brasiliensis*) to erase pencil marks, they did so using pieces of bread. (Perhaps this has something to do with the origin of the phrase "to eat one's words"?) Today, erasers are often made of synthetic rubber, primarily composed of two substances, styrene and butadiene, both derived from petroleum. Whether the idea of attaching an eraser to a pencil could be patented went all the way to the Supreme Court (which decided it couldn't, because it was really just the combination of two different inventions).

The metal cylinder that eventually came to hold erasers to pencils is called a *ferrule*. Ferrules weren't made of aluminum prior to 1964 because of its tendency to crush—they were made of more expensive brass. Then an inventor named J. B. Ostrowski strengthened the device by minutely corrugating the ferrule, a great example of structural engineering (recall corrugating paper in Chapter 3). Ferrules have been made of aluminum ever since. Aluminum is mined and processed out of bauxite ore.

Finally, the cheery yellow of pencil paint (or "lacquer") is made of the same things most paints are made of: pigments, resins, and solvents. Why yellow? Originally this was a marketing strategy. When a high-quality graphite deposit was found in northern Asia in the 1800s, pencil manufacturers using this graphite wanted a way to signal the quality of their pencils to consumers. Yellow was associated with Chinese royalty, so that's the color manufacturers used. Yellow pencil paint has gone through a number of recipes, as various chemical components have fallen out of favor for various reasons. Lead chromate, for instance, the pigment that used to give pencil paint its yellowness, has since been replaced with non-lead-containing pigments.

That's a very basic history of the pencil and its parts, which helps in doing an LCA of a modern wooden pencil—analyzing its raw materials and basic manufacturing processes, its use as it gets ground down into wood shavings and eraser bits, and what happens to its remains once discarded.

Life Cycle Analysis of a Pencil

A very brief LCA of a pencil can be summarized as follows: Pencil leads are made by mining graphite, adding clay, and then shaping and hardening the mixture in ovens. The leads are glued between two slabs of wood before being cut into individual pencils and painted. Erasers made of synthetic rubber are attached with corrugated aluminum ferrules. Pencils are then packaged in plastic or paper containers, shipped, and sold to consumers, who sharpen and write and erase with them and then discard the shavings, eraser crumbs, graphite marks (words and drawings on paper), and ultimately the used pencil stub into the trash, typically without recycling much if any of the waste.

But even with an object seemingly as simple as a pencil, an analysis of its physical components can get pretty elaborate. Every component of a pencil—the lead, the wood casing (and the glue in the wood casing), the eraser, the metal connector, and the paint—entails a separate manufacturing process, involving the extraction and transportation of materials, a physical factory and machinery, energy and chemical processes, and so on. So a complete LCA of even this most basic item can easily branch off into several "sub-LCAs" in no time.

For example, manufacturing the aluminum of the pencil ferrule necessitates clearing land above the mine; loosening the soil with explosives; transporting the bauxite-rich soil to chemical plants; treating the bauxite ore with caustic soda (sodium hydroxide), heat, and pressure to dissolve it from the rest of the soil; precipitating alumina (an interim substance); dissolving the alumina in molten cryolite (another mined substance) at 1,000°C (1,832°F); passing an electric current through the mixture; and filtering the result . . . all just to get the aluminum that connects your eraser to your pencil!

The life cycle framework is immensely helpful, because it takes thickly complicated phenomena and gives us a roadmap for disentangling it. Product LCAs help us better understand human-made items as *processes*, to whatever level of detail we choose to go. An LCA presents a relatively orderly sequence to the greatly intricate processes of making just about anything. An additional strength of LCAs is that they are general enough, conceptually, that they can be applied to basically anything and everything humans make. So learning to use this one single tool increases our analytical abilities enormously.

Building Our Better Future

Visually, humankind's general process for making just about everything involves a simple "cradle-to-grave" pattern of extraction, production, use, and disposal. A pattern that becomes clear after analyzing even just a few human-made objects is that the way we tend to make things is characteristically linear. That is, the beginning of the process (extracting raw materials) and the end of the process (disposal) generally don't connect. Except in

> **E**very science has for its basis a system of principles as fixed and unalterable as those by which the universe is regulated and governed. Man cannot make principles; he can only discover them.
>
> –Thomas Paine, 1794

the notable exception of recycled materials, pretty much everything we make ends up in a landfill or somewhere else in the environment, such as the ocean or atmosphere. This isn't very surprising, of course, because we're accustomed to it, but it is useful to boil our manufacturing procedures down into a single, generalizable process, in order to contrast it with the way the rest of Nature makes things. When using a Nature-inspired approach to teach students about sustainability, this contrast is your pedagogical game plan.

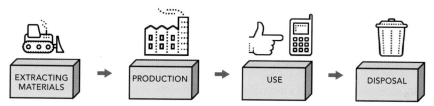

So how does Nature make things? Humans, of course, aren't the only species to make stuff. Where we create our tennis shoes, pencils, automobiles and cell phones, the rest of the living world makes trees, mushrooms, flowers, panda bears, ants, and salamanders. Surprisingly, the primary difference between human manufacturing and that of the rest of the natural world isn't the *amount* of stuff produced. Humans don't actually make as much stuff as the rest of Nature.

I find this to be a very interesting fact. If you put all of the bric-a-brac humankind makes in a year on a balance scale, and on the other side place the cornucopia made annually by the rest of the living world, the arm would tilt heavily toward Nature. Ounce for ounce, all of Nature's annual production of elephants, grasslands, bacteria, phytoplankton, octopuses, fungi, and its myriad other forms of life far outweighs our skyscrapers, automobiles, fidget spinners, and so on. Humans mine roughly 61.5 billion tonnes (metric tons) of material each year out of Earth's crust, from which we make everything. In comparison, Nature produces 210 billion tonnes of material each year *in cellulose alone*, over three times the scale of human manufacturing.

So, the important differences between the sustainability of humankind's and the rest of Nature's manufacturing processes aren't about the *amount* of stuff we each make. This is an important realization, especially because we often suggest to kids that sustainability is just a matter of conservation, that is, using less stuff. Reducing the amount of stuff we make and use *is* important, because it can slow humankind's negative effect on the planet. But conservation isn't a solution for finding a sustainable way of life by itself. It just buys us more time to do so.

This surprises some people, because it is common to hear that humankind isn't sustainable because there are simply too many of us on the planet. But this is misleading. Were we all to stand collectively on a bathroom scale, humankind's biomass would move the needle less than the other species living on this planet with us. The biomass of ants, for instance, likely exceeds that of humankind, and they have been living continuously on Earth for tens of millions of years. Ants are generally considered good for the planet.

The point is, it is not the number of humans, or the scale of what we make, that explains our sustainability problem. These are both important points to cover with your students, because they likely have the misconception that the scale of our production and the number of people on the planet are the fundamental drivers of humankind's negative environmental impact. They aren't.

There is a simple equation developed by Paul Ehrlich and his colleagues that really helps clarify the relationship among these factors:

$$I = P \times A \times T$$

where *I* stands for impact, as in negative environmental impact. It is equal to population, *P*, times affluence, *A* (i.e., consumption), times technology, *T*. You can see that increases in population or consumption exacerbate negative environmental impact. But even if you reduce population and consumption, detrimental technology is still going to cause negative environmental impact. Unless we can eliminate *T* (not likely), reductions in population or consumption only moderate the magnitude of our negative environmental impact; they don't eliminate it. They buy us time, but they don't get us to a sustainable world. Rather, the nature of the impact that technology has on the environment must change to become *positive*. That's the only way to create a world that thrives and endures, despite populations and levels of consumption that, if anything, are likely to continue growing. We'll circle back to these surprising points later on.

FIVE TO THRIVE

There are some truly fundamental ways in which Nature's approach to making stuff differs from our own. Considering these differences can be profoundly instructive, as well as interesting in their own right. This section takes up these differences one by one, in a logical, methodical sequence, using the framework of an LCA. These key differences in how Nature makes things can be summed up in one tidy graphic, which I call *Five to Thrive*. It consists of five elements Nature uses to generate and maintain this remarkably sustainable living world: mining without materials, power without pollution, benign by design, ingeniously effective, and infinitely useful. Teachers can use this as a framework to break sustainability down into logical pieces with their students and explore each principle in-depth through the associated lessons described below.

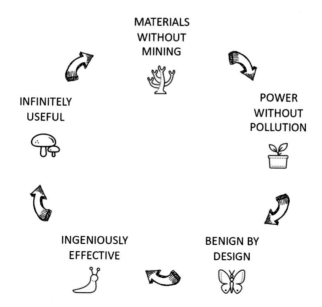

FIVE TO THRIVE: A framework for sustainability. By distilling a few key principles from how Nature thrives, engineers can learn from the rest of Nature how to design elements of a prosperous and enduring human-built world.

> **ACTIVITY: What Makes Nature Thrive?**
> Before presenting this framework outright to students, it's ideal if you begin this unit on sustainability by asking students to ponder: What makes Nature sustainable? What makes Nature thrive over time? Reflecting and writing on this question comprises an excellent homework assignment, where students can spend some time outdoors looking at things in Nature as they consider how to answer this question. Discussing the students' ideas afterward as a class is the perfect way to kick the unit off.

So, what does make Nature sustainable? What makes Nature thrive over time? You might want to take a break from reading at this point, go outside, and consider this question yourself.

Scientists looking at the fossil record don't all agree on exactly when Life on Earth began, but they do agree it began sometime around 4 billion years ago and has persisted continuously to the present day, even while suffering a handful of massive extinction events along the way. No matter how old one considers Life to be, it is clear that it has a sustainable operating system.

Any semiwild field, patch of forest, or full-fledged wilderness appears ably managed, despite not being managed at all. Vegetation grows abundantly, through its own powers, seemingly without inputs and certainly without the help of farmers. Organisms are born, live, and die, and in a matter of days their bodies disappear, as though these areas were fastidiously maintained by committed janitors. Life abounds, renews, and continues. Instead of chaos reigning over the area, it proceeds in a generally orderly way on an ongoing basis, without any apparent central command or control.

How does Nature do it? What makes Nature sustainable? More to the point, what are the most salient principles of Nature's evident thriving endurability, which engineers can draw inspiration from in our own pursuit to design a more sustainable human-built world? And how through education can we convey these vital, timeless ideas to young people? These are key educational challenges in tackling the subject of sustainability. The Five to Thrive framework can help address these challenges, as we'll see below.

Materials Without Mining

The first step to making anything is getting materials. For us humans, this is accomplished through the bulk extraction of physical materials from Earth's crust, to the tune of 68 billion tons per year. We keep our dozers and dump trucks busy! Mining for industrial starter materials seems like the most normal thing in the world (how else are you going to make things?) until one considers an overlooked fact: we are the *only* species to make things this way, the only one, out of millions of other species. The rest of Nature's first step to making things is strikingly different.

Nature makes every living thing—230 billion tons of blue whales, kangaroos, prairies, amoebas, dragonflies, fairy rings, boreal forests, and so on—*out of thin air*. You read that right: *air*. Nature's manufacturing processes begin with making primarily vegetation, out of which everything else in Nature is made. What is this vegetation composed of? All the world's grasslands and forests, and the ocean's phytoplankton, consist almost entirely of carbon dioxide (CO_2), extracted from the air. More than 90 percent of a solid tree comes from CO_2 (plants fix gaseous CO_2 into solid sugars and other woody substances), with another 7 percent coming from rain (H_2O), and the remainder, generally less than 1 percent, coming from the soil (N, P, K, Ca, etc.). If Nature can be said to mine anything at all from Earth's crust, it does so by sipping miniscule quantities of it. Nature doesn't bulk mine Earth. The vast majority of Nature's corpus is air.

Nature uses CO_2 molecules as the nucleus upon which to build other molecules. Plants fix fluid, gaseous carbon dioxide into solid sugars and other woody substances, such as all-important glucose. In the final analysis,

> **M**ore and more one comes to see that it is the everyday things which are interesting, important and intellectually difficult. . . . The materials which we use for everyday purposes influence our whole culture, economy and politics far more deeply than we are inclined to admit; this is, indeed, recognized by the archaeologists when they talk about the "stone age," the "bronze age" and the "iron age."
>
> –James Gordon,
> *The New Science of Strong Materials*

Northern California's grand forests of redwood trees are, essentially, magnificently crafted *compressed* CO_2. (Whereas atmospheric compounds are about 3 nanometers apart on average, the diameter of an entire glucose molecule is only a single nanometer wide.)

This is hard to square with our experience of air as an insubstantial substance. Much like fish, who presumably rarely notice the water that surrounds them, we humans forget we also live in a fluid. When the wind blows, or when we dangle our hand out the window while traveling in a car, we may briefly sense that air is, in fact, not "nothing." Indeed, our fluid medium is inconspicuously hefty. If you weighed the air extending above your head to the top of Earth's atmosphere, it would weigh in at a tonne (over two thousand pounds)—the mass of a (European) car. When a forest gets burned, virtually nothing but a small veneer of powdery ash remains on Earth's surface. Where did the forest go? It went back into the air from whence it came.

Add it up, and the total weight of Earth's atmosphere is a whopping 6 quadrillion tons—plenty of available raw material to make stuff out of. The airy carbon Nature spins into the world's vegetation then proceeds

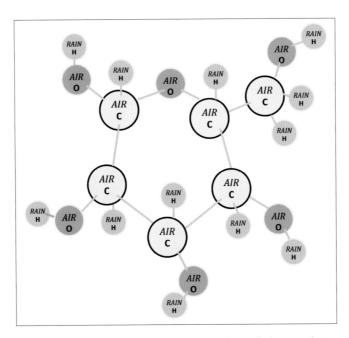

A MOLECULE OF GLUCOSE, a major product of photosynthesis, which is used by plants to create Nature's most abundant material (cellulose) and across the living world to fuel activity. Notice the origin of each atom in the molecule.

to nurture everything else, from munching herbivores through creeping carnivores to patient decomposers. The carbon that plants fix from the atmosphere rises up through the food chain like a fizzy drink up a straw. The carbon in us (about 18 percent of our body mass) isn't anything we fixed ourselves but comes completely from the atmosphere, via carbon first sequestered by plants or phytoplankton, transferred to our bodies when we eat salad, grass-eating cows, or plankton-eating sushi. Thus, the molecule most vilified by humankind today is the same one Nature uses to build its very existence.

Using What's Readily Available. Why does Nature choose to use CO_2 from the atmosphere as its principle building block? It's a fair question. The reason involves the unique combination of characteristics carbon enjoys as an atom, which make it a rich platform for developing the sophisticated chemical universe Life depends on. To begin with, acquiring carbon is literally a breeze: many other atoms are more prevalent on Earth, but carbon, when attached to superabundant oxygen, forms a gas at normal temperatures on our planet. Thus, it flows easily as a constituent of both the atmosphere and the ocean, making it readily available to any aspiring system of complex living chemistry. Types of atoms stuck immovably in Earth's crust, particularly those that don't dissolve in water, would never do. "The silicates which comprise the sandy deserts," wrote N. J. Berrill, in his eloquently fascinating 1958 book *You and the Universe,*

> *the feldspars of the mountains, the curbstones and headstones, all those irresistible natural objects that bruise and bury human flesh and hold it down, barely dissolve in water at all—which accounts for their bulky presence in the landscape and their virtual absence in water wherever we find it, whether in lake or ocean or the juices and tissues of living creatures. . . . Minerals that don't dissolve reach neither sea nor the salts in our bloods and, conversely, minerals which are rare in the earth, even if soluble, are rare in cabbages and kings as well.*

A Versatile and Gregarious Resource. Another prerequisite of an atom to be Life's building block is met by the fact that carbon can form multiple bonds with other atoms. Atoms limited in their potential attachments would never satisfy the expansive molecular diversity needed by living organisms. Carbon is rather uniquely suited to form bonds with itself (for a variety of reasons having to do with bond strengths and other factors), creating long molecules consisting of chains of interconnected carbon atoms (C–C–C– . . .).

Through the use of highly variable side groups, these chains of carbon atoms allow carbon to form molecules of sufficient complexity and distinctiveness, as well as significant size, giving these chemicals a nearly infinite repertoire of structural and behavioral possibilities. The paper this book is written on is made of cellulose, one of these very molecules. To date, over 9 million different carbon-containing chemical compounds are known. In contrast, there are but half a million inorganic (noncarbon) ones. Carbon, in sum, is versatile and gregarious. If Life had a dating profile, it's hard to imagine more accurate adjectives than these.

Using What's Reusable. We've zoomed in on carbon, to try to understand its role in Life's economy. Now let's zoom out briefly, too, to try to understand why its role in Life's economy also works with the planet's larger systems. The removal of atmospheric CO_2 by plants works as the foundation of Life because it is also manageable for the planet and can continue indefinitely. How can that be? Organisms sequester CO_2 in their tissues for a time, but when they decompose they release the molecule back into the atmosphere. So the resource is never depleted, just borrowed, like so many books from the library.

Self-Regulating Resource. Furthermore, the rate of sequestration is self-governed at the planetary scale. If the rate of CO_2 sequestration increases too quickly, the loss of CO_2 from the atmosphere has a cooling effect on the planet, slowing the rate of plant growth and allowing CO_2 in the atmosphere to build back up again. Conversely, if the rate of CO_2 sequestration decreases too much, the buildup of CO_2 in the atmosphere raises the planet's average temperature, and the rate of plant growth goes up accordingly, sequestering more CO_2. Hence, within certain tolerances, the rate of CO_2 sequestration is self-regulating, ensuring that the planet can continue growing vegetation at a nearly constant rate indefinitely. From a global resource perspective, CO_2 is the perfect molecule upon which to build a living world.

Unsustainable Use of Limited Resources. Bulk mining of Earth's surface to create physical products, our approach, is an utter anomaly across the millions of species we share this planet with. Why is that? The answer is partly just a question of supply. The surface of Earth is a highly limited resource. We have only so much surface area to go around. Any species that routinely maintains itself through bulk mining Earth's surface, in time, wouldn't have any surface left to live on. While modern humans have been around for some 200,000 to 300,000 years, most other species are far more ancient. Sharks are 450 million years old. Jellyfish are 550 million year old. Cyanobacteria have been on this planet for 2.8 billion years. If any of these species had made bulk mining of Earth's crust their primary means of production, there would no longer be an Earth's surface upon which to produce.

Taken to its logical extreme, mining Earth's surface for industrial raw materials is a technological dead end. But while long-term supply shortages are inevitable, near-term economic shortages of vital industrial resources are already

EXTRACTION ON A MASSIVE SCALE: Humans are the only species that bulk mine the Earth's crust for raw materials to make things.

relevant. In its mildest forms, shortages of industrial raw materials cause economic disturbances; in its worst forms, such shortages result in physical conflict. Meanwhile, day to day, mines are problematic in terms of their impact on water quality, soil contamination, loss of biological diversity, visual blight, and a host of other issues.

Why does this all matter? Because mining Earth's surface cannot continue indefinitely. If we're going to learn how to live on this planet over the long term, then we should consider examples of others who have already achieved it. And the industrial pattern we see when we look across Nature's many other species is that they construct their vast array of diverse materials largely by using CO_2 as a foundation.

MATERIAL ABUNDANCE: The airshed of the Los Angeles Basin provides the industrial feedstock for the production of plastics being made out of greenhouse gases.

Borrowing Reusable Resources from Nature. This may seem like a lesson with little applicability to the kinds of things we humans mine for, things like limestone to make concrete and petroleum to make plastic and fuel. But you might be surprised. Researchers and engineers inspired by Nature's ability to make materials out of thin air have been studying exactly how Nature achieves this bit of magic. They've been dutifully exploring whether we humans could emulate this practice, and lo and behold, they've been developing extraordinary, unprecedented manufacturing processes as a result.

Take plastic, for instance. To make it, we pump crude oil and natural gas from Earth's crust, four percent of the haul of which is transformed within the convoluted silvery pipes of oil refineries into the feedstock for crinkly grocery bags, slick nylon track suits, and glittery cell phone cases. It's a big job: 300 million tons of plastic get made each year out of the foul-smelling gases and black goop scooped and pumped from Earth's dark innards.

In 2003, Mark Herrema, the head of Newlight Technologies, Inc., wondered if humans could make all this plastic out of something less problematic. Worried about climate change, he wondered if we could make plastics out the same stuff trees make their own tissues out of: CO_2. The molecules comprising trees—the structural sugars and starches—are built on long chains of carbon atoms, after all, much like the petroleum-based plastics we make. Could we get the feedstocks for plastics from greenhouse gases, sucked out of the atmosphere, instead of petroleum pumped from the ground?

It took them a decade to work out the process, but Herrema and his colleagues discovered that they could. Newlight Technologies now makes thousands of pounds of plastic from atmospheric CO_2 annually, which they call AirCarbon. Moreover, their plastic costs less to produce than petroleum-based plastics. I've been to their factory in Costa Mesa, California. There is literally a pipe on top of the humble building, through which they collect the air from the Los Angeles Basin. That's their industrial feedstock and supply line. The air runs through a biocatalytic reactor, the heart of the company's technological innovation, and out the other end comes a plastic polymer they can process into nearly any kind of performance plastic desired, no petroleum required. They've made plastic for cell phone cases, furniture, and Dell computers.

When you hold a piece of Mark's plastic in your hand, it's a strange sensation: you're holding solid air. And you're holding greenhouse gases. Newlight Technology has recently signed deals with IKEA and other companies to replace *billions* of tons of oil-based plastics with AirCarbon. "Our hope," Mark explains, "is that AirCarbon starts a paradigm shift, where we start to view greenhouse gas emissions as a resource, a raw material that can be used to produce the highest quality, most cost-advantaged, most sustainable materials in the world."

The first time I heard about making stuff out of CO_2 was in reference to another material, cement. You may recall from Chapter 2 that Brent Constantz, a biologist now teaching at Stanford, figured out a way to make cement the way corals do: out of air. This may seem completely unintuitive and impossible, but corals actually make their bodies this way. The stony corals that make up the beautiful coral reefs of the ocean build their white exoskeletons by collecting carbon, oxygen, and calcium out of the surrounding seawater and, through a bit of relatively simple chemistry, using it to form molecules of hard calcium carbonate. As a graduate student, Brent was studying how organisms like corals make these biominerals when he began to wonder if humans could learn from the process to make their own industrial materials.

Humans make cement—the main adhesive component in concrete—not by precipitating the calcium carbonate molecule ($CaCO_3$) out of seawater like corals do but by finding deposits of calcium carbonate, otherwise known as limestone, in Earth's crust. We mine over 4.5 billion tons of limestone out of the earth every year. After locating a deposit, we blow the limestone up with dynamite and then transport the material to a cement factory, where we then cook the limestone at about 1500°C (2732°F), to transform the limestone into something that reacts with water (that way we can go down to the hardware store, pick up a bag of concrete, and mix it with water to make whatever shape we want). This cooking process drives CO_2 out of the material, where it enters the atmosphere. In fact, making cement accounts for about 7 percent of all the CO_2 humans release into the atmosphere each year, just to make this one single material.

What Brent did was to borrow the conceptual outline of the chemical process corals use to make cement. After all, it's the exact same material humans make, but it releases zero CO_2 into the atmosphere. Instead, corals pull absorbed CO_2 out of the surrounding seawater and use it to make the calcium carbonate molecule. Brent figured all he needed to try out the idea was a source of CO_2 and calcium. Brent's company, Calera, partnered with a coal-fired power plant in Moss Landing, California. They built an

CORALS AS AN INDUSTRIAL MANUFACTURING MODEL: Corals produce the same cementitious material we mine Earth's crust for, and they do it without mining a thing. They precipitate the calcium carbonate molecule directly out of seawater. Moreover, they do it at ambient temperatures, without releasing greenhouse gases. In fact, in manufacturing cement, corals clean the air, removing greenhouse gases and sequestering them in their hard skeletons.

apparatus that bubbled seawater and the gases leaving the power plant together and voila!, powdered limestone was the result! Tons of it, no cooking required. This cement sequestered CO_2 just like corals did in their exoskeletons. The cement, in other words, far from causing 7 percent of humankind's CO_2 emissions, was *carbon negative*. Making it scrubbed the air clean, and it required no quarries either. The process made materials without mining.

A year or two after I first heard about Calera, I had begun thinking that what we needed in education was a way to *show* students what was possible through Nature-inspired engineering. I didn't just want teachers to tell students about Calera's coral-inspired process for making cement, as great a story as it is. I wanted students to be able to *do* it, themselves. It was one thing to hear stories about sustainable technologies, but for students to really believe in them, I felt they needed to experience these technological processes themselves. It was a tall order in terms of curriculum development, to say the least. It would require coming up with an entirely original lesson plan. And it would work only if we could create a chemical process for making cement that was inspired both by corals and by Calera's process, which could be done in a typical high school chemistry lab, with safe, inexpensive, and readily available ingredients. That was my dream anyway.

Fortunately, I shared that dream with just the right person: Dona Boggs. Dona was a professor emeritus of physiology at Eastern Washington University when I met her, and very interested in Nature-inspired technological innovation. After explaining to her what I was hoping to do, she read a scientific paper about how corals are able to precipitate calcium carbonate out of seawater and then used some basic materials at home to see if she could do something similar. And it worked!

Dona and I then worked together to refine the process, and I wrote up the lesson plan, which I called "Concrete Without Quarries" and "Brainy Coral." The lab uses safe, inexpensive materials you can find at the grocery market and pet store. In fact, the process is so simple you don't even need a chemistry lab to do it. And most important, students get to see for themselves that, with a little help from Nature, we can completely revolutionize how we manufacture things like cement, one of the most important building materials of the modern world.

ACTIVITY: Making Cement Coral-Style

Since you're making calcium carbonate ($CaCO_3$) similar to the way corals do, this bit of chemical engineering requires only three reactants: a source of CO_2, a source of calcium, and a way to remove hydrogen atoms. In the ocean, corals increase the concentration of calcium ions and CO_2 from the surrounding seawater and expel any excess hydrogen ions that might "gum up the works" and slow down the reaction. (Specifically, the stony corals, order Scleractinia, collect calcium ions, Ca^{2+}, and carbonate ions, CO_3^{2-}, from seawater, and expel hydrogen ions, H^+ (i.e., protons), from the mixture, increasing the rate of calcium carbonate formation some 100 times over geological processes.) The result is the precipitation of calcium carbonate ($CaCO_3$), a mineral, from the seawater.

When you think about it, this is a magical-appearing process. You can show your students a glass of saltwater, and then drop a seashell into it. Would anyone ever believe you can create this seashell just out of that water that surrounds it? It's as unlikely and unintuitive a result as creating solid materials (like plastic) out of thin air, or pulling a rabbit out of a hat, but corals, mollusks, and many other aquatic creatures do it every day.

A ready source of CO_2 for the activity is dry ice, available from many grocery stores. But a more apt source—because we are demonstrating how CO_2, a greenhouse gas and pollutant, can be used to make something useful—can also easily be gathered from the tailpipe of a car (tailpipe emissions are roughly 15 percent CO_2). To gather it, use a Mylar balloon—regular latex balloons are semipermeable, and the gas will eventually escape. Gather it soon after turning on the engine—tailpipes get hot. Also make sure you don't inhale! This gas, then, is simply fed (via tubing) into the calcium solution. For this, you can use actual seawater, or a proxy for seawater available from any pet store that sells fish.

The final piece is to raise the pH of the calcium solution, in order to clear hydrogen ions from the reaction and keep the process humming. This is something corals do by expelling hydrogen atoms via a "proton pump," a complicated biological device that transports protons across biological membranes. For our purposes, we can remove hydrogen atoms and raise the pH of the calcium solution simply by adding something hydrogen ions crave, OH^-, which we can get from the base sodium hydroxide ($NaOH$).

You can buy sodium hydroxide from any chemical supplier, or simply go to the grocery store and buy something like Drain-O (household lye), which is the same stuff. (You want the clear, liquid stuff, so it mixes well and doesn't color the solution. Check the labels to make sure what you're getting is 100 percent sodium hydroxide, in liquid not gel form.) Use an eye dropper to add the base to the calcium solution before introducing the CO_2. Corals raise pH to about 9 or so, but any amount will accelerate and help maintain the reaction.

For reference, the reaction formula of the lab activity is as follows:

$$CO_2 + H_2O \rightarrow H_2CO_3$$

Add the base:

$$H_2CO_3 + NaOH \rightarrow NaHCO_3 + H_2O$$

$$NaHCO_3 + NaOH \rightarrow Na_2CO_3 + H_2O$$

This step needs to occur to allow

$$Na_2CO_3 + CaCl_2 \rightarrow CaCO_3 + 2NaCl.$$

MAKING CEMENT FROM CAR EXHAUST: These public school students are producing the raw material for making cement out of greenhouse gases, instead of by mining them from Earth's crust, by gathering car exhaust (top left) or using dry ice (top right), and bubbling the gas through seawater (bottom). The chemical engineering lab, inspired by corals, is simple and safe to do and uses inexpensive materials you can gather from your kitchen, grocery store, and pet store. In the process, students see that you don't have to mine the earth to acquire industrially important materials.

The reaction is silent, so to spice it up, I strongly recommend adding an aerator or foam bubbler to the end of the tubing where the CO_2 enters the calcium solution. This not only adds a soundtrack to the process but also speeds up the reaction by breaking the CO_2 into smaller bubbles with more exposed surface area.

Instantaneously students should see the calcium carbonate precipitate form in the solution, a whitish gossamer cloud that slowly begins to settle. When the reaction has gone on long enough and you have enough precipitate, drain the solution over a filter (a coffee filter will do) and let the material dry. When I sent some of this material to Calera, they used X-ray diffraction to confirm that the powder was 100 percent calcium carbonate.

You have just made solid powdered calcium carbonate, you can proudly announce to your students, *the same material we mine Earth for to make cement. And you made it using car exhaust!* Materials without mining—a revolutionary and sustainable manufacturing process, learned from our clever planet-mates, the corals.

ALTERNATIVE MANUFACTURING MODELS for industrial materials are everywhere we look. This marvelous yellow glass sponge (*Bolosoma* sp.) growing on the ocean floor is made completely of glass, which it precipitates out of the surrounding seawater at ambient temperatures.

Can humans produce industrial materials without mining them from Earth, like the rest of Nature does? You just provided your students with a concrete (pun intended!) example of exactly this. Having students experience the idea of materials without mining through their own tangible actions makes the reality of this possibility that much more believable and exciting. If the rest of Nature is any guide, a human society that can make its materials out of thin air is a species with a much better chance of living long and prosperously on Earth.

Cement is but one of many possible industrial materials that can be created this way, too. Plastics we've already discussed. You might have students research other materials made by organisms, which humans use in manufacturing, as well as the processes organisms use to produce them—this is the way Brent Constantz got started. Many species of marine sponges, for instance, create exoskeletons of silicon dioxide (glass). They precipitate the material out of seawater, whereas humans make the material by excavating quartzite sand from Earth's crust and then cooking it at high temperatures. The biological models are out there, and through activities such as these, you'll help create the next generation of aspiring material innovators that humankind desperately needs.

Power Without Pollution

The next step in our manufacturing process transforms the raw materials we mine from Earth into the refined materials of products, a step that requires the use of energy. The story of early humans being astonished by the power of lightning to set the African plains on fire, and then controlling that fire themselves, would be a thrilling history to know in detail. What we can infer, however, are largely the end points of this story and little in between.

What we do know is that, once humans acquired the ability to use fire, it has been our go-to source of energy for transforming materials ever since. Early hominids used fire hundreds of thousands of years ago to transform food in ways that made it easier to eat and to harden tools and weapons that made it easier to catch food in the first place. Later, fire was used to manufacture things like pigments (from wood and bone), glue (from bark), and pottery (from clay). The technological implications of this transformative new skill are why, when you see images of cavemen, they are so often depicted making fire.

Modern-Day Fire. What's less appreciated is how using fire for making things is not just a method from caveman times: it's exactly the same method we still rely on today for virtually everything we make. Instead of heating birch bark to produce glue for affixing spearheads to throwing sticks, we burn coal, oil, and gas to make the materials of modern life: concrete, steel, glass, and plastic. The materials we make have become much more varied and sophisticated, but the energy we use to make them is still caveman stuff. Eighty-seven percent of humankind's energy use comes from burning fossil fuels.

Scientists began warning of climate change due to CO_2 emissions from burning fossil fuels as early as 1965. Today, climate change has eclipsed all other global-scale human challenges for its array of negative impacts, which include ocean acidification, agricultural instability, exacerbated natural disasters, habitat destruction, and human impoverishment, migration, and violence. Nonetheless, the negative impacts of getting our energy from burning fossil fuels can still seem somewhat nebulous and ill-defined—it's not like getting hit by a bus, after all.

In fact, air pollution from burning coal *directly* kills over 13,000 people every year and results in 20,000 heart attacks, in the United States alone. Children raised near facilities that burn fossil fuel are at much higher risks for low birth weight, depressed IQ, asthma, attention deficit disorder, and other issues that will debilitate them for the rest of their lives. Mercury spewed from power plants burning coal has made as many as a third of

fish species unsafe for human consumption. Other changes to the ocean have resulted in the staggering loss of 40 percent of the world's phytoplankton since the 1950s, the basis of the entire ocean food chain.

These are not nebulous statistics—they are startling and frightening. Moreover, scientists have pointed out that global changes from greenhouse gas emissions can quickly become irreversibly catastrophic, from self-generating, "runaway" global warming—when, for example, the frozen peat soils of the northern hemisphere, which hold trillions of tons of the potent greenhouse gas methane, begin warming. Indeed, researchers have documented recent surges of methane coming from the Arctic. These facts are

FIRE is often thought of as caveman technology. What's less appreciated is that fire is still the dominant technology for making the things of modern life.

hard to receive. They may make you gasp, or they might just make you sigh. Either way, you should definitely care: the next gasp or sigh you take comes straight from phytoplankton, which produce 50–85 percent of the oxygen found in our atmosphere.

The point is that the impact of climate change is upon us and is in no way remote. How humans use energy for our various activities is profoundly consequential to our lives, to the lives of our children, and to the rest of Life on Earth. Hence, the pollutants entering the environment from burning fossil fuels have become *the* central issue in discourse about human sustainability.

Nature's Source of Energy. For a species hoping to learn how to live on Earth over the long term, Nature's approach to energy certainly deserves our attention. Even by our own economic measures, Nature's success is amply evident. To begin with, if gross domestic product were our measure, the natural world can't be beat for the amount of "product" that rolls off its assembly lines every day. Moreover, the natural world's production facilities are in their straight four billionth year. None of this enduring abundance is powered by a whiff of gasoline, drop of petroleum, or chunk of coal. And yet, the natural world uses far more energy than humankind. When you add up every charged cell phone, trip to the grocery store, and humming factory, world energy usage by people is about 18 terawatts per year, but the natural world uses more than *seven times* that amount of solar energy annually, in creating photosynthetic products alone.

The ways Nature has found to power itself don't destabilize the climate or pollute air and have never so much as suffered a brownout. That's why so many colleges, universities, companies, and government agencies have active programs in the research, development, and commercialization of Nature-inspired energy technologies (see the Additional Resources section at the end of this chapter).

Nature at Work. Possibly the best argument of all for ruminating on how Nature captures and uses energy is the sheer creative genius on display. The thorny lizard (*Moloch horridus*), for example, found in the arid scrublands and deserts of the Australian outback, can drink water out of the shallowest puddle: all it needs to do is step in it. The lizard's high-performance skin is designed with precision grooves and channels that capitalize on water's restless hydrogen bonds, drawing the cooling liquid up and over the outside of its body and then straight into its mouth—no

NATURE IS FULL OF INGENIOUS AND EFFECTIVE WAYS OF MAKING AND USING ENERGY. The desert-living thorny lizard (left) gets a drink just by finding damp soil and standing in it. Thanks to its clever skin, water flows uphill over its body and straight to its mouth, no effort required. Trees (right) power their chemistry and the movement of water through their tissues using the light of a star 93 million miles away.

pump necessary. A pine cone releases its seeds with scales that raise all by themselves, even if detached from the tree: contracting in dry weather with angled fibers, the scales lift themselves like garage doors, at just the right season for dispersal, no motor required.

Examples of the ingenious ways Nature does work are endless. Something that can fabricate a forest of 400-foot-tall redwood trees, all at ambient temperatures, powered by light from a star tens of millions of miles from Earth, is a virtuoso deserving of our attentive consideration, particularly as we grapple with how to run our economy without running ourselves into the ground.

Emulating Enzymes. Some of the most hopeful new energy technologies and innovations today are inspired by the natural world around us. Take enzymes, example. Chemical reactions in Nature run because of these specialized proteins, which bring reactants together and guide their interaction, speeding up chemical reactions by thousands or millions of times. Without enzymes, your hands literally wouldn't have the energy to hold up this book. In fact, without these clever shape-shifting molecules, your eyes wouldn't even have the spunk to slide across this row of letters, nor would your brain have the energy to understand them. Enzymes are used by creatures great and small to do the regular tasks of life, from giving a lion the gusto to pounce on a water buffalo to giving a bacterium the ability to digest the blood caused by the mess.

To achieve chemical reactions, humans generally substitute heat for enzymes: the motion created by adding thermal energy causes reactants to move around enough that they find one another—Nature creates chemical bonds through arranged marriage; humans throw a rave party. We wash laundry, for instance, by heating thermally voracious water, which when mixed with soap and clothes speeds reactions both chemically and mechanically. But laundry detergent companies have begun borrowing the idea of enzymes to design detergents that use natural and synthesized enzymes to augment their power to clean clothing stains and dirt. Using these detergents, clothing can be washed just as well at 60°F with the enzymes as at 90°F without them. At these cooler temperatures, in the United States alone, we could wash all our laundry without dumping 70,000 pounds of CO_2 into our atmosphere, equivalent to the annual electricity use of almost four million homes. We've barely scratched the surface of the energy we can save, simply by borrowing Nature's ingenious idea of enzyme-catalyzed chemistry.

As I write this, the 2018 Nobel Prize in Chemistry went to Dr. Frances Arnold, a chemical engineer who pioneered the development of enzymes by emulating something else from Nature: evolution. By repeatedly creating mutations in genes that produce enzymes and then selecting the most promising enzymes that result, a process she calls "directed evolution," Arnold has created enzymes that are even more efficient than their wild counterparts, in one case an extraordinary 256 times more efficient. The potential applications of this work are extremely hopeful. Arnold has been able to use this process, for instance, to improve the development of renewable biofuels produced by microbes.

Make Like a Fish. Nature's ideas have applicability at larger scales, too. Some of the most exciting developments in wind turbine technology come from Nature-inspired engineering. For example, turbine blades inspired by the shape of the flippers of humpback whales outperform traditional blades. Why? It has to do with the way humpback whales catch food. Though they're the size of school buses, humpbacks eat schools of prey composed of members as little as two inches long. To gather enough prey to maintain themselves, humpbacks fish using the same approach you or I would: they deploy nets.

Humpbacks cleverly make their nets out of strings of air bubbles. Swimming in collapsing spirals, humpbacks blow columns of bubbles in ever tighter nooses while encircling their prey. The whales then rocket upward, mouth agape, and gulp down the corralled prey all at once, securing the equivalent biomass of a giant fish dinner. All this turning in tight radii is achieved by the design of their flippers, whose leading edges uniquely sport large bumps, called *tubercles*.

When a similarly bumpy leading edge was tested on fan blades, they were a whopping 20 percent more efficient than straight-edged blades. Applying the whale-inspired tubercle shape on computer fans increases their efficiency by 12 percent or more. This is no small feat, given that just cooling down computers eats up some four percent of *all* electricity use worldwide.

And Stanford engineer John Dabiri has shown that, by arranging wind turbines in patterns inspired from schools of fish, positive interference from turbine turbulence can actually increase efficiencies of turbine arrays, by as much as ten times, a staggering amount. All of these innovations have come about in just the last few years, so we have likely only just begun discovering what Nature can teach us in the area of energy efficiency improvements.

Plant Power. Plants have probably inspired more dramatic innovations in energy than any other group of organisms. To gather hydrogen ions (protons), which they use to assemble larger molecules, plants cleave rainfall into its component parts, hydrogen and oxygen. The oxygen gets expelled—it's what you're breathing right now. For humans to do the same thing, we pass an electric current through water (i.e., hydrolysis).

Hydrogen makes a powerful, transportable fuel, which when run through a fuel cell can run a truck or car whose only effluent is water vapor. But when we make hydrogen using hydrolysis, we have to apply more energy to snap hydrogen and oxygen apart than we get out of the resulting hydrogen fuel. Not so with plants: they can do the same chemical magic using mere sunshine and enzymes. Engineers drawing inspiration from this ability of leaves have designed ever more economical "artificial leaves," similarly capable of producing hydrogen fuel out of water, sunshine, and metal catalysts—definitely a technology to watch.

Another talent of plants is turning CO_2 from the atmosphere into stored chemical fuel (e.g., glucose and starches). This ability has inspired engineers to try to do the same. The U.S. Navy has succeeded in converting seawater—with its dissolved CO_2 and hydrogen from the water—into *jet fuel*, literally, one of several successful and extraordinary efforts inspired by this "run-of-the-mill" plant ability.

Capturing Energy From Light. Of course, the most obvious Nature-inspired energy source, you might suppose, is solar energy. As far as we know, however, Edmond Becquerel (1820–1891), the French physicist who discovered the photovoltaic effect when he was nineteen years old, was not inspired by a plant's ability to

SCHOOL OF NATURE: Bio-inspired engineers have dramatically improved the performance of wind turbines by borrowing technological ideas from organisms like humpback whales, owls, and schools of fish.

create a flow of electrons from sunlight. The phenomenon of photosynthesis had been known at the time—Dutch scientist Jan Ingenhousz (1730–1799) had discovered it in the 1770s. Instead, Becquerel's influence appears to have come from the development of photography, which happened also to demonstrate the ability of sunlight to create changes in materials. (The observation that asphalt would harden in the sun inspired the French inventor Nicéphore Niépce (1765–1833) to make the first photograph.)

Solar energy is a mainstay of clean energy, but as currently designed, it has problematic environmental impacts of its own that are important to understand. To begin with, the quartzite sand that today's photovoltaic cells are made of must be mined and then cooked to create the electrical-grade silicon used in solar panels. Cooking quartzite sand at 2000°C results in a lot of CO_2 being released into the air, as you might imagine. It takes a solar panel an average of three years just to pay back that carbon debt, that is, to create enough clean electricity to compensate for the CO_2 released into the atmosphere during its manufacture (from then on, solar panels are vastly superior to burning coal to create electricity). There are significant toxic by-products from the manufacturing of silicon-based solar panels as well. And for this relatively new technology, the environmental impact of their disposal at the end of their lives is uncertain.

From the late 1950s to the early 1970s, what began as a way to study photosynthesis became the idea of developing a different kind of solar cell, based on the way plants capture sunlight and use it to create a flow of electrons. The idea of using dyes or other organic materials rather than electrical-grade silicon to capture light and produce free-flowing electrons is a big paradigm shift and had immediate material and performance implications. Freed of energy-intensive silicon, a solar cell could theoretically produce net clean energy from day 1 rather than after several years of operation. It might also be physically flexible. Exciting as these prospects were, however, the conversion efficiency of early devices (the amount of energy you get out of a solar cell in relation to the amount of sunlight reaching it) was relatively poor.

A pivotal innovation in the early 1990s mimicked another part of plant leaves, the thylakoid membrane, a high-surface-area structure within chloroplasts where reactions to light occur. Applied in the leaf-inspired solar cell, this structure is achieved using a three-dimensional mesh of nanometer-sized particles of titanium dioxide, which greatly increases the surface area across which photons striking the dye are converted into flowing electrons. For the first time, energy conversion efficiencies of plant-inspired solar cells approached ranges competitive with conventional silicon-based solar cells, particularly given the low production cost of leaf-inspired solar devices.

Plant-inspired solar cells, known as *dye-sensitized solar cells* (DSSCs), have a number of advantages over silicon-based solar cells, in addition to their production's low carbon footprint, low cost, and physical flexibility. For instance, like plants, DSSCs continue producing electricity in low light. Just like you can grow many types of plants in a windowless office under office lights, DSSCs can work under cloudy skies or indoors. One of my favorite applications of a DSSC is a small panel on a wireless computer keyboard. The keyboard doesn't need a battery (because the DSSC provides all the energy that it needs). Even in a black room with the lights off, the DSSC is able to produce electricity, simply from the light coming off the computer monitor next to it! Another neat aspect of DSSCs is that they can use various colors of dyes, even clear dyes, to capture photons. This allows DSSCs to be integrated into windows, which serve both to illuminate the inside of architectural spaces and to generate electricity at the same time.

Students can build a leaf-inspired solar cell themselves. The cell's materials are put together like a sandwich. The outside of the cell is any transparent, conductive material, generally a glass microscope slide or clear plastic coated in conducting indium tin oxide, which can be purchased or made yourself. If you use plastic, which can be recycled, the solar cell will be flexible, which adds to the cool factor.

The next layer is the dye, which absorbs photons of light. You can literally use chlorophyll from crushed leaves for this, or the juice from the skin of frozen blackberries, strawberries, or other fruit, which also work because they are designed to absorb light for other reasons (e.g., to protect the fruit and create color).

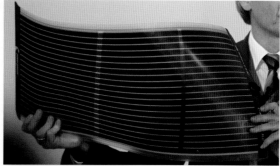

PHOTOSYNTHESIS-INSPIRED SOLAR CELLS: Because they don't need silicon, these solar cells are far less energy intensive to make. They can also be flexible, like a leaf (top). With the use of transparent or semitransparent dyes, they can be integrated with windows to transmit light while simultaneously generating electricity (bottom left). Teachers put together a dye-sensitized solar cell at a workshop (bottom right).

ACTIVITY: Making a Dye-Sensitized Solar Cell

An engaging way to have students get their hands into the engineering and innovation of Nature-inspired clean energy is to have them build their own dye-sensitized solar cell. This is surprisingly easy using juice and just a few other supplies, which you can collect yourself or acquire in pieces or through a kit (see the Additional Resources section at the end of the chapter).

The next layer is a paste of nanometer-sized titanium dioxide (TiO_2), a compound found in toothpaste, paint, even powdered doughnuts. The paste can be purchased or you can fabricate it yourself, which involves grinding with a mortar and pestle, which makes one feel delightfully like a nineteenth-century chemist. The titanium dioxide paste serves as a substrate for the dye, presenting a high surface area to the light source, analogous to the highly folded structure of the thylakoid membrane in the chloroplasts of leaves. This enables far more photons to interact with the dye, and because this is where the electrons first get dislodged by the incoming light to feed the electrical circuit, it's an important component of the system's overall efficiency.

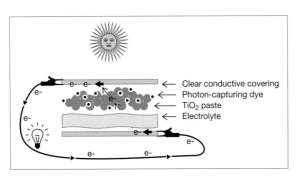

A DYE-SENSITIZED SOLAR CELL is a three-dimensional electrical circuit assembled like a sandwich. Dye is used to capture photons of sunlight, just like chlorophyll in a leaf. A nanosized mesh of titanium dioxide creates a large substrate for the dye, just like the high surface area of a leaf's heavily folded thylakoid membrane within its chloroplasts.

Now, add some electrolyte, such as iodide (to help keep the electrons in the circuit flowing) and sandwich it all together, and you're pretty much good to go. Attach alligator clips to the assembly, and students will immediately be able to see the volts of electricity on their voltmeter, even inside, just from the classroom lights above.

This activity is ripe for all sorts of STEM discussions about optical physics, electrical circuits, and materials, with no end of possibilities for experimentation and optimization in any part of the system.

Exploring the idea of power without pollution through a Nature-inspired approach has many advantages. To begin with, the approach fosters students' knowledge and appreciation of Nature's myriad abilities to do work, admirable for their ingenuity and for how they coexist peacefully and beneficially with the larger systems of which they're part. The college/career argument is strong as well, because so many postsecondary schools, companies, and government agencies have active initiatives in the research, development, and commercialization of Nature-inspired energy technologies. Slowly, it seems, we're catching on: a sustainable world can be just as productive and industrious as the current one, but like the rest of Nature, it must be powered by clean and enduring sources of energy.

Benign by Design

At one o'clock in the morning of December 3, 1984, in the Indian city of Bhopal, a storage container of methyl isocyanate gas at a manufacturing plant leaked the deadly chemical into the surrounding neighborhoods. Four thousand people died within minutes. Over the next weeks and years, some 20,000 people died from their injuries. Thousands more suffered permanent respiratory and other disabilities, in what has become known as one of the worst chemical accidents in history.

Methyl isocyanate isn't rare: humans still produce tons of it every year. An intermediate chemical produced in the manufacture of carbamate pesticides, methyl isocyanate is used to kill insects in agricultural fields. You have very possibly used these pesticides in your own garden or purchased fruits or vegetables grown with them. Methyl isocyanate is not unusual, as far as human-made toxins go—and it is but one of thousands humans make.

In just a few centuries, we humans have come to excel at manipulating matter at the chemical scale. Databases documenting the chemicals we synthesize or isolate now have an astonishing tens of millions of entries—an average of 4,000 new entries per day. The rate of new chemicals we are producing is increasing exponentially. At the same time, we understand very little about the toxicity of the chemicals we invent. For the vast majority, we have no toxicity information at all. Relatively complete toxicity data exist for only about 10 percent of the 5,000+ chemicals we use in very high volumes (i.e., 1 million pounds or more per year). For the other 90 percent, we know next to nothing.

And, as the Bhopal tragedy only too clearly shows, even knowledge of a chemical's toxicity doesn't prevent its production or ensure its effective control. Indeed, repeated evidence is clear that it is the "normal" use of chemicals that deserves our greatest scrutiny for the health of humankind. Doctors Philippe Grandjean of Harvard Medical School and Philip Landrigan of the Mount Sinai School of Medicine, after helping identify chemicals commonly found in food, clothing, furniture, and the environment that are associated with lowered IQ levels and increased attention deficit disorder and autism in children, put it this way: "Our very great concern is that children worldwide are being exposed to unrecognized toxic chemicals that are slowly eroding intelligence, disrupting behaviors, truncating future achievements and damaging societies." Nor are children the only people affected: as I write this, new research has shown that people worldwide now lose an average of over two and half years of their life spans because of toxins produced by human industry and dumped into the air.

Chemicals are a major component of how humans transform raw materials into everyday products, so they are just as important to consider as the mining and energy involved in manufacturing. And just as with acquiring raw materials for industry and transforming them with energy, it probably comes as no surprise that Nature can help us with the myriad complexities surrounding the production and management of toxins.

BOTH HUMANS AND THE REST OF NATURE MAKE TOXIC CHEMICALS, but there are some crucial differences. Nature's toxins generally serve a purpose, rather than being by-products; they're spatially limited, rather than spreading throughout the environment; they break down into harmless component parts, rather than persisting; and the rest of Nature has had time to come up with ways to cope with them.

Your students might be under the impression that humans are the only ones to make toxins, that "natural" inherently means nontoxic. That would be an oversimplification. It's important to clarify to students that Nature makes and uses toxic chemicals too. Think of spider venom, for instance. There are, nonetheless, real differences between humanity's use of toxins and that by the rest of Nature:

- To begin with, Nature's use of toxins generally serves a purpose (e.g., paralyzing an insect meal), while humankind's are frequently waste by-products from manufacturing processes.

- Second, Nature's toxins are also generally constrained spatially (e.g., a single unfortunate insect caught in a spider's web), rather than spreading throughout the environment.
- Third, Nature's toxins break down into nontoxic components, and quickly. Your own body produces hydrogen peroxide, for instance, a toxic compound, but it breaks down into harmless water and oxygen.
- Finally, the rest of the natural world has had time to come up with strategies for managing Nature's toxins, hydrogen peroxide being a case in point. In contrast, human-made toxins are new in the scheme of things. They frequently cause so much destruction because the rest of Nature hasn't had time to come up with ways to cope with the chemicals we make.

All of these differences can be explained partly by the fact that, for the rest of Nature, toxins are made within or near living tissues. There are no "industrial zones" in Nature, remote from Life, where toxins can be manufactured and stored without consequence. Life has thus had to develop toxic chemicals within very strict design criteria, to ensure that these chemicals, at the systemic level, are safe for living tissues. Organisms are occasionally harmed by toxins, wildlife species occasionally go extinct, and ecosystems occasionally disintegrate over evolutionary time, but the stronger pattern, by far, is a system in which, despite occasional counterexamples, the natural world generally operates in ways that are ultimately safe for all of the members that comprise it, from individual biological cells to entire ecological systems. Life, overall, thrives, despite some amount of disruption, offering a model for a species wishing to design a benign overall impact on the world around it.

Benign by design means consciously designing things to work with the rest of Nature, rather than against it, especially when it comes to the material of Life itself. Toxic chemicals are one way humans can disrupt the healthy functioning of Life on Earth, by being detrimental to living tissue. The activities described in Chapter 5 under "Indomitable Drops," which explores a Nature-inspired approach to creating hydrophobic surfaces using leaf-inspired texture, rather than chemical hydrophobic surfaces using toxic perfluorinated compounds, is one of many examples of the idea of benign by design. Here are some more examples of how we can use Nature's designs to improve well-being for ourselves and all of Life.

Benign Adhesives. If you are reading this in a house, or any structure built using plywood, you are likely surrounded by toxins right now. Formaldehyde, for example, is a compound in the adhesives used in plywood that can be given off as a gas. Today, we know that formaldehyde is a carcinogen, resulting in nasal or lung cancer, rates of which have been rising along with the increasing amount of time we all spend indoors. A few years ago, a new formaldehyde-free plywood entered the marketplace, called PureBond. Its thin sheets of alternating wood fiber stick together without a formaldehyde-based adhesive, thanks to studies of marine mussels.

NEW BIO-INSPIRED PLYWOOD made with mussel-inspired adhesives contains no toxic formaldehyde.

Dr. Kaichang Li, of the Department of Wood Science and Engineering at Oregon State University, first made the connection between plywood manufacturing and the abilities of these humble creatures that cling bravely to seashore rocks amidst pounding ocean waves. These indomitable snail relatives tether themselves to stone using an extraordinarily strong adhesive, which is free of formaldehyde (and also, miraculously, cures under water). Mimicking the chemistry of the proteins used on the ends of these tethers allowed scientists and engineers to make a strong formaldehyde-free adhesive for the very first time. The plywood resulting is competitive in both performance and cost, and you can now buy it at the largest home building supply store chains, build a house with them, and breathe easy at night.

Benign Footprints. Humans also cause disruptions to Life at larger scales. Consider the development of cities, which can degrade, separate, and gobble up the habitat of wildlife populations. It seems extraordinary to realize, but wolves used to howl across the island of Manhattan, before the now-ubiquitous sirens of ambulances and police cars. Bison used to roam throughout grasslands now paved over in Dallas. Grizzly bears used to romp across the Hollywood hills of Los Angeles. Urban sprawl has already wiped out millions of acres of habitat around the world, and it's set to get much worse, much faster. Growing exponentially, we now add about a quarter of a million people to the planet *every day*.

We are not the only species to reach such high population numbers, however. Certainly there are more ants on the planet than people. A single colony of ants may contain millions of individuals. And despite ants' small size, Earth's biomass of ants is higher than the biomass of humans. And yet, ants are generally considered good for the planet, aiding the biodiversity of Earth, not harming it. Could ants teach us something about living at such high numbers, yet in a less harmful, even beneficial way? Might ants teach us how to design our cities more benignly?

I developed this activity in part because of the extraordinary research and images made by Dr. Walter Tschinkel. Using plaster and liquid metal, Tschinkel, an ant researcher at Florida State University, has cast actual nests of several ant species, excavated them out of the ground, and has revealed to the world the outsized efforts of these diminutive architects. We are familiar with ant nests as small mounds of excavated dirt particles ringing a hole in the surface of the ground, but the real story extends underground, sometimes for twelve feet or more. After looking at several of these ant nest casts, a pattern quickly becomes evident: ants live in vertically oriented dwellings.

This may not be a particularly unexpected realization, but the reason for the ants' architectural habits is what's enlightening. Living at high densities across Earth, ants can't afford to design their cities to sprawl improvidently across the landscape.

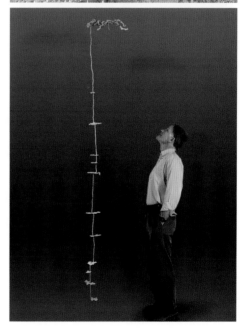

BUILDING VERTICALLY: Human cities spread over Earth's surface. By building vertically, ants also house millions, yet with a very small footprint on Earth's surface. Ants rely on the habitat of the surrounding earth for their sustenance.

ANT-INSPIRED ARCHITECTURE could completely transform the urban environment of many places, enabling high densities of people to live in immediate proximity with Nature, greatly minimizing the negative impacts of urban life.

After all, ant colonies rely on the surrounding landscape for sustenance. But they also rely on their large colonies to be able to find enough food to survive (as you'll see in Chapter 7). Ants' reliance on the surface of Earth for food yet inescapable condition of living in high densities is much like the situation facing modern humankind.

Ingeniously, ants have developed a pattern of vertical architecture that can house their immense colonies, in which the only disruption to Earth's surface is a tiny hole surrounded by a modest donut of dirt. A more humble indicator of genius is perhaps hard to imagine. As Nature-inspired engineers, we are sometimes like trackers, seeking the profound meaning of exceedingly subtle signs, and here, for sure, is one worth noticing.

Just imagine if humans more steadfastly utilized vertical architecture where we otherwise opt for urban sprawl. Humans are now capable of making extraordinary skyscrapers. The Burj Khalifa, you may recall from Chapter 3, is one of the tallest buildings in the world, about half a mile tall. It can house 5,000 people with a footprint of only two acres. Skyscrapers like that can contain not only housing and offices but also schools, hospitals, bowling alleys, movie theaters, grocery stores, and (vertical) agricultural systems.

What happens when we imagine applying ant-inspired urban planning to Mexico City, one of the densest concentrations of humankind in the world? I calculated that if people there lived in skyscrapers like the Burj Khalifa, all of the 84,000 people per square kilometer could be housed in just 16 buildings, on merely 32 acres. That would mean only 5 percent of each square kilometer in Mexico City would be required to house people. The rest of the landscape, 95 percent, would suddenly become available for agriculture, recreation, wildlife habitat, ecological services (like fresh air and water), and so forth.

ACTIVITY: What's Your Footprint?

Ant architecture presents an opportunity for your students to imagine what ant-inspired urban planning would do for their local area. Ask your students, if people in your area lived in skyscrapers the size of the Burj Khalifa, how many buildings would be needed to house everyone? (If your students live in a rural area, you could consider having them focus more on vertical agriculture rather than vertical housing, or have them use a nearby urban area as their case study.) How much area would this take up? How much more area would this make available for other uses, like recreation and wildlife habitat? What was the native habitat of your local area before development? What organisms lived there?

Have your students calculate the numbers, make a visual representation of what this kind of urban plan might look like, and discuss what the positive implications would be. You could have them present their work to the class, and even to the planning office of the local government. There are lots of spin-off benefits to this kind of urban planning, which you can explore with your students. People in urban areas spend an increasing amount of time in their cars, commuting. What happens to our quality of life when we live, work, shop, and go out to lunch all in the same building? Roads and pavement create major issues because of runoff, which can pollute waterways. How much pavement would this new urban plan avoid? How much might this improve issues related to runoff and water pollution?

Vertical living at this scale has many implications worth exploring. What might be the social issues of getting suburbanites to live in skyscrapers? What's possible through vertical agriculture? How can biophilia (see the next section) be used to design life and work in skyscrapers to be as fulfilling as possible? What are the physical and mental advantages of having large outdoor recreation and wilderness areas easily accessible to everyone?

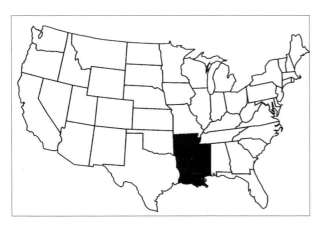

SMALLER FOOTPRINT: The amount of area that would be covered by human cities, if all of humankind lived at the density of Paris.

You can even do this activity with very young students. Using Legos, students can make models of two contrasting urban plans, sprawl and ant-inspired, and then calculate the amount of area the ant-inspired plan saves.

This kind of ant-inspired urban planning is extraordinarily powerful. At the density of Paris, all of humankind could actually live on an area covering no more than the states of Louisiana, Mississippi, and Alabama. Even given the additional footprint from agriculture, humanity could, in theory, largely live in a world as full of wilderness and wild animals as it was before we transitioned from hunter-gatherers to hedge fund managers. A wild world is possible, in other words, even in modern, populous times.

These are but a few examples of how consciously designing more benignly can improve living conditions not just for humans but for all Life on Earth. Humankind has a profound influence on the rest of the millions of species we share this planet with, through the construction of our products and places. But from the scale of chemicals up to the scale of cities, Nature also provides us with models for transforming modern human life into one exerting a much more benign influence on the planet, even at the high population densities that appear to be our destiny.

Ingeniously Effective

This aspect of Five to Thrive corresponds to the step in the product life cycle involving the actual operation or use of a product, rather than the extraction and manufacturing processes that bring products into being. Effectiveness is the aspect of a product that we tend to think about and focus on when we're not thinking about a product's sustainability.

The ideas in Nature that can inspire us to invent something new or improve a product's actual operation are literally endless. Several of these ideas have already been discussed in this book, for example, the development of airplanes inspired by birds, gecko-inspired materials enabling people to climb walls, and energy-efficient cell phone screens inspired by butterflies. Nature is full of ingenious ways to be effective at what it needs to do, a vast resource for us to draw upon in the development and optimization of our own technologies and designs. The point should be crystal clear by now that Nature can inspire extraordinary innovations in what technologies can do and how well they can do it.

What examples of Nature-inspired engineering are good to explore in a unit on sustainability, at this juncture in the product life cycle? Anything that bears on humankind's or the planet's well-being related to the actual operation (not manufacture) of products is your target. This might involve innovations that make products more energy efficient to use. For example, battery-wise electronic screens that use ambient sunlight, inspired by structural color in butterflies. Or, good examples here could involve innovations that relate to human health and safety. For instance, a medical supply company recently developed surgical thread with backward-facing projections, inspired by the pernicious quills of porcupines, that help hold the thread in place. This allows surgeons to tie sutures with one hand and speeds up operations for patients. Yet other innovations make products more reliable, like self-healing roads, inspired by the way living tissue like skin heals itself. Adding pockets of a liquid substance within the concrete or asphalt that hardens in contact with air allows it to repair cracks by itself—just imagine, pot holes that fix themselves!

Other good examples of Nature's ingenious effectiveness inspiring innovation in product performance include the tree-inspired fillet (Chapter 3), which can strengthen material notches and make things like bridges safer, and hydrophobic coatings inspired by the surface textures of superhydrophobic leaves (Chapter 5). Below are a few more examples of Nature-inspired engineering that can improve human-made things during their operation, in ways that help humankind thrive.

Antibiotics Without Resistance. Due to its washboard texture, the skin of sharks turns out to be difficult for bacteria to colonize. By mimicking this texture in a plastic film applied to surfaces in hospitals, bacteria can be controlled without relying on chemicals to kill them. This is huge, because destroying microbes with antibiotics inadvertently breeds resistant bacteria, which already kill hundreds of thousands of people every year. This shark-inspired, nonlethal approach to controlling microbes has worked for sharks for 450 million years. And now, thanks to people studying sharks, it's begun to work for us, too.

TEXTURES REDUCE BACTERIAL GROWTH. The spread of staph bacteria over three weeks on a textured surface inspired by shark skin (top, and top row) is much slower compared to a smooth control surface (bottom row). Slowing bacteria down through texture alone, without the use of any chemical biocides, reduces the development of resistance.

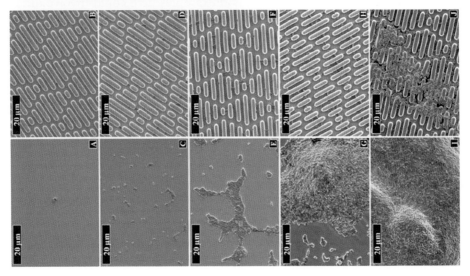

Storage of Biological Samples at Room Temperature. A microscopic animal known as a *tardigrade* (or water bear) can replace virtually all of the water in its cells with a special form of sugar, trehalose, and remain in a near-dead state for years before springing back to life unharmed with the next cloudburst. Inspired by the tardigrade's example, researchers are now able to use trehalose to preserve biological material without refrigeration, with profound implications for blood platelet availability, vaccine spoilage, and organ transplantation. One study found that, if Stanford University's 350 labs all stored their biological samples using the water-bear-inspired technology instead of refrigeration, the university would save $1.6 million and avoid emitting 1,800 tonnes of CO_2, every year.

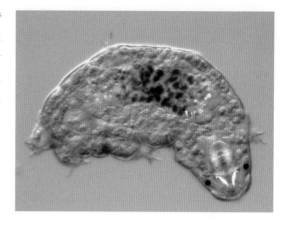

Biophilic Designs. Products are not the only type of thing Nature can help us improve. A concept with wide applicability to the improved performance of human-made *places* is biophilia. *Biophilia* (which means "love of Life") relates to the various positive inborn responses people have toward the living world. Our love of pets is an example of this phenomenon. Astronauts often become acutely aware of biophilia when they look through the windows of their spaceship back at Earth.

One of the fun things about biophilia is how it can help us understand some of our seemingly built-in yet arbitrary reactions or behaviors to the world around us, but which make sense in light of human safety and survival over evolutionary periods of time. From elementary school, I fondly recall reading a well-known book *Shane*, by Jack Schaefer, about a cowboy. One of the things that struck me was how Shane always chose a seat in the very corner of the saloon, so that he could see all the goings-on and nothing could surprise him from behind. A 2010 study by research psychologists Matthias Spörrle and Jennifer Stich at the University of Munich found that people tend to position their beds so that they are as far as possible from the bedroom door, while still being able to see it.

From a number of studies of people from different cultures, a pattern of human landscape preferences has emerged that includes things like a general appreciation for bodies of water and good vantage points for seeing the surrounding terrain. These widespread preferences are explained by evolutionary factors that would favor responses to landscapes that generally support human safety and well-being. Since these responses are inborn, engineers and designers can capitalize on them to improve the design of what we make. Architects, for instance, have applied these understandings about human psychology in a wide variety of ways that can improve our experience of the human-built world, an entire field known as *biophilic design*. Designing buildings to have lots of natural sunlight and fresh air is one simple example, which research has shown makes people happier, healthier, and more productive.

One of my favorite examples of biophilic design is applied to the art of sculpture. The concept is a robotic object placed in a high-traffic area of a building, such as the lobby, made of various materials and shaped in the basic form of a tree. Sensors placed outside the building record weather information such as wind speed and direction, which are radioed to the sculpture indoors. In response, the robotic tree, with its actuators and other mechanisms, bends and moves and sways, as though in direct contact with the weather outdoors. In this way, the inhabitants of a building are kept in implicit contact with the outdoors, through an artistic engineered object/system.

The following activity offers a range of ways to introduce students to biophilic design. For more information about Nature-inspired innovation in architecture and urban planning, see the Additional Resources section at the end of the chapter (and notes at the end of the book).

ACTIVITY: Exploring Biophilia

You can explore the fascinating topic of biophilic design with your students in a number of engaging ways. Because the subject is based on humans' emotional responses to their surroundings, it's a great topic to approach through self-observation and reflection. You can have students keep a journal in which they note their emotional reactions to physical environments and postulate the cause.

A more technical approach to the topic of biophilia is to have your students test their galvanic skin response to various landscape stimuli. Used in polygraph tests, galvanic skin response (a.k.a. electrodermal activity or electrical skin conductance) is a change in the electrical resistance of the skin in response to emotional stress. Electrical skin conductance is effected by sweat. It's not the most reliable tool for understanding *why* people react the way they do (one reason lie detector tests have their detractors), but for our purposes it can be a great tool.

To use skin conductance to explore biophilia, you need two things: contrasting physical environments as stimuli (the "treatments") and a way to measure skin conductance. You can use real physical environments for this (for example, a city park or schoolyard vs. an urban environment like a busy traffic intersection) or, much easier, videos of contrasting physical environments. One of my favorites is to compare students' responses to videos of the busy streets of Manhattan versus the green walking trails of Central Park, just a couple blocks away. To measure students' galvanic skin response, you can buy a detector or have students make their own (see the Additional Resources section at the end of this chapter).

Lastly, have students use their research on biophilia to design or redesign something. How would students design their ideal home, or a school, based on their research of biophilia? Biophilia is one of Nature's ingeniously effective ways of making us love and enjoy Life; biophilic design is a promising way we can get inspired by Nature to create beauty in the world and improve the human-built world's effect upon us.

In addition to the major categories of acquiring materials without mining, and manufacturing benignly and with clean energy, Nature is full of clever ways of doing things well. Several examples of Nature's ingeniously effective strategies for doing various things have been mentioned throughout the book and in this chapter's section. You can address this step in the product life cycle through hands-on activities, or, because you'll likely have already covered it elsewhere in the curriculum, elect just to make reference to these as examples of Nature's clever competence. The key point to make is that, by observing and understanding the genius of Nature, we can borrow these ideas to make our own world work better for all.

WHAT HUMAN-MADE ITEMS CAN BE DESIGNED TO BIODEGRADE? Much more than commonly appreciated. Cars used to be made of wood, as can modern-day versions (top). High-performance electric circuits that run cell phones (bottom) can be made from cellulose and biodegrade in soil.

Infinitely Useful

One of the fundamental reasons Nature's "products" are sustainable is because they biodegrade and then recycle an essentially infinite number of times *(i.e., "upcycle")*. This is a critical feature for things made on a finite planet. In order for human technologies to become sustainable, they will ultimately have to be designed to behave in this same manner.

Recycling: Turning Waste into Resource. Recycling is such a normal part of our culture that we sometimes don't examine the concept closely. The idea of recycling is both commonplace and radical. In its current form, we are complacent with submitting our plastic bottles and some other items to be recycled and are resigned to the fact that, at best, we can only reduce solid waste and slow its detrimental effects through limited recycling. But in its radical conception, the idea of recycling is far more enticing: what if *everything* we made was designed to be recycled? Could we pursue such a goal? Could we design such materials?

What if, when we were through using our products, we could just throw these reimagined plastic bottles, old cell phones, and what-not *on the ground*, to be biodegraded by decomposers back to their original, useful elemental components? This may be possible with many more materials and products than we realize. Engineers today have already succeeded in creating biodegradable electronics, wind turbines, and even cars.

While it's no secret we have a serious solid waste problem, we also don't worry about it much on a daily basis either. Indeed, humans go to great lengths to deal with this problem psychologically, through the old out-of-sight, out-of-mind approach. The only time I have to confront my garbage is during a short walk on Tuesday mornings from my garage to the curb, when I drag my garbage bin out for collection. It would be quite different if we had to live in close proximity with the garbage we made. The average person in the United States produces 4.4 pounds of garbage a day, 31 pounds in a week, 124 pounds in a month, or nearly 1,500 pounds in a year.

What if, instead of hauling it to the curb every week for its magical evaporation, we had to store our own garbage in our home? Then the absurdity of producing permanent waste might strike us. After all, we'd have to devote an entire room in our house to store it. In a few years, we'd have to move out altogether for lack of space. In the United States alone, we produce over 250 million tons of garbage a year.

Worldwide, humankind produces some 2.2 billion tonnes of solid waste annually. And somehow, it doesn't strike us as embarrassing that, to get rid of it, we actually just dig holes in the earth and bury it there, or dump it in the ocean, behaving as though that takes care of the problem.

When I was a Peace Corps Volunteer in the Philippines, one of the first field trips we took during our three-month in-country training was to visit a community living at the city dump. The families we met there lived in the dump full time, with shacks literally built on the topmost strata of garbage. While we were there meeting the mothers, fathers, and children of the community, a truck rumbled up and dumped a load of garbage. The youngsters immediately sprang into action, rushing toward the new refuse, picking through every piece of it hunting for anything of value. I watched them in a sort of paralysis; I had never seen anything like what I was witnessing. A child lifted something up and I suddenly saw tubing full of red blood and the familiar biohazard symbol displayed on some of the garbage. It was waste from the local hospital.

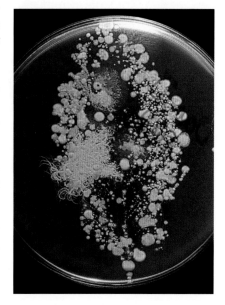

THE TIRELESS, INVISIBLE BIODEGRADERS FROM THE SURFACE OF A LEAF. Nature doesn't make anything for which there isn't an enzyme to break it back down, a valuable idea and challenge for engineers to figure out how to integrate into their work. Simply pressing a leaf into an agar plate can help students see that biodegradation is happening all around us and better appreciate its significance for creating a technologically sustainable world.

ACTIVITY: What Is "Waste"?

Why is making things that don't break down a problem? Set your students minds upon this question. From a sustainability perspective, nonrecyclable and nonbiodegradable waste is problematic in part because it means resources are constantly being removed from the planet's stock and literally thrown away. It's like drawing from a savings account but never putting any money back in.

Notice that the term *break down* doesn't just mean becoming smaller. Some plastics that manufacturer's claim will "decompose" simply break into smaller pieces of plastic. How is that different than biodegrading? Set your students' minds upon this question as well.

The question is really about designing products so that the resources used to make them can be reused again and again, indefinitely. Products that just get smaller by breaking apart are actually more problematic, because they become harder to find and use yet more easily travel to places where we don't want them to be.

These are surprisingly simple yet effective questions to get your students thinking, and can be expanded into reports and class presentations on numbers and types of recyclable or nonrecyclable materials in the classroom, school, or home.

The Breakdown on Litter. Another important question has to do with the concept of littering. Anti-littering campaigns are one of the most common solutions we hear about to address the issue of solid waste. I grew up with the classic, "Give a hoot, don't pollute." Littering is definitely a problem, but we need to back up for a moment and ask, when does littering actually *happen*? What I mean is, at what point does littering occur? When someone throws garbage on the ground?

That's what we typically think of as littering. But that's not really when littering happens. From a life cycle perspective, *littering happens when we make something that can't or won't be completely recycled or decomposed.* That's when the planet gets littered. Everything else is about where you put that garbage.

The polystyrene foam we make to ship things, for instance, doesn't

SHIPWRECK: We need impact-resistant shipping materials to last for just a few days or weeks. Ones made of polystyrene last thousands of years.

readily break down. We need it usually for only perhaps 3–5 business days, but it lasts for thousands of years. University students Eben Bayer and Gavin McIntyre created a polystyrene substitute by using agricultural waste, such as grass stalks, over which they grow mycelia, the thready root-like structures of fungus. The result is a biodegradable foam material they call MycoFoam, which they can grow into any shape needed. When you throw it away, it becomes food for your soil and garden. MycoFoam is now used to protect Dell computers and IKEA furniture during shipping.

ACTIVITY: Egg Drop With A Nature-Inspired Twist
A fun activity to do with students is to have them compare the impact resistance of polystyrene and MycoFoam, in a modified version of the classic egg drop activity. All you need is a block of each material about 6 inches square, enough to surround a raw egg. You can even have students grow their own fungal foam (see the Additional Resources section at the end of this chapter).

WELL PACKED: In a variation of the classic egg drop activity, teachers at a workshop prepare two containers for protecting an egg, one made of polystyrene and the other out of a fungi-based foam. They then compare the containers for impact resistance at different heights.

Have students hollow out enough space in each block of material to place a raw egg, insert the unfortunate object, and use rubber bands to secure each material around its respective passenger. Then work your way up to more and more perilous heights, checking the condition of each egg after every toss. I've seen eggs survive falls from upward of thirty feet in both types of packaging material, though the one in polystyrene began showing hairline fractures.

Now that students have seen for themselves how fungus-based foam works as well or better than polystyrene, top the experience off by having students crumble up the materials loosely into two different containers of soil. Water and monitor the soil for a time, and then check each for the presence of their respective foams. What do students see?

What other human-made materials could we substitute with materials that biodegrade? This could form the basis of a terrific design challenge, in which students try to identify natural materials that would work well as substitutes for otherwise nonbiodegradable human-made objects. Then students could craft prototypes using the biodegradable materials and test their performance, just as in the above activity.

Technological Recycling. In their path-breaking book *Cradle to Cradle*, authors Michael Braungart and William McDonough describe the two independent systems involved in recycling and reusing: one organic, where products are designed to biodegrade (used as raw materials by Nature), and the other technological, where nonorganic, human-made materials are designed to be recycled forever into new human-made products. The idea with technological recycling is that materials comprising every part of a cell phone, for instance, could be used again and again, with none of it ever going to a landfill.

Conceptually and aspirationally, this idea makes a lot of sense. There are some products, perhaps, that we can't or wouldn't want to make out of organic, biodegradable material (e.g., airplanes). But once the materials for these objects have been mined and refined, it would be ideal if we could continue recycling them 100 percent, reducing the need to mine or dispose of these materials ever again. A variety of things would need to be in place for such a system to actually work, however. Put the question to your students: how could a relatively closed-loop system for technological materials be established? What would it entail? Would it be effective? (Consider, for instance, the toxic leak disaster at Bhopal.) All great questions for your students to consider.

One feature of such a system would be the necessity of separating the various components comprising products into their constituent materials. Human-made products are frequently composites, made of completely different materials joined in various ways. This can present a problem for would-be recyclers, from whom separating a product's various components may be difficult or impossible. Think of the time and expense involved in separating a cell phone into its many different components, just so that its various materials could all be recycled.

Lilian van Daal, a designer from the Netherlands, became intrigued by the fact that plants create so many differently behaving structures out of essentially one material, cellulose. Think of a tree, with its brittle bark, solid trunk, flexible branches, and plastic-like leaves. You can really appreciate this fact by spending some time exploring a houseplant with your hands. Close your eyes and feel its different parts carefully. Some are stiff, some flexible, with various ranges in between. Different parts of the same plant have completely distinct textures, properties, and behaviors, even though it's composed of just a single material. Lilian, intrigued by

COMPLEX FUNCTIONALITY FROM SIMPLE MATE-RIALS. Like these various parts of a conifer tree (top), plants achieve a wide range of material behavior from limited source substances. Designer Lilian van Daal borrowed this idea to 3D-print furniture out of a single recyclable plastic (bottom). The structural requirements of different parts of the chair perform as needed by varying not the kinds of material used but the density of a single material, thereby cleverly eliminating the classic recycling problem of separability.

how plants achieve this spectrum of behaviors by varying the structure of essentially one material, realized that this ability of plants could help inspire solutions to a long-standing difficulty with recycling, in this case furniture.

Furniture is a classic case of a human-made object that is hard to recycle because its various materials are difficult to disassemble. The couch I'm sitting on right now is composed of a wooden frame, with metal springs, foam, cloth, and leather glued, stapled and sewn together into the functional shape of a couch. How are you going to disassemble that? You pretty much can't. Perhaps that's why couches are such a frequent and iconic object at city dumps.

But inspired by what plants can do with a single material, van Daal designed a chair out of a single type of recyclable plastic. To do so, she had to carefully vary the density of the material at strategic points to ensure the chair was comfortable to sit on yet with enough structural rigidity that it would support the weight of a human body. Using a 3D printer and her recyclable plastic, she simply printed the chair out.

This is far too valuable a planet to throw away, or to treat like a trash can. What logic is there in that? By studying the underlying designs of Nature's materials and the processes by which the rest of the natural world biodegrades and recycles them, we will be able to learn how to better create materials and products ourselves that do what we want and need our technologies to do. The important conviction is that a 100 percent recyclable world of varied and high-performance materials is possible. Indeed, Nature is already such a world, and an edifying example for us to follow.

> **ACTIVITY: Closing the Loop**
> We've covered a lot of territory in a relatively short period of time. Your students may have trouble holding it all together in their minds. Here is good synthesizing activity that helps wrap up this unit on sustainability and bring all this conceptual work down to Earth in a tidy way.

Write each Five to Thrive idea on its own piece of paper, along with a concise explanation of the principle:

MATERIALS WITHOUT MINING: Nature acquires raw materials for manufacturing without bulk extraction from Earth's surface.

POWER WITHOUT POLLUTION: Nature powers its manufacturing using clean and enduring sources of energy.

BENIGN BY DESIGN: Nature's processes and products are ultimately safe for living tissues, wildlife populations, and ecological systems.

INGENIOUSLY EFFECTIVE: Nature meets its functional requirements through ingenious and resilient designs that deploy resources efficiently.

INFINITELY USEFUL: Nature's manufactured materials recirculate fully, creating no waste, maintaining the planet's promise and productivity forever.

Lay the slips of paper with the principles on them in a circle, in the order of a product life cycle. Then place a different natural item (a leaf, a feather, a twig, a seed, etc.) next to each principle.

Have students look at the setup, quietly considering each object next to the corresponding principle: Does each natural item work with its respective principle? How or how not? After students have had a few minutes to think individually about the connection (or lack thereof) between each natural object and corresponding principle, have them discuss their thoughts together as a group.

After they've had a few minutes to do that, physically pick up and rotate each natural item one principle over, either clockwise or counterclockwise. Now each natural object is next to a different principle. Ask the students again, does each natural object work with its (new) corresponding principle? Have students consider the question individually again and then discuss as a group.

Now completely switch things out: replace all of the natural objects with human-made objects (a pen, a paperclip, a cell phone, etc). Once more, have students look at the setup and quietly consider each human-made item next to the corresponding principle: Does each object work with its corresponding principle? How or how not? Again have students consider these questions individually and then discuss as a group.

Some things about this exercise are predictable. The natural objects should work well with any Five to Thrive principle (that's why these principles emerged, after much thought, as essential aspects of a sustainable world). The exercise ideally won't seem predictable but, rather, will reinforce the ideas of the unit. And there may be some surprises too. For example, human objects next to the "ingeniously effective" principle very often fit nicely together. A paper clip is clever and functions well for its intended purpose (even if it doesn't work well with the other principles). Humans tend to be pretty ingenious themselves when it comes to making things, which is something we definitely should feel good about.

This exercise is a nice way to synthesize the main ideas of the unit and still yields some interesting new insights. You can also use this activity as a summative assessment of students' learning.

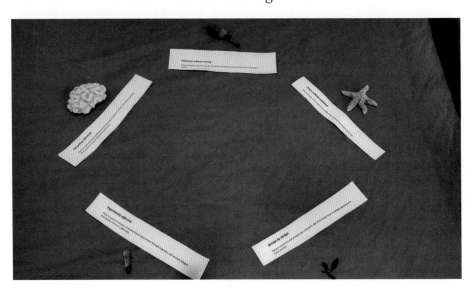

Five to Thrive is a simple framework for teaching sustainability through a Nature-inspired approach. Many who have been teaching sustainability to their students for years have adopted it, and many others who've never taught sustainability to their students have started by using it. Does it cover everything that sustainability entails? No, of course not. But it is a reasonably comprehensive approach to a challenging topic. And, as important, it's an accessible approach to this challenging topic for young people (and many adults alike). Ideally your students will use it themselves in their self-directed projects (see Chapter 8). A Nature-inspired approach to teaching sustainability can turn what seems like a heavy, complicated subject, one that many ignore or mangle, into a logical, engaging, solution-oriented, and optimistic exploration of issues and concerns vitally important to young people—and to the future of humankind.

Additional Resources

About sustainability in general

"Story of Stuff" video: https://www.youtube.com/watch?v=9Gorqroigq M&vl=en

See also the Story of Stuff Project's website: https://storyofstuff.org/

Hawken, P. 1993. *Ecology of commerce: How business can save the planet.* Weidenfeld and Nicolson.

McDonough, W., and Braungart, M. 2010. *Cradle to cradle: Remaking the way we make things.* North Point Press.

Benyus, J. M. 1997. *Biomimicry: Innovation inspired by nature.* Harper Perennial.

Curricula about sustainability

See the middle/high school version of *Engineering Inspired by Nature*, at The Center for Learning with Nature: www.LearningWithNature.org

See also the work of the Ellen MacArthur Foundation: https://www.ellen macarthurfoundation.org/

Materials Without Mining

Curricula

A lesson plan for the coral-inspired cement lab, called "Brainy Coral," can be found in the middle/high school version of the *Engineering Inspired by Nature* curriculum at The Center for Learning with Nature: www .LearningWithNature.org

Real-world examples of materials without mining

Plastics from CO_2: https://www.newlight.com/

Cement from CO_2: http://www.calera.com/; see also http://www.blue planet-ltd.com/

Energy from CO_2: https://www.energy.gov/articles/new-leaf-scientists -turn-carbon-dioxide-back-fuel

Power Without Pollution

Curricula and activities

A lesson plan for the dye-sensitized solar cell lab, called "Largesse of Leaves," can be found in the middle/high school version of the *Engineering Inspired by Nature* curriculum at The Center for Learning with Nature: www.LearningWithNature.org

Making your own conductive glass: http://www.teralab.co.uk/ Experiments/Conductive_Glass/Conductive_Glass_Page1.htm; see also https://simplifier.neocities.org/optglass.html

DIY enzyme detergent: https://www.reviewed.com/science/diy-make-your -own-enzymatic-laundry-detergent

Cameras that detect carbon dioxide
Modified Camera Exposes Alarming CO_2 Emissions. https://www.youtube .com/watch?v=iH-W3gYx8vY

Example initiatives in Nature-inspired energy technologies (colleges/universities, companies, government)
Umeå University's Solar Fuels Research Environment: https://solarfuels .eu/

Dr. Daniel Nocera's research at Harvard: https://chemistry.harvard.edu/ news/artificial-leaf-named-2017-breakthrough-technology

The Canadian Institute for Advanced Research on bio-inspired energy: https://www.cifar.ca/research/programs/bio-inspired-solar-energy

Center for Bio-inspired Energy Science: http://cbes.northwestern.edu/

Research Frontiers in Bio-inspired Energy: https://www.nap.edu/ catalog/13258/research-frontiers-in-bioinspired-energy-molecular-level -learning-from-natural

Benign by Design

Curricula
A lesson plan for ant-inspired urban planning, called "Ascendant Cities," can be found in the middle/high school version of the *Engineering Inspired by Nature* curriculum at The Center for Learning with Nature: www.LearningWithNature.org.

Hydrogen peroxide and liver enzymes: https://www.scientificamerican .com/article/bring-science-home-liver-helping-enzymes/

Biophilia
Wilson, E. O. 1992. *Biophilia*. Harvard University Press

Time lapses for any location: https://earthengine.google.org—try your local area, and fast-growing places like Las Vegas, Nevada

Galvanic skin response
Making the wires: http://www.instructables.com/id/Making-Galvanic -Skin-Response-Finger-Electrodes/

The app to download to a cell phone: https://play.google.com/store/ apps/details?id=com.GSR.gasperi

More info: http://www.extremenxt.com/blog/?page_id=168

POV (point of view) walk through Central Park: https://www.youtube.com/ watch?v=jGjr3FHtoko

POV walk through New York City: https://www.youtube.com/watch?v =5JrhTbcrD48

Designing Sustainable Places
The Genius of Place: https://synapse.bio/blog/ultimate-guide-to-genius -of-place

Infinitely Useful

Curricula
A lesson plan on waste and biodegradation, called "Counsel of Mycelium," can be found in the middle/high school version of the *Engineering Inspired by Nature* curriculum at The Center for Learning with Nature: www.LearningWithNature.org

Great examples of infinitely useful products and systems
MycoFoam: https://ecovativedesign.com/; see also the TED talk: https:// www.ted.com/talks/eben_bayer_are_mushrooms_the_new_plastic

Biodegradable electronics: https://www.nature.com/news/biodegradable -electronics-here-today-gone-tomorrow-1.11497; https://www.bbc.com/ news/health-19737125

Cardboard to Caviar project: https://www.ted.com/talks/michael_paw lyn_using_nature_s_genius_in_architecture?language=en

Other examples: https://www.greenbiz.com/blog/2011/02/16/companies -learn-close-loop

Information on industrial ecology
One can focus on the infinite usefulness of individual products but also on entire systems, referred to as *industrial ecology*.

Wikipedia entry on industrial ecology: https://en.wikipedia.org/wiki/ Industrial_ecology

Book on industrial ecology by the National Academies Press: https:// www.nap.edu/read/4982/chapter/4

GreenBiz article on the topic: https://www.greenbiz.com/article/we-will -close-loop-waste-2030

See also the Ellen MacArthur Foundation: https://www.ellenmacarthur foundation.org/circular-economy/concept

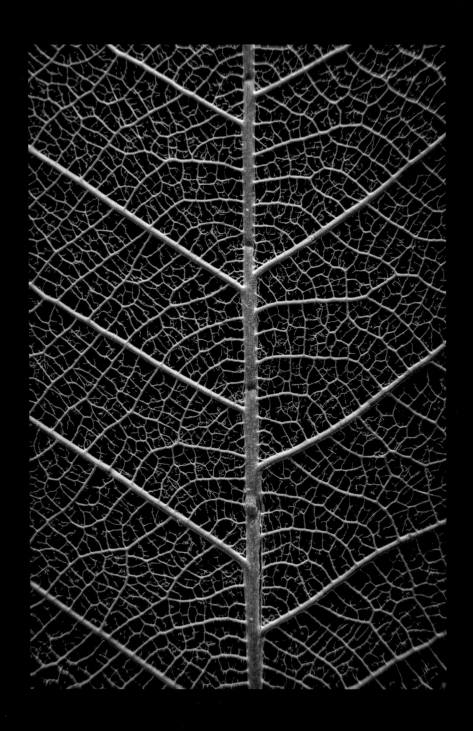

7

TAKEN BY SWARM: NATURE-INSPIRED COMPUTER SCIENCE

In the case of all things which have several parts and in which the totality is not, as it were, a mere heap, but the whole is something beside the parts.

–Aristotle, 350 B.C.E.

Like any broadly applicable technology, the advent of computers opened up a whole new horizon of engineering activity for humankind. Computers aren't actually just a technology; they're a technological *platform*: multitudes of technologies rest on its fundamentals, with new technologies springing up all the time. In part, computers are so useful because there are so many things to compute. How much steel is likely needed for this bridge to support the weight placed on it during rush hour twenty-five years from now? What week during the summer tends to have the best weather for an outdoor wedding in Missoula, Montana? Should my car change lanes now or not? Computing technology can be applied to any number of questions that humans ask.

Just think of all the things we use computers for today: predicting the weather, analyzing scientific data, keeping track of store inventories, online dating, word processing, games and entertainment, communicating with others, and on it goes. A few decades ago, I would have been writing this book on a typewriter, using something like Wite-Out to fix mi$takes the same way one paints a picket fence. Computers find mistakes automatically and correct them with a push of a button. Our cell phones are really pocket-sized computers, which make phone calls as but one function. From the Internet to the International Space Station, computers are integral to modern life, as are the engineers that create the computer hardware and programs that run them. Along with the invention and extension of computers into human life, computers have created an increasing demand for engineers who can design and build these contraptions, as well as software programmers who envision new things computers could do and then implement these behaviors through computer code.

Computer science is a major new branch of engineering and design, being taught today to people of nearly every age. And while computers may seem like the epitome of a technology created solely through human ingenuity, without help from Nature, and computer science may seem like the last subject you'd think of teaching with a Nature-inspired focus, you just might be surprised. That's because from their very origin to their most modern form, computers have been inspired by the living world.

The development of computers has a long, complicated history, but at the very beginning there was Claude Shannon. A bright child who grew up in a rural part of northern Michigan in the 1920s, by graduate school Shannon found himself at MIT, trying to figure out the subject for his master's thesis. He had just finished taking a class about deductive logic, the system first described by Aristotle that humans implicitly use whenever we reason. For example, when you look out the window and see the roads are icy, you know it might be dangerous to drive; you don't need to be on the roads that day to know this, because you know *all* icy roads can be dangerous to drive on. That's logical reasoning in action. Same thing in math: if you know A = B and B = C, then you also know A = C—logical reasoning again. So Shannon, fresh off this college course, had deductive logic spinning around in his brain at the time. Meanwhile, to help pay for school, Shannon ran a very large machine developed by his academic adviser, a giant calculating device that preceded digital computers. Eventually, Shannon became intrigued by the machine's relay switches, the magnetic armatures that predate today's silicon transistors and routed electrical current through the machine to make it run.

One day, Shannon had a startling thought: what if the relay switches could be arranged to mimic human logic?

In their essence, computers are machines that use logical operations to transform information. Press the caps button on your keyboard *and* the letter t: a capital T appears on your screen. Press one shift button down *or* the other, and then the number 5: you get a percent sign on the screen. Simple electrical circuits perform these instructions in your computer. Combine and multiply these circuits, and you start to be able to compute responses to very involved, complicated questions. But the individual circuits are elemental, and they are designed as models of how humans reason.

As Aristotle and later philosophers first described, humans think by combining small bits of information according to implicit rules in order to produce new conclusions. When Shannon wrote his master's thesis on using relay switches to model human thought, he shared an epiphany with the world that sparked the computer revolution. Widely considered the most influential master's thesis of all time, Shannon's work as a young graduate student in his twenties demonstrated for the first time that we could design machines that, in their mechanics, *reason*. That's why the electrical loops in the central processing unit (CPU) of your computer are known today as *logic* circuits. They carry out logical processes that are literally models of what happens in the human mind. At their core, the inspiration for computers is a biological phenomenon. Just as cars are the automation of horse-powered transport, and e-mail the automation of snail mail, computers are the automation of human logic. They are an abstraction of the process of human reasoning, carried out in silicon instead of gray matter.

Today, engineers of hardware and software continue to revolutionize computing through inspiration from the living world. Artificial intelligence, for example, has made leaps and bounds in recent years by creating computers that don't just carry out software programs but write their *own* programs, in order to solve challenges—in other words, they *learn*. Known as machine learning, deep learning, or other related terms, these new approaches to artificial intelligence all rely on computational software inspired by how neurons in our brains process information. These new software designs are known accordingly as *artificial neural networks*, and they are responsible for the recent extension of computers into everything from the way the stock market runs to the suggestions Google gives you when you type something into its search box. After being stymied for decades, the recent artificial intelligence explosion is due to computer scientists mimicking the information processing arrangement of neurons in the brain.

MODELING COLLECTIVE BEHAVIOR

One of the most interesting developments in Nature-inspired computing comes from computer scientists learning from the collective behavior of social insects, such as ants and bees. Social insects like bees solve very sticky problems every day, such as finding pollen and nectar in an ever-changing, prairie/forest/asphalt landscape.

The Rules of Foraging Ants

Or consider ants: how are they so good at finding the proverbial picnic basket? As entomologist Jean-Louis Deneubourg figured out, the key is how ants work *together*. In the late 1980s and early 1990s, people like Deneubourg were beginning to figure out that social insects like ants use their large numbers to advantage to solve very complex problems. In a classic experiment, Deneubourg and his colleagues placed a colony of Argentine ants (*Iridomyrmex humilis*) next to a food source, separated by a bridge. On the way to the food, the bridge branched into two options. Branch A was twice as long as branch B. Which branch did the ants use? Both, at first. But after a little while, nearly all the ants switched to using branch B, the shorter bridge to food, every time. How were they learning which way was the shortest path to the food?

How Ant Colonies Find Food. In the real world, where picnic baskets live, or a drop of honey, or a dying beetle, the challenge for ants is much more difficult, of course. Instead of two possibilities, there are infinite possible pathways they can theoretically take toward a food source. In addition, the ants have no prior knowledge about where a food source may be, no maps to get there, and no one to help them organize the colony into a search party to figure it all out. Ants would appear to be the least qualified things possible to find *anything*. And yet, there on your picnic blanket they appear, first one, then another, and soon half the colony.

Ant colonies perform the daily, miraculous feat of finding food, it turns out, using a small set of simple rules, in connection with information supplied by the individual ants themselves. Here's how it works:

- **STEP 1:** Ant scouts march out of the colony individually ("one by one," as the song goes), searching their surroundings for food, moving more or less randomly over the ground. As they travel, they deposit a chemical behind them (called a *pheromone*), leaving a scented trail.
- **STEP 2:** When an ant discovers food, it collects some of the bounty to bring back to the nest. How does this lottery winner find the nest again? Rather cleverly, the scout simply follows its own trail of pheromones back, like a spool of string. What's key here is that this trail of pheromones is now roughly *twice* as strong as before, because the ant first walked along it one way, and then along it back, depositing pheromones the entire time.
- **STEP 3:** The ants have a simple rule: if you find a trail of pheromones that's stronger than yours, *follow it*. So now the other scouts, walking more or less randomly along, that bump into this double-strength pheromone trail ditch their own single-strength trail to follow the new one. As a result, the other ants eventually discover the route to the food source too, without the first ant having to tell them where it is or say anything at all. Pheromone strength and a simple rule do all the communicating necessary.
- **STEP 4:** In their trips to and from the food source, ants travel the shorter pathway more often in the same amount of time, reinforcing the shorter pathway with pheromones at a faster rate than the longer pathways. By always choosing the more pungent trail, in time more ants follow the shorter pathway than the longer ones. Thus, the ants automatically converge on a more optimal pathway to food.

That's it. Its brilliance is its simplicity, yes, but also the way it uses the resources at hand: random searching, pheromone trails, scent strength, and many ants. That's the way an ant colony converges on a food source, without prior knowledge, a map of the area, or a leader to organize them. Not only that, but pheromones don't last on the ground very long: these

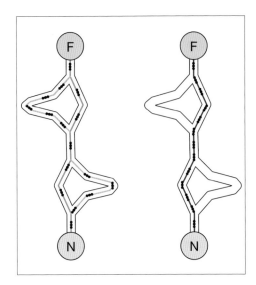

OPTIMIZING ANT TRAILS: Ants (left) have recently found food (F) and move along several trails carrying resources back to the nest (N). Ants travel the shorter pathway more often in the same amount of time; as its strength increases relative to the longer pathways, more and more ants choose the shorter pathway—a great example of optimization in Nature.

short chains of hydrocarbon molecules break apart and float away in minutes. This also helps shorter pathways to food (upon which pheromones of passing ants are more frequently applied) to smell stronger than longer pathways, speeding up the process of optimized travel. It's as though the pheromone trails were bridges that are constantly evaporating; only those that are continually reinforced by traffic remain for the rest of the colony to follow.

Ant-Inspired Robots. In the summer of 1990, an engineering graduate student named Marco Dorigo sat in the audience of a computer science conference in Bonn, Germany, listening with interest to entomologist Jean-Louis Deneubourg explain how ants forage successfully. Marco was intrigued. He had been working on programming robots to solve problems in the most optimal ways possible, and here was an example in Nature where individual "agents"—the ants—used an approach to solving a problem that was both optimal and novel. As far as Marco knew, "this was the first time anybody had made a connection between ant behavior and computer science." By learning from each other's information, and by following a simple set of clear rules for making decisions about that information (what computer scientists would call an *algorithm*), ants come up with reasonably good solutions to complicated problems, and do so efficiently. The path to food settled on by the ants might not be the very shortest path to food possible, but it is *one* of the shortest, and they discover it quickly. "So at that time," Marco explained, "I came back to my university in Italy, and I told my supervisor that I had seen this talk, and that it might be interesting to use it to find a good solution to optimization problems."

TABLE 7.1

Set of Simple Rules Governing Ant Foraging Behavior

Condition	Rule
Not carrying food, not on pheromone trail	Walk randomly, deposit pheromone
Find food	Return to nest with food following pheromone trail, laying down more pheromone
Not carrying food, find stronger pheromone trail	Follow stronger pheromone trail
Reach home without food	Turn around, follow strongest trail in opposite direction
Reach home with food	Deposit food, turn around, follow strongest trail in opposite direction

The kind of optimization problems Marco was thinking about were of immense complexity. The best known of these, the so-called traveling salesman problem, had bewitched computer scientists for a long time. The theoretical challenge for a traveling salesman is finding the most efficient route to take between various cities. That's easy to figure out when there aren't that many cities. Between New York City, Los Angeles, and Dallas, for example, there are only six possible routes to compare (these are easy to figure out in your head: NYC → LA → Dallas; NYC → Dallas → LA; LA → Dallas → NYC; LA → NYC → Dallas; Dallas → NYC → LA; and Dallas → LA → NYC).

As the number of cities increases, however, the possible combinations among them rises exponentially. Between New York City, Los Angeles, Dallas, Seattle, Louisville, Baltimore, and Detroit—just four more additional cities—the number of possible routes the traveling salesman has to consider rises from 6 to 5,040! Between only ten cities, there are over *3 million* routes possible! That's because when you add just one additional city, you introduce far more than just one additional possible route. One additional city changes the entire network of possible routes among the cities. So while the number of cities added increases *linearly* (i.e., arithmetically), the number of possible routes among them increases *exponentially* (linear growth is slow and steady; exponential growth gets faster and faster).

The reason computer scientists think about problems such as these, called *combinatorial problems*, is because they are very common in real life. Whether it's figuring out a bicycle lock, remembering a password, or determining an entire student body's schedules for classes on a college campus, combinatorial problems are all around us. And the hardest combinatorial problems are given to computers to figure out. For some of these problems, computers take days or weeks to come up with answers, if they can find a solution at all. If there were an entirely new way to program a computer to figure out complex combinatorial problems more efficiently, that would be big news.

"So I started to think about how to extend, to apply the ideas from the ants to more complex problems," Marco explained when I interviewed him, "and I came up with this algorithm." The algorithm, now a whole group of algorithms, is formally known collectively today as *ant colony optimization* algorithms. "It seemed like a crazy idea in the beginning," said Marco, yet when he started to test his algorithm on the traveling salesman problem, and some other combinatorial-type challenges, he got promising results. After tweaking the algorithm further, he got *very* promising results. The computer didn't always come up with the very best solution possible, but it came up with one of the best solutions—and in a fraction of the time. "That was the first algorithm that was solving difficult mathematical problems, taking an approach inspired by the ants."

Marco published his results, and soon hundreds of other engineers and computer scientists started adapting and applying ant colony optimization algorithms to all sorts of challenges, moving from theory to practice and from computers to real life. Today, a growing number of companies manage their delivery logistics, for example, using ant-inspired software. These logistics can be daunting. Taking just one company as an example, each day Barilla, the global pasta maker, has to plan out regional deliveries from central hubs to scores of local retailers, taking into consideration the delivery destinations, quantity of product, road conditions, available drivers, available trucks, and delivery windows, all variables in constant flux. Managers used to work out the best delivery plan they could with pen and paper, but the number of possible combinations of options is immense. The plans they produced were suboptimal at best, took a long time to figure out, and were quickly outdated once conditions changed. Now, a computer running an ant-inspired algorithm calculates optimal or near-optimal delivery plans just before the trucks head out. For over a thousand trucks, all going to different places, it takes the computer each morning all of *fifteen minutes* to make a solid plan.

Not only does the approach save companies time, but it also can save them money. Another company, Air Liquide, which delivers oxygen to hospitals, carbon dioxide to soda drink companies, and other products to over 15,000 customers in the United States, used ant-inspired computer programs to help with its delivery plans and to figure out which products to produce in which factories around the country. In Air Liquide's case, using the ant-inspired software has saved them some $20 million dollars *each year.*

How Digital Characters Evolve

Students may not care so much about delivery schedules and saving companies time and money, but fortunately, Nature-inspired computing has other kinds of applications young people do care about. For instance, when I was a kid, video games had what today is almost an endearing feature: they were clunky. Not only were the graphics flat and blocky, but the action was stiff and predictable. That's because the underlying software was based on a code that told the computer what to display in each of a few limited situations. Your tank was hit? Play the explosion sound and show the enlarging cloud of smoke. Quarterback sacked? Cue the roar of the crowd and referee's whistle. Every time, the action was canned, with just a few possible routines. Then, in the early 2000s, a graduate biology student named Torsten Reil started to think about the intersection of biology and computer science. In particular, he wondered what would happen if, instead of writing computer programs, he let them *evolve*—literally. "One thing that we found in our original research," says Torsten, "is how powerful evolution is as a system, as an algorithm, to create something that is very complex."

Torsten arrived at this conclusion after creating a digital character that could do something normally requiring a surprising amount of computer code: he created a character that walked on the screen. But Torsten accomplished this in a very unusual way. Instead of writing out the step-by-step instructions for the virtual figure to walk across the screen, he made one hundred random computer programs with incomplete instructions for digital figures to walk. Essentially, these programs were rudimentary "brains" to control the computerized figurines. Then, he wrote a *master* computer program that evaluated the results of these different computer programs.

Those programs that created digital figures relatively more successful

SLIME MOLDS are independent single-celled organisms that live much of the time on their own. However, they can also aggregate to accomplish certain things, such as form stalks to disperse spores for reproduction (top) or search an area for food (middle). By working together, aggregated slime molds are able to solve many kinds of challenges, such as finding the way through mazes (bottom) and determining the optimum network pattern for rail lines across the city of Tokyo.

at walking were "mated" with one another, producing new generations of computer programs ("offspring"), which were then evaluated and the most successful combined again, and again. "The algorithm then takes those individuals that do the best," explains Torsten, "and it allows them to create offspring." In other words, the "fittest" computer programs in each generation were recombined to produce the next generation of computer programs. Each subsequent computer program was a little different from its parent computer programs, but similar, just like what happens with evolution.

After running the program for just twenty generations, the results were shocking. "Eventually, miraculously, you actually end up with something that works . . . you don't know why it works and how it works. You look at that 'brain' and you have no idea actually what's going on, because evolution has optimized it automatically." The process resulted in an optimized computer program on its own, in other words, guided by the goal set for it: a digital character that could walk.

Then Torsten started changing the goal. What about a digital figure that could catch a football? Dodge bullets? Dance? The evolution-inspired master computer program could develop code capable of all these things. In time, the video games created by Torsten's company, NaturalMotion, were unlike anything the world had ever seen. Borrowing further from biology, Torsten crafted his digital figures with unprecedented anatomical and behavioral accuracy, not unlike Leonardo da Vinci's careful study of bone and muscle in cadavers in order to paint more lifelike figures than any painted before.

These startlingly lifelike computerized characters have since revolutionized video games. They not only look like and move as do real people, but they even *behave* like real people in real situations: they're unpredictable, and they learn. A quarterback that gets sacked during one play may throw the ball faster the next play, or protect an injured arm. "Even though we program these algorithms," says Torsten, "what actually then happens when it unfolds live, we don't control anymore, and things happen that we never expected, and it's quite a funny feeling that you create these algorithms, but then they do their own thing." That's the power of evolution, mimicked in the process of software creation.

In 2014, Zynga, one of the largest video gaming companies in the world, acquired NaturalMotion for over half a billion dollars.

Flocking Crowds

Not into video games? Nature-inspired computing has also changed the face of what we see on television and movie screens. Scenes involving large crowds, like battles or sporting events, used to require film companies to hire hundreds or thousands of extras, filming complicated scenes in enormous studio or outdoor environments. Understanding the behavior of swarming insects, flocks of birds, and fish schools has changed all that. Now, by programming virtual figures using simple rules about how to interact, scenes involving large crowds are done entirely with computers, without sacrificing realism.

One of the first movies to try this out was the *Lord of the Rings* films, directed by Peter Jackson. Jackson hired graphic designer and computer programmer Stephen Regelous, who had developed his computer programs by studying how groups behave in the natural world, such as flocks of birds. In one scene for Jackson, Regelous programmed virtual elves to react to hordes of attacking orcs by encircling them. But some of the elves couldn't "see" around the elves in front of them, so instead of creating a circle, they stood there shuffling—fidgeting, not knowing what to do until they finally saw the orcs and then got into position. "We didn't put in any rules for them to do that," says Regelous. "It was just an emergent property of the very simple rules that we'd given them to approach the Orcs in this horseshoe shape. But it looked really cool. It was like, wow, look what that guy's doing!"

Biologists are still unraveling the mystery of how bird flocks fly. One extraordinary example of this are flocks of European starlings (*Sturnus vulgaris*), known as *murmurations*. Even a few decades ago, it was understood that these large, seemingly coordinated groups of thousands of individual birds were able to fly in tight, ever-changing formation without colliding due to the use of simple rules. In 1986, computer programmer Craig Reynolds created the first computer program inspired by them.

"The whole point is," explains Regelous, "to model a crowd, you model lots of individuals, and the crowd is an emergent property of them reacting together." The approach has transformed how scenes of crowds are created in the motion picture industry. Since *Lord of the Rings*, Regelous's software has been used to create scenes in the Ben Stiller comedy *Night at the Museum*, in commercials for Honda, Verizon, and Budweiser, and much more.

Many, many other examples of Nature-inspired computer software abound. Ant-inspired software has been applied not just to company delivery schedules but to how phone and Internet signals are routed most efficiently through networks. Regelous's flock-inspired software has been used not just by the entertainment industry but by engineering firms to model how people evacuate from buildings (e.g., during a fire), to help architects redesign structures to facilitate safety. Marco Dorigo now programs robots that work together for rescue and space missions.

NATURE-INSPIRED COMPUTING IN EDUCATION

Nature-inspired computing is not just a fascinating, widespread, and impactful approach to modern software engineering—it's a great entry point for students to start learning about computer science. Nature-inspired computer science programs (sometimes called bio-inspired computing) now appear in colleges and universities across the United States and the world.

Moreover, the approach helps integrate the K-12 curricula (especially life science with the rest of STEM) and enables young people to learn about computer science not just in high school but starting in grade school if desired. And to top it off, Nature-inspired approaches enable kids of every background to learn computer science, whether a school can afford computers or not.

There are lots of resources online to explore Nature-inspired computing (see the Additional Resources section at the end of the chapter). But do you need computers to teach about computer science? To a large degree, no. Dr. Michael R. Fellows (Department of Informatics, University of Bergen, Norway) and Dr. Ian Parberry (Department of Computer Science and Engineering, University of North Texas, USA), put it best: "Computer science," they said, "is no more about computers than astronomy is about telescopes." In other words, computer science is a way of *thinking* and *creating*, foremost, *before* it is about anything to do with the tools of its trade. And that's the most important part, particularly when introducing the subject.

Introducing computer science by starting with coding on computers can even be a disservice to new students, distracting them from the science's essence, and perhaps ultimately limiting their creativity and interest in the subject. Vincent Van Gogh drew for years with pencil before

Computer science is no more about computers than astronomy is about telescopes.

–Michael Fellows
and Ian Parberry

he ever took up the colorful oil paint he is known for. In general, it is likely far more productive to tell poets to go take a walk outside then it is to thrust pen and paper in their hands. The extraordinary computer programmers described above, Dorigo, Reil, Regelous, and many others like them, all had their breakthroughs because they spent significant amounts of time exploring how the natural world works, before they brought any of it into the realm of computers.

So, while there are many online resources, curricula, and computer-based programs for exploring computer science, the activities presented here explore Nature-inspired computing without any computers at all.

To begin exploring how ants forage, one of my favorite activities is the simplest. It begins by finding a relatively clear patch of ground through which ants are occasionally passing. Using a piece of paper to represent that patch of ground, have students draw the trail they see an ant taking through the area. Every couple minutes or so, have students draw on their piece of paper any other trails they see ants taking, using a different color for each ant's trail.

Then, introduce a drop of sugary liquid on the patch of ground. Have students mark this spot with an X on their paper. Students continue drawing the pathways they see ants taking through the area, using a different color each time. A pattern should soon emerge: the number of pathways going to the sugary food should begin to increase, slowly at first and then more rapidly. In the end, students have observed and recorded on paper a time-lapse movie of ant colony optimization in action.

ACTIVITY: Smelling Your Way

Why not give your students the experience of trying to smell for themselves how ants discover and self-organize to exploit a resource? The activity here involves having students use their noses to try to follow a path, just like ants follow a trail of pheromones.

The setup is easy. Soak an untreated cotton string a few feet long in some pungent essential oil (peppermint oil works well). Blindfold your stu-

dents, and then lay out the string outdoors or on the classroom floor. For starters, I advise using a more or less straight line—gradual curves are fine, but nothing too extreme (it's easy to get thrown off the scent). Lead blindfolded students to one end of the string and have them kneel on their knees with their hands far apart, so that the beginning of the string lies somewhere between their two hands—have them grip some foam or wadded up T-shirts so they don't feel the string with their hands inadvertently. Now they're ready to get started. The goal is for them to use their nose to follow the string to the other end.

It's harder than you think, but not impossible: just the right level of challenge. Many students will find their way along a portion of the trail, if not get all the way to the end. But it isn't easy, and the going is slow. Consider videotaping students so they can see their relative progress later on. Students should come away feeling some sense of personal achievement and, at the same time, a much greater empathetic appreciation for the abilities ants have to follow smells so quickly and accurately.

Complex Behavior From Simple Rules

One of the most important ideas underpinning Nature-inspired computing is that things that look very complex in Nature often are actually the result of something quite simple. This is one of Nature's most admirable achievements. Solving complex problems using a simple set of rules is something beautiful to behold—it is one more way Nature exemplifies grace under pressure. Understanding that complex biological phenomena often emerge from simple rules of interaction was the key translation biologists made that allowed computer scientists to then take this insight and begin creating the tremendous Nature-inspired software unfolding today. So, having an activity that helps students begin to appreciate how Nature uses simple rules to achieve complex behavior and problem-solve is a great way to explore this pivotal idea.

ACTIVITY: Simple Rules Game

Of the many possibilities, one of my favorite Nature-inspired computing activities is easy to implement with nothing more than a classroom of students and an open area, like a parking lot, schoolyard, or gym. In this simple rules game, the challenge is for all the students in the class to arrange themselves equidistant from two other students in the classroom.

One way to do this is to appoint someone to carry this task out ("central command"). This student either physically moves all the other students into such an arrangement or tells students where to go. If you have enough time, you may want to try out such an approach, before doing it the way ants would solve this challenge.

How would ants solve this challenge? They would use simple rules of interaction, of course. To show students how to solve this challenge the way ants would, have each student mentally (privately) choose two other people in the class. Explain that when you say "go," each student needs to form a triangle with the two other students selected, such that they are equidistant from both of them (i.e., forming an equilateral triangle). The triangle can be of any size, but you must be an

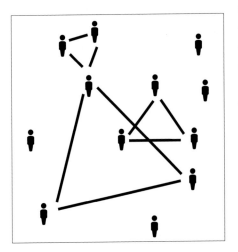

SCHEMATIC OF A SIMPLE RULES GAME: Each student finds a position equidistant from two previously chosen classmates.

equal distance from both students you've selected. Once you are in an equilateral triangle with them, you can stop moving. Oh, and there's no talking throughout the process (giggling is fine).

Then say "go" and enjoy the action as it unfolds. The group of students will start to move around silently, as each student, keeping an eye on the two other students selected, tries to settle into a stable arrangement and stop moving. Each student has likely selected *different* students to form a triangle with, however, so you can see that a stable arrangement isn't easy. The fun of the activity is that the mass of students will move about silently, and a stable arrangement will emerge from what seems, at first, like chaos. Getting there will entail a great deal of adjustment, but the adjustments happen "automatically" due to the simple rules each student is following.

It could take a few minutes, more with more students. But in the end, all of the students will in fact be arranged equidistant from two other students. It's a sophisticated pattern to impose on a group of people, but it can be achieved readily with each individual student simply operating from a simple rule, no "central command" required. In fact, using a central command to achieve the arrangement is generally a much more difficult and inefficient way to do it.

Brute Force Computing Versus Ant Colony Optimization

As Marco Dorigo discovered, ants can help humans learn how to solve complex combinatorial challenges in effective, expedient ways, whether the traveling salesman problem, scheduling deliveries, routing Internet signals efficiently through various servers, or any number of other situations where computing a large number of possibilities can consume a large amount of time and effort. A computer can, theoretically, figure out the very best solution to the traveling salesman problem or how to route an Internet signal the quickest way through which combination of available servers. But often there isn't time, or the expense for such computation isn't worth it. Trucks have to get going, signals have to be sent. Besides, conditions could change in the very next moment, and then the calculations have to start all over again.

In computer science, an exhaustive search through all the theoretical possibilities to find the best solution is known, aptly, as the *brute force approach* to computing solutions. In a brute force search, a computer literally goes through every single theoretical possibility, calculates the best one (e.g., quickest routing), and spits out the answer. The brute force approach for an ant to find food would mean it walks over every each inch of ground until it finds food, calculates the length of every possible route back to the nest, and finally chooses the very shortest path between nest and food. In the end, this will be the very shortest path possible, to be sure, but the food will be gone, or the ant will be dead from exhaustion, long before the very shortest theoretical path possible is calculated.

That's what's so handy about how ants actually solve this problem: they arrive at a *good enough* solution, and they figure it out *quickly*. Before we learned the nifty ways in which creatures like ants indeed solve complex problems, computer scientists largely took a brute force approach to computation.

ACTIVITY: Algorithm Search Game

A really neat activity to illustrate the value of something like ant colony optimization algorithms is one that compares and contrasts ant-inspired versus brute force-style searches for solutions. One could do this using a computer, of course. Another approach that does not require computers is to create a *physical* model comparing the two search approaches.

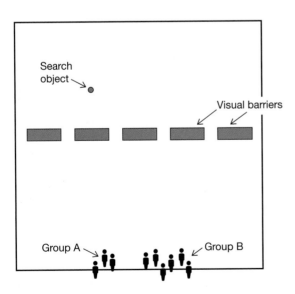

SETUP FOR THE ALGORITHM SEARCH GAME

In a large space in the schoolyard or gym, imagine a square or rectangle (about the size of a volleyball court). This area represents the computer's search space. Through the middle of the area, position five to seven equally spaced self-standing barriers that partially block the students' view of the far side of the space. Freestanding display boards (e.g., the kind restaurants put on sidewalks) work well, which you can fashion out of cardboard, or you can use chairs with blankets on them or similar barriers. The height of the barriers depends on the size of your area, but ideally students would be blocked from seeing 50–100 percent of the other half of the area from their position on the opposite baseline.

Before students arrive, place on the far side of the area a small object of some kind, like a penny, on the floor (the "search object"). What is important is that students cannot see the object from their starting position on the opposite baseline but can see it once they pass between the barriers bisecting the area.

Line students up along one baseline, separating them into two groups of students: group A (composed of three students) represents the brute force computational strategy, and group B represents the ant colony optimization strategy—the size of this group should equal the number of gaps between the self-standing barriers (i.e., if you have five barriers, group B would comprise six students). The other students are the timekeepers.

Explain to students that they are inside a computer right now, and they are part of the computer about to perform a search using two different methods, brute force and ant colony optimization. Since they perform the searches, they'll actually be able to see how these two search strategies compare. Explain that group A represents brute force search and group B represents ant colony optimization search. Neither group knows where the thing they are searching for is (that's why it's a *search*).

Give Group A, representing the brute force strategy, a measuring tape and explain that they will try to find the fastest route to the search object by measuring each pathway from the baseline to the search object on the other side, and back again, through each gap in the barriers bisecting the search space. To prove

INSPIRED BY SOCIAL INSECTS, robot designers like Marco Dorigo design robotic systems of individual units that communicate and work together. This gives robots unparalleled flexibility to accomplish a wide variety of tasks that would be difficult or impossible to achieve individually.

which pathway is the shortest, group A must measure each possible route (i.e., between each barrier) and compare the distances (even if they find the search object before they've measured each possible route). Three students should suffice for this group, one to do the searching and the other two to measure and record the distance traveled.

Group B, representing the ant-inspired algorithm, will try to find the fastest route to the search object by each member of group B walking each possible route—one student through each of the gaps—simultaneously, returning to their starting position on the baseline by the same outgoing route. So, when members of group B get to the search object through their individual pathway (i.e., one through each gap in the barriers), they will simply turn around and retrace their steps back to their starting point. Whoever returns first to the baseline has found the fastest path.

We need a way to ensure the speed at which each "algorithm" works is the same. To ensure the members of both group A and group B all walk at the same speed, you can use a metronome or regular sounding device (e.g., regular clapping by the other students, the timekeepers). To add still more standardization, you can tie each individual member of the groups' ankles together with the same length of rope (one stride length) and ask them to walk using this length stride.

Remind the class that group A represents the brute force search, and group B ant colony optimization. When everyone is clear about the directions, begin. Group A and group B should begin at the same time.

At least one member of group B should return to the baseline before group A has completed measuring all the possible pathways to the search object. As soon as the first member of Group B returns, the other members of Group B can stop searching. Record the time when the first member of group B returns, and record the time when group A has completed their measurements and determined which pathway is shortest. That difference in time helps emphasize the difference in time efficiency between brute-force and ant colony optimization search strategies.

So did both groups arrive at the same answer? What differences did the students notice between group A's and group B's strategies for search? You're looking for the following:

- Group B finished faster.
- Group A's analysis was linear, while group B's analysis was parallel, that is, with multiple "agents" going out at the same time.
- Unlike Group A, group B was not exhaustive in their search. Most members of group B don't even finish their searches, but group B was not trying to consider every possible solution, only to find a relatively fast solution.

These are just a few of the many ways you can begin introducing students to the idea of Nature-inspired computing. The first goal is to make students aware that the living world can inspire computer scientists in the first place, a trend in computer science of which many students are completely unaware. Humans may be the first species to type a word into a search box, but we are not the first to search. We may be the first species to develop computers, but we are not the first to compute. Computer science began its development in the mid-1900s; species like ants have been optimizing computation for 100 million years.

The numerous ways in which various phenomena in Nature carry out their many activities are often analogous to the same tasks humans need or want to do. And the solutions we find when we look at Nature are just as often completely different from what the human mind would ever think to imagine or design.

Additional Resources

Excellent, accessible book on swarm intelligence

Miller, P. 2010. *The smart swarm: How understanding flocks, schools, and colonies can make us better at communicating, decision making, and getting things done.* Avery.

Good articles about computer science education

Fellows, M. R., and Parberry, I. 1993. SIGACT trying to get children excited about CS. *Computing Research News, 5*(1), 7. http://archive.cra.org/CRN/issues/9301.pdf.

Computer Science and Mathematics in the Elementary Schools. http://larc.unt.edu/ian/research/cseducation/fellows1991.pdf

More about NaturalMotion's Nature-inspired video game development

TED Talk by Torsten Reil: https://www.ted.com/talks/torsten_reil_studies_biology_to_make_animation?language=en

Article on Torsten Reil's work: https://www.wired.com/2004/01/stuntbots/

Try out Clumsy Ninja! https://en.wikipedia.org/wiki/Clumsy_Ninja

See also: https://www.wired.com/2014/01/zynga-natural-motion/

Math connections

Bird flocking behavior: https://www.khanacademy.org/computer-programming/birds-flock-together/940061217

Ant foraging simulations

Simpler: http://www.searchamateur.com/Play-Free-Online-Games/3D-Ant-Farm-and-Pheromone-Simulation.htm

More complex: http://users.sussex.ac.uk/~tn41/antAppletFull/war/AntAppletFull.html

Very complex: https://www.mathworks.com/matlabcentral/fileexchange/52859-ant-colony-optimization-aco

Good websites about Nature-inspired algorithms

Algorithms in Nature: http://www.algorithmsinnature.org/

https://en.wikipedia.org/wiki/Natural_computing

8
STUDENTS INVENT!

Children are the research and development division of the human species.

–Alison Gopnik

Humans are natural engineers. We wonder how things work and tinker from an early age. It is profoundly meaningful that wooden blocks are still one of the most common toys in preschools and kindergartens around the world. With educational standards like the Next Generation Science Standards, it's easier than ever to continue fostering these instincts and abilities as young people mature. Including engineering as a thread that weaves throughout a child's education is a wonderful way to nurture a natural, rewarding, and vital ability in future generations.

The technological capacity of humankind is one of the wonders of our planet. Those of us whose lives have straddled a time period before and after a transformative technology has emerged perhaps have an easier time appreciating this fact than others—for me, I'm thinking of personal computers, digital word processing, and the Internet; My children's great grandmother remembers a time before penicillin, television, and microwave appliances.

The word *tinker* comes from the Middle English word *tinkere* (literally, "keepers of tin"). It refers to craftspeople who traveled the European countryside fixing tools and objects made of tin. The word is also onomatopoetic, mimicking the sound of repairers tapping on metal.

And our children will no doubt have extraordinary before-and-after stories about human technological innovation too. They may even be part of making those stories come true. That's what this chapter is all about.

What exactly are the outcomes of a Nature-inspired engineering education, and when do they occur? These may culminate in their fullest form toward the end of a lesson, unit, or curriculum, but they actually should be designed to happen all along the way. Nature-inspired engineering doesn't manifest only once students finally stand next to a design concept or prototype of their cricket-inspired Gigglyhopper X4000—it happens all along the journey to getting to that final project, and then beyond. That's because, more than what students design or make in the end, it's the *cognitive processes* that matter most: How do Nature-inspired engineers think? How do they see the world and make connections? These are the things that you, as their teacher, are building *in them*.

At the end of the day, the Gigglyhopper goes into the recycling bin or on a shelf at home; what stays with students, potentially for the rest of their lives, is what they learned: how to recognize innovation needs and opportunities, how to discover Nature's abilities, and how to draw inspiration from the natural world to design and engineer a better world. The observational, cognitive, and modeling abilities students demonstrate throughout an education in Nature-inspired engineering are the outcomes, and they are nurtured throughout the educational engagement, whether that lasts for an hour, a week, a semester, a year, or across K-12.

The preceding chapters have explored just a few of the engineering topics and activities with scads of opportunities for students to think and learn about design challenges, Nature's many talents, and how to draw inspiration from the latter to inform the former. This chapter zeros in on the design process of Nature-inspired engineers, to give you the theoretical and practical background needed to guide students through their own Nature-inspired engineering projects. So what is the process by which engineers actually learn from Nature to innovate?

ANALOGICAL THINKING

Foremost, Nature-inspired engineering is a cognitive process involving *analogical reasoning.* Analogies are simply when someone makes a connection between two different things, based on a similarity between them. For example, in the famous analogy from Shakespeare, "a rose by any other name would smell as sweet," Juliet compares a flower to her Romeo—Shakespeare makes an analogy between flowers and people, two very different things, and the basis of the comparison is *beauty.*

Analogies can be powerful, because literally and figuratively they enable us to see a connection between apples and oranges. They also can be transformative: making an analogy can suddenly reveal to us another way to understand the world we thought we knew. Instead of seeing just two different, unrelated things as we did before, what is unveiled to us is something new *in the way they're connected.* A fresh picture of things comes into focus, and the world can seem more united, interesting, and meaningful. With this new perspective, the old way of understanding things falls away, and new possibilities and options can appear.

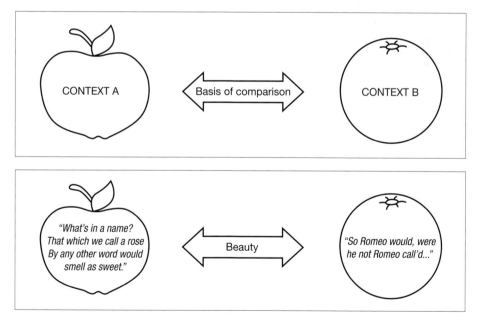

ANALOGIES connect two different things based on a similarity (top). In Shakespeare's *Romeo and Juliet*, Juliet makes an analogy between a rose and Romeo on the basis of beauty (bottom).

PART OF THE FUN OF NATURE-INSPIRED ENGINEERING is seeing the world in new ways. Nature-inspired engineers use analogies to make fruitful connections between the biological and technological worlds. Researchers, for example, have studied the way animals shed water to design more efficient laundry machines.

For example, the *Gaia principle*, formulated by chemist James Lovelock and microbiologist Lynn Margulis, makes an analogy between planet Earth and a self-regulating biological system, like a cell. The Gaia principle says that organisms modify Earth to be more conducive to Life, in a positive feedback loop. For instance, plants help regulate the amount of carbon dioxide in the atmosphere, helping keep Earth's temperature within a range conducive to plant growth. Thinking this way can completely transform how one perceives planet Earth and how Life works. Simply through analogy, we see Earth in a new way, not just a venue for Life but as alive itself.

Or consider a boy who grew up with a speech impediment and spent a lot of time alone in his room, listening with fascination to the bursts and snippets of broadcasts from his dad's CB radio and police scanner. Now a billionaire, Jack Dorsey invented an entirely new way for people to communicate by broadcasting their thoughts: Twitter. The analogy between Twitter and CB radios makes us appreciate something different from either Twitter or CB radio, namely, the idea of communication by general broadcasting.

Analogical thought is a common and effective cognitive practice used by all kinds of engineers. But in Nature-inspired engineering, analogies are particularly central, because here the engineering practice is driven specifically by connections made between the abilities of the natural world and the technological aspirations of humankind. How can we foster this kind of analogical thought in young people?

INDUCTIVE REASONING

To teach children the ability to use Nature-inspired engineering, first we need to know how professional engineers actually do it themselves. But how do we figure this out? There is no manual. All we have are a bunch of individual instances of people using Nature-inspired approaches to innovation. What we need to know is a generalizable process.

My kids sometimes play a card game called mao (or mau) that I find fascinating. No one is ever told the rules of the game, except that the object is to get rid of cards. Instead of being given the rules before playing, new players must observe players who already know how to play the game and participate as best they can. When new players make a mistake, they have to draw a card. When they do something correctly, they get to keep playing. I'm always amazed that it works, but it appears that in a relatively short period of time just about everyone learns through trial and error how to play the game correctly.

This is how we learn to do lots of things, actually. Our native language, for example, we learn primarily through observing how others use the language and by attempting to use the language correctly ourselves. No one usually sets out to show us how to sip from a glass, sled down a hill on a snowy day, or use a remote control device. These are classic examples of *inductive reasoning*, where people derive general rules and patterns from specific examples or experiences, often by watching others try something, or through trying it out ourselves (it's the opposite of *deductive reasoning*, where we first learn the general rules for something, and then apply them to specific instances). Series completion problems are based on inductive reasoning, such as this one:

$$2, 4, 6, 8, ?$$

Inductive reasoning seems perfect given our situation here, because we want to derive general guidelines for how to do Nature-inspired engineering, when all we have are individual examples of people using it. Perhaps we can use inductive reasoning to try to derive general principles for how to do Nature-inspired engineering, and then from this develop ways to teach it to children.

Calming of Birds

In 1981, Mr. Eiji Nakatsu, an engineer for the Japanese National Railways, was mentally exhausted by protracted labor union negotiations. To relax, he began watching birds. It became a hobby that would make him one of the best-known Nature-inspired engineers since Leonardo da Vinci and the Wright brothers (also bird-watching engineers).

Fast forward to 1989, and Eiji is the chief engineer of JR West, the corporate owner of the fastest train in the world, the bullet train. JR West wished to speed up its already rapid train, the front of which was literally rounded like a bullet. Eiji knew that the most difficult technical issue with speeding up the train, however, was noise. The train already traveled well over the speed of the fastest baseball pitch; now the company wanted to push the train to travel *twice* that speed! But the company was already receiving complaints about the train's noise from residents up and down the lines. Eiji was expected to figure out how to quiet the train, and quiet the complaints.

During this time, Eiji went to hear a presentation titled "Wild Bird Flight and Aircraft" by aeronautical engineer Seiichi Yajima at the Osaka branch of the Nippon Wild Bird Society. It was there that he learned from Seiichi about owls' remarkable ability to fly silently, and how they do so. Inspired by the birds' abilities, Eiji went back to his team and led efforts to redesign a critical piece of the train's hardware: the pantograph. A major source of turbulence-induced noise, the

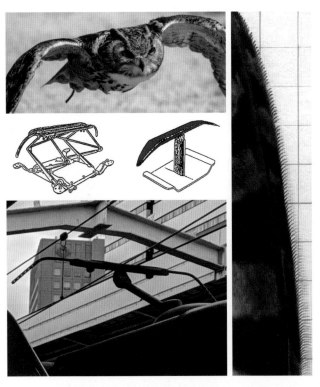

SERRATIONS on owls' flight feathers (right) break airflow into small vortices, reducing noise produced during flight. Engineer Eiji Nakatsu borrowed this idea and the shape of owl wings (left, top) to change the traditional pantograph design (left, middle and bottom) and reduce the noise caused by the bullet train.

pantograph connects the train to the electrical lines above. Eiji's concept was to redesign the pantograph to be shaped like that of a soaring bird.

Humans cannot hear the flight of most owls, nor, crucially, can the owls' prey. Normally, we can hear birds soar by because the air passing over their wings creates turbulence, which we hear as a low *whoosh* (or *fffff*). Owls, uniquely, have tiny serrations along the forward and aft parts of their primary flight feathers. This doesn't eliminate the wings' turbulence, but it does cut it up into smaller vortices, too small for us to hear. Eiji borrowed this idea and placed tiny projections on his pantograph to mimic the owls' serrated feathers. He also redesigned the round post supporting the pantograph based on the more elongated cross-sectional shape of bonito fish (a tuna relative). The idea worked exceptionally well, all but eliminating noise from the pantograph!

These things helped greatly, though they didn't eliminate the noise completely. The bullet train also suffered from noise when it exited tunnels, which created a large sonic boom. Air inside tunnels didn't flow smoothly around the train but instead piled up on its front end, like snow on a plow. It then released explosively at the tunnel's exit, just as an inflated balloon suddenly pops on a pin. Eiji again thought of a bird that copes with something similar. Kingfishers dive into water in order to catch fish. Fish feel the smallest disturbance and flee, so kingfishers have to be able to enter the water smoothly.

Eiji surmised that if the train's front end were redesigned to be shaped more like the bill of a kingfisher, which creates little splash when entering water, the air would flow smoothly over the train in tunnels, reducing the build-up of air

DIFFERENT TRAIN MODELS were shot through tunnels to assess the effect of train shape on noise (top). The quietest shape converged in shape with that of a kingfisher's beak (bottom, shown with Eiji Nakatsu).

pressure. Models of trains with different front-end shapes were tested in the lab, and the quietest model indeed turned out to be one with a wedge-like front end, much like a kingfisher's beak. The train's front end was redesigned accordingly, and the sonic boom was eliminated. Though Eiji didn't directly study kingfishers to inform the design of the train (as he had with owls), the fact that the front end of the quietest train model converged on the geometry of a kingfisher's beak greatly validated Eiji's belief that Nature can be a powerful source of engineering solutions.

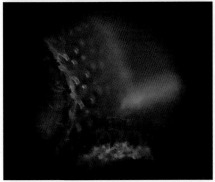

A BUR PLANT, the inspiration for perhaps the best-known example of Nature-inspired engineering, the hook-and-loop fastener.

Hooked on Nature

Perhaps one of the most famous Nature-inspired engineering examples is the story of Velcro. George de Mestral, a Swiss electrical engineer, came up with the hook-and-loop fastener after taking a hunting trip in 1941, where he examined the seeds stuck to the fur of his dog, Milka. Perhaps you've pulled similar seeds off your pant legs after hiking, too. Intrigued by their perniciousness, George studied the seeds closely and discovered the seed coat had hooks projecting from it in all directions, which effectively snagged the fur of a passing animal to hitch a ride. George spent years perfecting the hook-and-loop fastener made famous under the Velcro brand, which he first patented in 1955.

What can we learn from these classic examples of Nature-inspired innovation? A lot. Remember, Nature-inspired engineering involves analogical insight and reasoning, which there's plenty of here. Eiji recognized analogies between how owls fly and kingfishers dive and the movement of his train through the air and tunnels. George de Mestral recognized analogies between cocklebur seeds and fasteners that humans want. We'll return to analogies in a little bit.

RECOGNIZING CHALLENGES AND OPPORTUNITIES

One thing that stands out in these stories is that both Eiji Nakatsu and George de Mestral already had a *challenge in mind* before they found its solution in Nature. For Eiji, he explicitly was given the task of quieting the bullet train. For George de Mestral, just shortly before his trip his wife had asked him to help with a zipper that was stuck. Implicitly, then, de Mestral had troublesome zippers on his mind as he first observed and then examined the bur seeds stuck in his dog's fur. This leads us straight to our first key insight into the process of Nature-inspired engineering.

> **F**irst of all it is to have a problem consciousness.
>
> *–Eiji Nakatsu*

To retell the joke, an engineer, a holy man, and a criminal are each sentenced to death by guillotine. The holy man is brought out first. He asks the guards to allow him to lie in the guillotine face up, so that "I might face toward God at my final moment." The guards allow it and place his head through the slot. The executioner pulls the lever and the blade drops. Lo and behold, the blade gets stuck just inches shy of the holy man's neck. This is regarded as so extraordinary, the guards let the holy man go free. Next comes the criminal, who says, "Geez, it worked for that guy! Put me in face up too." The guards allow it, pull the lever, and again the blade stops just inches from the criminal's neck. The overjoyed criminal is given a pardon and set free. Next comes the engineer. "Can you please put me in face up too?" the engineer asks. The guards agree once more and place the engineer in the contraption, face up. The executioner grabs hold of the lever, but just before he can pull it, the engineer pipes up: "Oh, you know what? I think I see where the problem is."

Engineers, first and foremost, are alert to the many design challenges and opportunities around us to make the world better. They notice when a door creaks, when shoes on a shoe rack could be organized more efficiently, and when the world is putting too much carbon dioxide into the atmosphere. Most engineers, another classic joke goes, are so introverted they'll only stare at their own shoes; then there is the rare extroverted engineer, who will stare at *another* person's shoes. Cute joke, but the truth is, successful engineering is characterized by being *outward facing*. That is, engineers whose work improves peoples' lives observe and interact with people and information to know *what* to engineer, as well as how to design what they make.

In that sense, engineering is a kind of technical exercise in empathy. Engineers from MIT working on improving the design of low-cost prosthetic legs, for instance, traveled to India to interview amputees and observed how they use their prosthetics in real time. This approach even has its own name, *responsive design*, though really all effective engineering is implicitly if not explicitly responsive.

Famous stories of responsive design are everywhere, from the demand and subsequent development of the disposable diaper to the upside down, squeeze-type plastic ketchup bottle. When the best-selling Toyota RAV4 SUV was first launched in the United States, it didn't have any cup holders. The U.S. distributors knew this was a mortal design flaw. When Toyota's chief engineer visited the United States, the distributor driving him around in a RAV4 stopped by a local convenience store and bought his guest a cup of coffee. He gave it to the chief engineer, who was delighted with the quintessential American-style gift. Then the distributor got back in the RAV4 to continue driving. He didn't have to say a thing. One drive in another person's shoes, so to speak, was all it took for Toyota to correct the design for U.S. markets.

Many engineering and design companies now even have social scientists on staff to help hone in on what people need and want and how they expect things to function. Huzaifah Khaled did his own social science: during his many hours commuting on trains to classes as a law student, he got to know some of the homeless people in the stations and on the streets. "I essentially developed a very deep understanding of their needs," Huzaifah explained, and he realized that the locations and hours of homeless shelters could make it difficult for homeless people to plan their movements or hold down a job. So he developed vending machines designed to give homeless people much more convenient access to necessities like water, toothbrushes, fresh fruit, and even books. He now runs a nonprofit that installs and stocks them.

Developing a capacity to spot design challenges and opportunities is fundamental to engineering and engineering education. The Next Generation Science Standards enshrines this in its performance expectations across K-12:

GRADES K–2: "Ask questions, make observations, and gather information about a situation people want to change to define a simple problem."
GRADES 3–5: "Define a simple design problem reflecting a need or a want."
GRADES 6–8: "Define the criteria and constraints of a design problem."
GRADES 9–12: "Analyze a major global challenge."

As important, a focus on building this capacity makes the world more interesting, and students more active and empathetic participants in it. Just like political awareness makes one more likely to vote, a "problem consciousness" makes one more likely to identify problems, sympathize with the needs of others, and work toward solutions.

Architect Bill McDonough quips in his excellent TED talk that it took humans 5,000 years to put wheels on luggage. It's not that it wasn't a problem before people thought of it; luggage is heavy, and it would have been easier if luggage had had wheels during those several millennia! But it was just an inconvenience to be suffered; it wasn't recognized as *fixable*.

Some people react to problems like annoyances and try to ignore or avoid them; engineers react to problems like challenges, literally like they are *being challenged*, and rise up to solve them. That's the switch in attitude and awareness. Heavy luggage is both a problem and an opportunity. This is an important point: when we speak of design challenges, we shouldn't forget that engineers also demonstrate a capacity to spot design opportunities. In fact, engineers tend to see problems *as* opportunities.

Necessity isn't always the mother of invention; sometimes opportunity is as well. The line between challenge and opportunity can be thin. Very often, innovation can be more about opportunity than problem. Richard Belanger, the inventor of the sippy cup, filled notebooks with inventive ideas like fog-proof bathroom mirrors and haircutting machines before settling on making a spill-proof cup. Yes, he decided to focus on the problem during a time when his own child frustratingly spilled everything, but he was already actively looking for a way to apply his inventive skills.

Before Reed Hastings and Marc Randolph cofounded Netflix, they were in a commuting group to jobs that were soon disappearing because their employer had been acquired by a larger company. During their final commutes together, they explored their next move with questions like "What's the criteria for something that is going to be successful?" and "What's a trend that we could leverage?" They didn't even *have* a problem (other than impending unemployment); they were just trying to discern the "next big thing." The point is, anything that engineers can do to make the world a better place is what we want to give our students the ability to start recognizing themselves.

ACTIVITY: Challenges and Opportunities Journal

How can you encourage students to become more aware of the design challenges and opportunities around us? One great place to start is to try to become more aware of the design challenges and opportunities around yourself, and then reflect on that process. What do you wish worked better at work? At home? The other day there was no ice cream left in the freezer . . . wish there was a way to be alerted when important food items are getting low! What if dishwashers were designed *as* cabinets, so one never had to put the clean dishes away? What if an entire refrigerator was designed to be horizontal instead of vertical, and mounted at eye-level like a cabinet, so you never had to squat to find things in it? What is actually helpful and good to give to homeless people? How can you best introduce a new idea at work so that your coworkers will be more likely to embrace it? How could you make it easier to get up in the wintertime when mornings are so dark? How do you hear the dreamy sounds of rain and thunder at night but not have to worry about things on the windowsill getting wet?

Challenges and opportunities are everywhere. They flow through our minds all the time, and we let them pass by like the breeze. But with a little intentionality, we can stop and recognize them passing through our fleeting consciousness, pick them out of the flow, and give ourselves the chance to notice, ponder, and address them more substantially.

A simple and effective technique to use for this purpose is to have students keep a journal of the design challenges and opportunities they notice. Since these often strike us in fleeting ways, a journal can help students capture their ephemeral thoughts and observations whenever they have them,

DEVELOPING A CAPACITY TO SPOT DESIGN CHALLENGES AND OPPORTUNITIES is fundamental to engineering and engineering education. A poorly designed water fountain damages the floor (top left). A simple, playful park bench brings people and Nature closer together (top right). A snowed-in house presents an opportunity to the creative occupants (bottom).

especially outside the classroom. Have students start the journal early on: if you are exploring engineering for a week, a month, or a semester, have students begin keeping their journal of design challenges and opportunities from the very beginning, so they can fill it up with observations and thoughts. Give them assignments to write down one each day or at least three per week. Have them share what they write down with the rest of the class. The point is to get students in the habit of noticing design challenges and opportunities. In some people noticing design challenges and opportunities is a predisposition; in others it has to be learned. But we all have the ability.

We can also learn to notice patterns hidden in things we encounter every day. I listen to a lot of music with my kids, and I like to point out patterns sometimes in the music. I've noticed a lot of songs I like use seventh notes: a note seven notes away from a root note on a scale. They can give a slower song a bluesy feel, but in a faster song they can add a sense of urgency (car horns often contain seventh notes). The staccato chords of the Beatles "Taxman" are chords with seventh notes; 50 Cent sings nearly the entire "In Da Club" song at a seventh interval, as does Bob Dylan in "Subterranean Homesick Blues." When they listen to these songs, my kids heard the seventh notes, in the sense that they experience them, but they weren't conscious of it—they didn't necessarily pick them out from the rest of the song. But once I'd pointed out seventh notes enough times, my kids could recognize them in other songs.

Experiencing design challenges and opportunities by *personally* noticing them, through journals or otherwise, is crucial to developing a predisposition for this. The personal observation aspect is vital because otherwise all you may get is students regurgitating challenges they hear about from their parents or the news, such as those concerning international conflicts or climate change. This doesn't give students a chance to develop their own abilities at identifying challenges or opportunities.

ACTIVITY: Design Challenges

That said, there is also a time and place for simply providing students with design challenges to try to solve. Giving students preset design challenges lets them focus on other aspects of Nature-inspired engineering. Having students redesign their cities based on ant-inspired architecture (Chapter 6), for instance, gives them the opportunity to dive deeply into comparisons and contrasts with urban sprawl. By simply giving students the challenge of urban sprawl and ants as the inspiring biological model, you shift the focus to the implications of ant-inspired urban planning.

Another reason to give students preset challenges is to give them lots of practice discovering inspiring natural models (see also the next section). Crafting design challenges for students to work on using Nature-inspired approaches is limited only by your imagination. Here are a few examples:

- *Don't blow it.* An airplane company has asked you to design a bomb-resistant cargo hold for its new line of airplanes.
- *Green is the new roof.* Your local city has asked you to provide specific design guidelines for implementing green roofs across the entire city, taking into account the city's need to insulate buildings against rising temperatures while keeping the weight of green roofs to a minimum, reducing flood risk and polluted water runoff, and improving the habitat availability of wildlife native to the area.
- *UNpassable.* The United Nations has asked your team to use Nature-inspired engineering to address the fact that one in seven people around the world lack all-season access to passable roads, making trips to the market or the doctor impossible for much of the year.
- *Outside in.* Conventional window screens are great for keeping insects out of houses, but they also obstruct the flow of fresh air. A large window manufacturer has put out an RFP (request for proposal) for a new window screen design that better enables the flow of fresh air. Come up with a design and "sell it."
- *Lessons from planet A for planet B.* General interest in colonizing Mars raises a number of design challenges that could be addressed through Nature-inspired engineering, including astronauts' health during the voyage, a sustainable industrial system on Mars (materials and energy), and a sustainable agricultural system. Choose one or more challenges associated with colonizing Mars and use Nature-inspired engineering to address it.
- *Pitch it.* Some research suggests that the quality of tent a person owns influences how often they go camping. A major camping supply company has asked you to use Nature-inspired engineering to design a tent with qualities that will attract more people to camping because of its functional brilliance.
- *Should be a ballast.* Cargo vessels take on water as ballast for stability while traveling, and discharge it upon arriving at their destination. This has resulted in the movement of invasive aquatic organisms into many areas where they weren't found previously. A large shipping company has asked you to come up with a new design for its container ships to eliminate this problem.
- *Sizing fashion.* A major children's clothing manufacturer has put out an RFP seeking designs for clothes that grow along with their wearer. How would Nature design a pair of pants? Coat? Gloves?

In addition to the value of these exercises where students are provided a specific design challenge, there is also value in helping students further refine design challenges within larger, well-known issues, such as a challenge within the broader problem of climate change. This is an opportunity to develop important skills in narrowing focus to address smaller problems within a broader challenge, which is essential to being able to tackle large, difficult problems in effective ways. You can't fix a problem like climate change in one fell swoop, but you can, for example, improve the efficiency of computer fans, or develop new ways to isolate hydrogen fuel, or better reduce heat lost through hot water tanks.

Have students identify an area of interest within technology and society and deeply research the various challenges found there. Giving students the opportunity to more narrowly define a challenge within broader problems helps them better understand the big picture and rationally choose what to focus on, which improves their chances of success. Ultimately, this can help them feel more empowered to take action in an often overwhelming, complicated world.

Younger students need help identifying challenges and opportunities that are less worldly but still relevant and just as important in terms of learning to have a "problem consciousness." How to avoid getting tagged at recess even if you're not the fastest kid? How not to get car sick? How to keep a younger sibling from taking your stuff? How to put more power into your throw or kick? How to make friends or to be a good friend? How to get out of bed in the morning? The challenges are everywhere, wherever students find their interests and concerns.

The switch in attitude you're aiming for is seeing that inconveniences aren't to be suffered but, rather, can be fixed. When we think a problem can be fixed, or when we're asked to identify it and try to solve it, we are suddenly in a very different position with respect to the issue. Likewise, when we ask students to envision the ideal, we give them a reason to imagine how the world could be better. And we certainly don't encourage students to use their imaginations nearly enough in education. We tend to look down at the trail in front of our feet unless we are given a reason to look up toward the horizon.

History is full of examples of missed opportunity and lack of vision. Darryl Zanuck, a 20th Century Fox executive, infamously said in 1946, "Television won't be able to hold on to any market it captures after the first six months. People will soon get tired of staring at a plywood box every night." Similarly, Thomas Watson, IBM president in 1943, remarked, "I think there is a world market for maybe five computers." We don't even know all the missed opportunities and failures of vision our world now suffers, because we become inured to our world's shortcomings. In a sense, the difference between our world as it is and our world in a more ideal state is the exact quantity of lack of vision there's been so far. Asking students to notice challenges and opportunities to make the world a better place is simple, but it's also radical. Do this enough, and obliviousness and complacency can be replaced with critical awareness and ambition. Even if students come away with nothing else than this new predisposition, you'll have done something transformative.

> **Y**ou miss 100 percent of the shots you don't take.
>
> –Wayne Gretzky

DISCOVERING NATURE'S GENIUS

One of the grandest joys of Nature-inspired engineering is having an excuse to focus on the endlessly intriguing natural world we are fortunate enough to live in. In Nature-inspired engineering, Nature is your box of inspiration. And what a large, mighty box it is. There are millions of types of creatures in our world, some as big as bowling lanes and others as small as 1/40,000th of a grain of sand. Some are powered by hydrogen sulfide billowing out of Earth's crust at the bottom of the ocean; some are activated simply by a sunny day. Each species has a theoretically infinite number of attributes that could inspire technological innovation, features of their molecules, cells, tissues, organs, internal systems, and characteristic interactions with the environment around them.

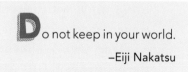

> **D**o not keep in your world.
>
> –Eiji Nakatsu

And in addition to the sheer magnitude of ideas represented by Nature, is their novelty. Nature vastly enlarges the solution space for engineers because organisms accomplish things through so many original means that the human mind would be unlikely to think of on its own. Who would think of rendering perilous bacterial threats impotent simply by changing the texture of a surface . . . until one sees how shark skin functions? Or making a retractable thumb tack, until looking at cat paws? Or making a surfer invisible with light, until learning that marine organisms use counterillumination to obscure their silhouettes? The English poet William Blake (1757–1827) put it best when he wrote, "Nature is imagination itself."

> **M**r. Dursley stood rooted to the spot. He had been hugged by a complete stranger. He also thought he had been called a Muggle, whatever that was. He was rattled. He hurried to his car and set off for home, hoping he was imagining things, which he had never hoped before, because he didn't approve of imagination.
>
> –J. K. Rowling,
> *Harry Potter and the Philosopher's Stone*

Fortunately for us, the human mind seems particularly well designed for the capacity to take this imaginative world in. We have superb senses of sight, hearing, and touch, as well as senses of smell and taste. We react viscerally to the natural world (e.g., biophilia) and are quick to form connections in our minds. Young children, in particular, seem to react to the living world with natural fascination and openness—think of the iconic youngster crouched over an ant nest.

True, with age many of us can become less likely to actually perceive the natural world, as we rush on by to other needs and concerns. We see Nature, but our minds do little with the experience. We observe a tree, in the sense that the light reflecting off the object hits our retina. We may at some level register the object as a "tree" and move on, the process taking mere milliseconds, while intellectually we derive no value from the interaction. We've seen trees a thousand times before, after all. Why should we stop and think about it?

This efficiency on our part is actually normal and often healthy. It doesn't make sense to linger about, staring fruitlessly at an object we already "know." Naming familiar objects and moving on quickly is a time-saving measure. If we didn't do this, we would hardly get out the front door for the fascination of the hallway rug. And yet, when it comes to learning how to see Nature as an engineer might, this efficiency is a major pitfall, for it constitutes a kind of debilitating blindness. It's like when you read an entire page of a book and then realize you have no idea what you just read. Your eyes passed over the words, but you extracted no meaning from the experience. You are just going through the motions of reading, without the purpose.

What is the difference between person A, who on passing a tree in the front yard, a tree walked by a thousand times before, thinks "tree" and keeps moving, and person B, who sees the same tree and stops, thinking, *Wow! How do trees make themselves out of thin air? How does this thing not fall over when the wind blows? Why is bark cracked? Wouldn't it be cool to have a ceiling fan that mimicked the relaxing sounds of leaves blowing in the wind?* Person A has walked by Nature blind to the possibilities latent there, essentially illiterate, while person B has read deeply between Nature's lines and found riches of curiosity, meaning, and potential inspiration. The difference between these two scenarios is not the tree—the tree is the same physical object for both person A and person B—the difference is in what person B *brings* to the observation of the tree.

WE LIVE IN AN AMAZING AND TALENTED WORLD, where everyday phenomena of extraordinary magnitude and significance often go unnoticed.

Reading Nature

When we observe something in Nature, we actually engage in a process that has many similarities to the physical and cognitive processes involved in the act of reading written language. Our visual system, for example, comes equipped with a high-focus area for our eyes (the fovea, in the center of our retina, with its high density of cone cells), as well as a parafoveal region, and still further peripheral region. If you've ever stopped along a trail for no apparent reason and then suddenly noticed a snake sunning itself along the path just ahead of you, you have your parafoveal and peripheral visual systems to thank. They are the eyes of our subconscious, and they save us from snakes, thrown balls, lone Lego pieces left on the carpet, and a host of other perils that we become conscious of only after the fact.

As we get better at reading, our speed increases because we employ the same visual systems to scan ahead along a row of letters. As we read (like you are doing right now), we are actually seeing fourteen or fifteen letters ahead of where we are consciously focused. By the time our fovea gets there, we have a head start on the linguistic processing necessary to understand what we read, even though we are not yet aware of having done so. Looking at Nature and reading are so similar because reading, a newly acquired cultural ability, co-opts the same visual and cognitive systems we evolved to observe the natural world. Where before we used this visual system primarily to recognize things like marauding bears and nutritious mushrooms, we now use it to also literally recognize the words *marauding bears* and *nutritious mushrooms*.

When we read, we do more than recognize words, of course: we construe meaning from them. Similarly, Nature-inspired engineers construe meaning out of the natural world they look over. What these engineers focus on, and the meaning they derive from the experience, will determine if they obtain the insights needed from the biological world to drive technological innovation.

How does one learn to "read" Nature the way a Nature-inspired engineer does? The process is vital. If you are illiterate, no amount of showing you the word *cat* will conjure a furry, purring feline in your mind. Instead, you will just see a set of black lines that yield neither information nor meaning. Similarly, if you are Nature-illiterate, no amount of waving a leaf in front of your face will conjure for you new revelations of how to design a solar cell, air freshener, or traffic network. Instead, you will just see a plain old leaf, as you've seen them a thousand times before, inspiring nothing in your creative brain at all.

Typically, if we are led to look at Nature at all, it's usually a largely semantic exercise in recognizing and naming. As youngsters, our parents point out to us "tree," and "cat," and so on. When we are older, a bird-watching expedition entails spotting a bird, consulting an expert or book to obtain its name, and then moving on. Learning that the bird at our feeder with a black-and-white head is a "black capped chickadee" can be a death sentence for curiosity—it's all about the *what*, as in, "What is that?" This is like reading a book by pronouncing the words correctly in your mind, carrying out the mechanics of reading, but deriving no meaning from the activity.

Just as we are encouraged to read deeply, to read as critical thinkers—quite different from merely seeing the words on the page—reading Nature like an engineer is a very different type of experience. The text of Nature dissolves into a massive mystery of fine details, unexpected connections, and plot twists. An engineer reading Nature this way is like a plumber abducted onto an alien spaceship. The "guts" of the ship are all exposed, but the pipes look misshapen, the spigots appear absent, and the valves aren't valves at all but something else entirely that you don't recognize. How do you react to this bizarre system of pipes? You react by leaning in, by trying to understand what you are looking at. You react by wondering and formulating questions.

Nature-inspired engineers react to seeing the natural world the same way. They react with wonder and ask questions that often begin with *why* and *how*. Why are the veins of a leaf in that pattern? How does the body detect tumors? Why do grass stalks bob back and forth? How do mosquitoes fly in the rain? Why do cantaloupe melons have that pattern on their skin? The only "what" involved here is in terms of *what does it do?* What does the shape of our outer ears do? What purpose do our toes serve? What does the hair on a bumblebee achieve? What role does the bird with the black-and-white head play in the ecosystem of my yard?

Biologists refer to many of these kinds of features of organisms as *structures* and *behaviors*, and what these structures and behaviors do as their *function*—not in the sense of a purpose but, rather, what a feature does for the organism. Biological structures and behaviors don't come about "on purpose," the way a person might design something for a purpose; they evolve because having that structure and behavior achieves something beneficial, performs a *function*, for the organism.

But *function* is an awfully dry word. It's also easily misunderstood, so with students (and definitely with younger students) I often refer to biological structures and behaviors as Nature's *talents*, *abilities*, or *ideas*. The fact that geckos can walk straight up walls is one of Nature's talents. Nature's abilities also include the more familiar concept of adaptations, but the emphasis of *adaptations* is what the biological structures or behaviors do for the organism (their function). The emphasis of biological *ideas* is what the structures or behaviors could teach *us*. Also, Nature's abilities go beyond adaptations. The fact that corals make their bodies out of seawater isn't what we normally regard as an adaptation, but it is one heck of a biological idea.

We actually know much less about the function of many biological features than we often presume to know. And we often assume less design in Nature than there actually is. When I was growing up, the human appendix was considered just a vestigial organ that served no purpose, for example,

not the vital reservoir of gut microbes it's now understood to be. Discovering functional design in Nature is a journey that begins with open-minded inquiry. For example, I have often wondered why the canopies of trees reach their summit along circuitous rather than straight paths. If an engineer were to design a tree, it would likely look like a series of straight tubes, shortening in length with height from the ground, changing angles only as necessary, rather than the often tortuous, contorted shapes we commonly see in tree branches. One day while passing such a tree, whose branches snaked wildly before reaching top, I asked my eight-year-old son why he thought the tree's branches were so twisty, instead of just being straight. He looked for several moments at the canopy of the tree and then said: "More space for birds?" I was floored—rarely have so few words created so much joy in me.

Sometimes people involved with Nature-inspired innovation get hung up on the actual biology of Nature. But what actually occurs in Nature in terms of function isn't, surprisingly, the most important part. If a feature one observes in Nature may *potentially* do something, *might* serve a function, that's the primary thing you're looking for to inspire innovation. As we've seen, scientists are rarely certain of the precise functional roles played by the various aspects of Nature, anyway, or how they work.

Biological accuracy matters if one can find it, but inspiration matters more—*never* squash the latter for the former. This is what makes Nature-inspired engineering so creative. It's what one can *see* in Nature that matters. It's driven by vision. Facts, where they exist, come into play only insofar as they inspire further vision. But the lack of facts, or clarity about them, shouldn't constrain the creative process. An innovative design is an innovation, by definition, wherever and however the inspiration comes.

Two Key Lessons

There are two key, overarching lessons for budding Nature-inspired engineers to learn about Nature when discovering its genius:

1. Nature is a formidable engineer itself, full of solutions to myriad different challenges.
2. The challenges Nature solves are relevant to the kinds of challenges human beings face.

Implicit and explicit in all of the exercises described so far in this book is that Nature is a formidable engineer itself. This is not the kind of thing you can realize all at once. It's an understanding and conviction that take time to form, after repeated meaningful, personal experiences arriving at this conclusion again and again. Eiji Nakatsu saw that an owl could help him reduce the noise caused by the bullet train's pantograph; when he subsequently saw that a kingfisher could help him reduce the noise of the entire train, he was sold. This is partly why a Nature-inspired approach to engineering education involves many lessons where students see firsthand that Nature can provide a superior solution to a problem.

That's part of the underlying logic to the architecture of such a curriculum. That way students get to explore lots of engineering topics and simultaneously discover in a lasting, meaningful way that Nature-inspired engineering really works. Trees are effective models for structural engineering and material toughness. Bones are paragons of lightweight design. Coral reefs are inspiring mentors for radically different manufacturing processes. Ant colonies are exemplary for fresh urban planning ideas and efficient computer algorithms. Lesson by lesson, students come to realize that Nature addresses thousands of difficult challenges with novel, elegant, and highly optimized strategies—a masterful and prodigious engineer to learn from.

ACTIVITY: Nature's Learning Stations

While each of these activities conveys the underlying message that Nature is full of talents and abilities, there are more direct ways to convey this message too. At the University of Louisiana, for instance, preservice and in-service teachers learn how to set up short stations through which elementary students rotate, each station conveying in a quick, engaging way something Nature is good at doing. At one station, students learn that polar bears can remain in icy water for hours or even days at a time; the students are then invited to see how long they can keep their hands in a bowl of ice water. At another station, upon learning that grasshoppers can jump twenty times their body length, students are challenged to hop as far as they can, with the equivalent distance a student-sized grasshopper could hop marked out on the floor for comparison—some 65–85 feet for an elementary student. (And fleas can jump some 220 times their body length, but for that you'd need an outdoor venue with a landmark some 800–900 feet away!) Dung beetles use their back legs to roll a ball of dung fifteen meters or more, 500 times their body length (at night, they often use the Milky Way to orient their direction); after learning this, students see how far they can roll an exercise ball with their back legs, pushing against the floor with just their hands. Whether it's trying to stand on one leg for as long as flamingos do (twenty minutes or more), holding your breath for as long as do sperm whales (two hours), or slowing down your heart beat as much as some bats can (by 33 percent), students come to appreciate how Nature is full of extraordinary capabilities. The physical engagement with the content moves the ideas from being merely informational to being fun, memorable, and emotionally impactful. Students acquire more than cold fingers, for example, at the polar bear station: they acquire empathy and esteem.

CONNECTING WITH NATURE'S ABILITIES through simple physical activities.

ACTIVITY: Nature-Inspired Research

For older students, deepening the understanding that Nature is full of awesome proficiency and creative genius can be approached in a number of ways. The book report approach has its virtues, with students reading about a biological talent or functional ability in Nature and writing a report on the topic.

My preferred option is to have students conduct their own research project on Nature's functional abilities and do something more authentically engaging. Here's a recipe, in four steps:

1. Ask students to spend time observing the natural world until struck by some interesting or curious feature.
2. They then hypothesize a function served by this biological feature: Why is it that way? What does it do? (the mantra of a Nature-inspired engineer).
3. Next, they devise a way to test whether the feature indeed serves this function.
4. Finally, they conduct the test and present the results.

A similar process can also be followed to answer the question, how does it work? (another mantra of a Nature-inspired engineer). It's an ambitious approach, yes, but it comes with proportionate rewards.

Let me give you an example of this approach to discovering Nature's genius. For many years, people thought that our fingers get wrinkly in the bathtub from simple osmotic swelling—it served no purpose. Then someone along the way noticed that if a nerve to the fingers is severed, no wrinkling happens. Hmm . . . so, finger wrinkling is not a simple physical reaction, like a sponge sitting in water. It's *caused* by a response in our nervous system; our bodies control it. Now things are starting to look interesting. Why would our bodies want our fingers to get wrinkly when we're in a bathtub?

Mark Changizi, a researcher on the evolutionary origins of biological and cognitive design, hypothesized that this behavior might actually serve a purpose in helping us grip slippery things. To examine the intriguing idea, Kyriacos Kareklas and colleagues at Newcastle University devised a test in which subjects with smooth fingers transferred wet marbles from one bowl into another, while other subjects with fingers wrinkled by soaking in water attempted the same. The result? Wrinkly fingered subjects transferred wet marbles substantially faster than smooth-fingered subjects. Our fingers wrinkle in the bathtub, it now appears, because it helped our ancestors not slip on wet creek bottoms while grabbing hold of fish dinner. Mark Changizi and his colleagues' research suggests that the specific topography of a wet fingertip is what makes the adaptation work, by whisking water away from the tips of our fingers, much like the treads on car tires whisk away water gathered from rainy pavement.

This research example is a model investigation of functional biology. To have students conduct a similar project, from observation through hypothesis and testing to reporting test results, is the kind of authentic engagement that drives the realization of Nature's ingeniousness deep, and it comes with many ancillary benefits, such as nurturing direct observation and question formation, creative and reasoned thought, and the kind of carefulness required to conduct research. There is also perhaps no better way to integrate science with engineering.

ACTIVITY: Nature-Inspired Flash Cards

Some teachers have used picture cards in a simple yet valuable in-class approach to fostering an appreciation for Nature's talents. Each card contains an image of something in the natural world—bee honeycomb, a bunch of bananas, a chameleon with its tongue rocketing forward, and so on. Students work in groups, first writing down individually anything they can think of that the natural element depicted is good at doing. To get them in the mood, tell students they are aliens from another planet, sent to Earth to study its creatures. These aliens have to prepare a report about each organism they look at, explaining what they discovered about its abilities.

The trick is to provide a mix of content that stretches students to recognize Nature's talents that they might otherwise overlook. Chameleons are easy: for one, they have long, quick tongues that shoot out and grab things. But what's a bunch of bananas good at doing? Well, for starters, fruit can change the color of its skin, telling us when it's ripe.

When students are done, they share their lists with the group and discuss. If they get stuck, the back of each card has prompts to help students think up some of a natural object's abilities. It's not the same as walking through a rainforest, or even the schoolyard, but using cards has its advantages. It's contained, students can consider any natural element you place an image of on a card, and the modality of cards makes it seem like a game. With little mess, the activity achieves its goals of getting students to think about what Nature is good at doing, and with good

I thought that the course was extremely fascinating. I enjoyed learning about the extent to which we can apply nature to humankinds' problems. I would say that this course has influenced me in that I now realize that science can be as ingeniously creative as it is methodical and about experimentation. Before this class I typically thought of science as all experiments and equations or discoveries. Biomimetics opened up a different side of science for me.

—Natalie, age 17

content and mentoring, it works. Most of us don't tend to recognize that bananas, for example, are good communicators!

ACTIVITY: Using Our Other Senses

At an even more elemental level, students need ways to fight against the familiarity they feel when they see natural things. We need ways to avoid thinking "tree" and just moving on but to actually stop and see Nature as though for the first time. We need help to begin wondering again. This can be surprisingly simple to achieve. Our sense of familiarity with Nature is mediated primarily by our eyes. When we are first carried around by our parents who point out "grass," "tree," "bird," and so on, it is through our eyes that we take in this information. Remove sight, and these objects become unfamiliar again.

Try having your students put on blindfolds and place a familiar natural object in their hands (the Exploring Material Shapes activity described in Chapter 3). You will suddenly see them intently explore a pinecone or feather as though they had never encountered the item in their lives. With very young students, blindfolds can be seen as an invitation to "cheat," so place the natural object at the end of an athletic sock and have students reach in to feel it.

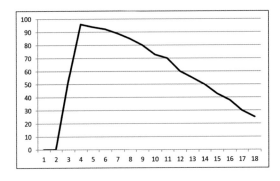

PERCENTAGE OF CHILDREN WHO ASK QUESTIONS, by age, based on an analysis by the Right Questions Institute of data from the U.S. Department of Education's 2009 *Nation's Report Card.*

There are infinite variations to this theme. My favorite is an activity Joe Cornell relays in *Sharing Nature With Children*, called "Find Your Tree." You need a safe patch of trees to work with, with a relatively clear understory. Students are paired up, and one starts with the blindfold. The blindfolded students are turned around several times and then led by their partner to a tree, which they explore with their hands, smell with their nose, whatever they like. They're then led back to their starting place, twirled around again several times, and the blindfold is removed. The challenge is now to go find their tree. You don't have to use trees: plants in a school garden could work too. You can even do this activity indoors (with blindfolds or athletic socks): once students explore a natural object, say, a pinecone, without their eyes, mix the object in with several similar but not identical pinecones, remove the blindfolds, and then see if students can pick theirs out from the bunch.

ACTIVITY: Nature's Talents Journal

Noticing Nature is a first step; asking questions about what you notice is next. Children are naturally very good at asking questions—research shows that, by the time children reach about five years of age, they will have asked about *40,000* of them! But after that age, the number of children who ask questions starts to fall—precipitously. It is like a great chorus whose members are silenced, one by one. By middle school, the percentage of students asking questions is down to about half, and by the end of high school, just one in four.

Nature is a Nature-inspired engineer's how-to manual, and just like a technician studies manuals to know how to fix any and all manner of problems that might crop up, Nature-inspired engineers study Nature. But Nature is written not like a how-to manual but more like a bunch of coded messages, which is what makes trying to understand it fun. Where a technical manual is written to be as literal as possible, the manual of Nature is suggestive, mysterious, and infinitely alluring.

Learning to see Nature, and to see that Nature is not just something pretty, "out there," disconnected from "real life," but directly relevant to the things we make and dream of making is a core skill for Nature-inspired engineers. And as a skill, it's not something you achieve once in your lifetime. No milestone awaits the aspiring Nature-inspired engineer in this endeavor. It's something you develop over time, a practice you get better at with effort.

So, as with discovering challenges and opportunities, have students keep a journal from the very beginning of your engagement with them on the topic of Nature's talents, where they can write down their thoughts and observations in and out of the classroom and throughout the curriculum. What about Nature impresses you? What in Nature makes you wonder? Assign a number of observations, questions, and thoughts each week.

Students don't have to live near a national park to do this—there is a natural wonderland out there in the schoolyard. Mysterious gallery forests run along the cracks in the pavement all the way between home and school. A zoo resides in the soil of every houseplant. That's what Eiji Nakatsu means when he says "read and touch the real nature with five senses." Or, as George de Mestral put it, "If any of your employees ask for a two-week holiday to go hunting, say yes."

The point is to look at Nature with fresh eyes, to see Nature not just as aesthetic but *instructive*. The first step to this kind of perspective is seeing that Nature isn't just pretty—it's instrumental. It *does* things. In a rose opening there is both beauty and mechanical actuators. In a common cold there is a system excellent at distinguishing foreign objects. And out your window an entire economic system is bustling along, gobbling up resources, manufacturing materials, trading, discarding, and somehow thriving over the long haul.

Yes, the more biological ideas we are familiar with, the greater the chance we will think of a helpful biological inspiration when confronting a design challenge. But discovering Nature's genius has far more importance than just its instrumental value to engineers. Remember, not every student will or should become an engineer. Even if you simply help your students reconnect with the natural world, and deepen their admiration for what they discover there, you will have enriched their experience of existence for the rest of their lives. The reward is a lifetime of intrigue and more.

CONNECTING ENGINEERING CHALLENGES
WITH BIOLOGICAL IDEAS

No one knows all the millions of things Nature is good at doing. The question for an engineer is less whether Nature holds a good, novel solution for any particular design challenge, and more whether the engineer can figure out how to *access* these biological ideas.

The first obstacle isn't usually difficulty finding a solution—it's finding a solution too fast. Once students have defined their engineering challenges, they will often immediately leap to a solution concept in their mind, before fully considering Nature's options. But coach your students not to rush to a solution and to set aside for now any solution concepts that strike them immediately. This is critical: people are sometimes very quick to think of a solution to a problem, but inspiration from Nature needs a little time to work its magic. Brains rewire slowly. Students have to stave off or put aside thoughts of how to solve a problem long enough to let promising biological models inspire fresh ideas. A persistent risk is that a student will short-circuit the design process by thinking of a solution concept before exploring biological inspiration, and then try to "backdoor" it, thinking of a biological model to justify a knee-jerk design solution. Don't let that happen!

Remember, at its heart Nature-inspired engineering involves *drawing analogies* (itself a rather nice analogy, reflecting the fact that making analogies is a creative activity, akin to making artwork). By connecting two things from different realms to each other, we can transfer the way we think about or understand one phenomenon to the other. That's the power of analogies: like Gaia theory, thinking of Earth as a biological cell, they transform how we think about something, often by leaps instead of increments, opening up entirely new, dramatic possibilities in the process.

In 1632, Galileo described butterflies flitting about the rafters in the cabin of a moving ship. He pointed out that by just looking at the butterflies, a person would have no idea the ship was in motion. Galileo's analogy was a clever way of dispelling arguments made against a Copernican world, that if indeed Earth were rotating around the sun (instead of vice versa) we should feel Earth moving. By using common experience (looking at butterflies) as an analogy to what was at the time an uncommon idea (a sun-centered solar system), Galileo helped people imagine how the seemingly impossible could be possible. Insight through analogy is powerful and fascinating stuff.

An Analogical Challenge

Let's see the power of analogy in action. Consider the following common problem in cancer treatment:

Radiologists struggle with how to radiate deep tumors and those in vital areas, like the brain, which are difficult or impossible to reach safely. Why? Radiation kills healthy tissue all the way through a patient's body to the targeted tumor. The situation seems irresolvable.

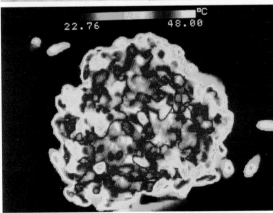

A BALL OF JAPANESE HONEYBEES: In the center is a Japanese giant hornet, being cooked to death.

Let's leave the world of radiology for the moment and consider the diabolical Japanese giant hornet (*Vespa mandarinia japonica*). The largest hornet in the world, it has a body 4.5 centimeters long and a wingspan greater than 6 centimeters. Invading a hive of European honeybees (*Apis mellifera*), a Japanese giant hornet can sting forty members of the colony to death in a single minute. A handful of hornets will destroy an entire colony of tens of thousands of European honeybees in a few hours. The hornets aren't even after honey: once they kill the bees, the hornets dismember them, removing their thorax, and then fly back to their nests to feed their own larvae.

The Japanese honeybee (*Apis cerana japonica*), however, has a defense against this fiendish foe. Unlike its European cousin, the Japanese honeybee has evolved alongside the Japanese giant hornet. When a hornet enters their hive, Japanese honeybees immediately surround the intruder from all directions, forming a tight ball around it. The balled bees then beat their wings rapidly, which raises carbon dioxide and temperature levels. A single bee's efforts raise CO_2 and temperature only a little bit, but together their efforts concentrate CO_2 levels and temperature in the very center of the ball where the hornet is located. In the middle of the ball of bees, the temperature reaches 46°C (115°F). The interloper is effectively asphyxiated and cooked to death.

Let's return now to the problem of radiating tumors. Can you think of a way to radiate a tumor deep inside a patient's body, or in a sensitive area, such that the tumor would be killed, yet the intervening tissue might be spared? . . . Perhaps a different approach that radiologists could take has started to dawn on you: what if radiologists directed multiple beams of less intense radiation from different directions, all converging on the tumor? That way, perhaps the power of any one beam could be reduced to safe levels for intervening tissue, yet combined they still have enough power to kill the tumor. Indeed, this is exactly how radiologists have begun approaching some difficult-to-target tumors.

This is an example of the power of analogies. When we first hear about the difficulty of reaching some tumors with radiation, the problem seems hopeless—we feel stuck with a situation, unable to get out of it. Just imagine how the outgunned honeybees feel when a massive and deadly giant hornet enters their colony! But Japanese honeybees developed a different response. They innovated. Like the honeybees confronted by a hornet, we too can solve what may seem like impossible problems, and we can use the power of analogies to help us do it.

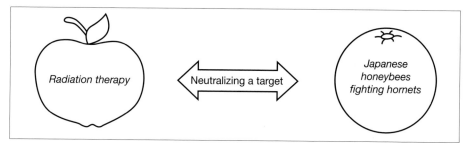

Connecting how Japanese honeybees kill giant hornets and tumor radiation strategies is pretty conceptual, but sometimes analogical insights don't require much abstract thinking at all. Bernie Sadow was hauling two suitcases through an airport in 1970 during a family vacation to Aruba when he saw a workman using a dolly to effortlessly push a heavy machine. Sadow recalled that, as he stood in line at customs, "I said to my wife, 'You know, that's what we need for luggage.'" Back home, Sadow made a prototype, and that same year he applied for a patent for the world's first rolling luggage.

Similarly, Dr. Annick Bay wondered if fireflies might hold secrets for improving the energy efficiency of LED lights. After noticing a pattern of overlapping scales on the fireflies' abdomens, she and her colleagues etched the cover of an LED light with a similar pattern. The result? A whopping 55 percent increase in light emission, meaning you could pump *half* as much electricity into LEDs with this kind of cover and get the same amount of light out of it. Thinking that fireflies may hold ideas for how to improve lighting technology doesn't require a great leap of abstraction, but it nonetheless can result in completely fresh and dramatic approaches to innovation.

Sometimes analogical insights are more abstractly spun, like our honeybee example. When Eiji Nakatsu related the diving of a kingfisher to the sonic boom created by a train exiting a tunnel, there was clearly a fruitful analogy to be made here, but it was awfully subtle. Kingfishers go from a less-dense medium (air), into a higher density medium (water) causing very little splash. Similarly, the bullet train goes from a less-dense medium (air before a tunnel), into a higher density medium (air inside a tunnel). As Eiji correctly surmised, a train shaped more like a kingfisher should likewise travel more smoothly into the higher density medium, and hence create less of a sonic disturbance on the other end. But to make this connection, Eiji had to see that the differences between water and air here were superficial, not to mention the differences between birds and trains.

But *how* do Nature-inspired engineers find analogies to biological models that will help them solve problems? Is there a methodical process, or is it just intuition and luck? To some extent, luck and intuition are part of the process, which can make the experience of doing Nature-inspired engineering fun and surprising. Clearly, we increase our chances of finding useful biological models by having a problem already in mind, either consciously, like Eiji's noisy train, or subconsciously, like George de Mestral's wife's stuck zipper. And, all else being equal, the more biological structures, behaviors, processes, and systems we are familiar with, the greater chance we have of connecting a biological model with an engineering challenge, particularly if these biological inspirations present themselves in close temporal or spatial proximity to the engineering challenge. But can we improve our odds still further by striving for more than serendipity? To do this, we need to move from a process conducive to flashes of analogical insight, to a process of steady analogical reasoning.

Using Wine to Make Pizza

Imagine you are drinking wine and making homemade pizza with a friend, when you discover the wooden rolling pin is not in the baking drawer. You can't find it anywhere. You try to spread the dough out with your fingers, but it doesn't work very well; your pizza looks like a fat starfish when you get done with it. Your friend just shakes her head. Grabbing the wine bottle, she covers it with flour and turns it sideways, rolling out the dough into a perfect flat circle. "You suffer from functional fixedness," she explains.

Later that evening, as you make the salad and start to run out of counter space, she opens a drawer and lays a cutting board on top of it: presto, more counter space. Then, at the end of the evening, while you are making cookies to polish off a great meal, you just hand her the stick of butter. "I suppose you have a unique way of softening butter, too?" After a beat, your friend takes the cheese grater off the dry rack and, with an alarmingly fast chopping motion, shaves the entire stick of butter into confetti.

The term *functional fixedness* was coined by psychologist Karl Duncker in 1945. The term describes a common impediment to problem solving, in situations where one is required to think differently than accustomed about an object's purpose. In Duncker's experiment, subjects were given a candle, a book of matches, and a box of thumbtacks and challenged to attach the lit candle to a wall so that it didn't drip wax on the

A GAS PUMP HANDLE is held in place with something we associate with serving a different function. Preestablished ideas about the purpose of things can constrain creative thought.

table below. Duncker found most people tried (unsuccessfully) to attach the candle to the wall directly, using the thumbtacks. Tacks, after all, are *for* attaching things. Very few people emptied the box of thumbtacks to use it as a shelf to hold up the candle, a solution that worked easily. Duncker interpreted the impediment to solving the problem as a difficulty in transforming one's understanding of the accustomed function of the thumbtack box from that of a container to that of a shelf.

In Nature-inspired engineering, we have to discern functions in the natural world to which we're not accustomed. Who thinks of kingfishers as holding ideas for making trains quieter? Or ants as containing solutions to computer problems? Or coral reefs as providing new approaches to manufacturing? We don't tend to think of the natural world as containing answers for humankind. Nature is pretty. It's just "out there," a backdrop to life. It has nothing to do with humankind's problems. Because we think of Nature this way, we don't seek solutions in that realm.

Instead, we need to learn to think of Nature as a problem-solving resource. Students need to be able to look at a rose and see not just something pretty but also a possible folding protocol for packaging or unfolding solar sails for powering satellites or ships in outer space. *That's* how Nature-inspired engineers think. Why wouldn't they? Plants have optimized the packaging of leaves and flowers inside buds over millions of years, through countless variations and trials. But efficient packaging is not what we tend to think of when we see a rose, and certainly not what we celebrate on Valentine's Day.

For students to learn the skills of Nature-inspired engineering, they need to be able to look at a natural scene and see *answers*. And to do that, nothing works like coming to Nature with questions. Sometimes those question are formed by an existing challenge. What in Nature has a large surface area but packs down into a small space? How would Nature design a shoe? And so on. And sometimes that question is formed by wanting to know what Nature can do. Why are the undersides of leaves so often whitish? What purpose do our fingerprints serve? . . .

Nature-inspired engineers understand that the challenges Nature solves on a daily basis—how to get materials, energy, information—are relevant to the kinds of challenges humans face. People can easily be led to admire the way a gecko can climb straight up a wall. But a Nature-inspired engineer relates that special ability to human needs and desires—this, you might say, is a Nature-inspired engineer's special ability. Recall that Nature-inspired engineers have a "problem consciousness," so they see a gecko climbing a wall and can associate that ability to human challenges and opportunities. A strong yet reversible adhesive—a technology geckos have perfected—would be a useful feature of medical bandages, quick-release ski bindings, picture hooks, carpet tiles, billboard posters, and electronics that can be easily separated into their component parts for recycling. That's how Nature-inspired engineers think.

It makes perfect sense that other species would have solutions for the things that matter to people. True, other species may not talk on cell phones, drive cars, or drink sodas. From that perspective humans can seem very different from the rest of the species on our planet. But our needs and wants are not that different from those of the caterpillar going by on the sidewalk. We all need clean water. We all need food and shelter. We all use and discard materials. We all strive for companionship and safety. We all must survive and find a way to live successfully on this planet over the long term. Our similarities are far more relevant than the superficial distinctions upon which we tend to focus.

Humans aren't the only species that stand to benefit from adhesives, or from protection from bacterial infections, or from flying. Over time evolution has tended to produce solutions to these and many other kinds of challenges in various species. That's why, to a Nature-inspired engineer, Nature's numberless talents are highly pertinent to addressing human opportunities and challenges. Moreover, Nature has more than one solution to any one of these challenges. There are mounds of different strategies for adhesion in Nature, bunches of different methods for coping with bacteria, gobs of different approaches to repelling liquids, dissipating heat, sequestering carbon dioxide, cleaning water, producing color, filtering sound, and on and on.

We can help students understand the relevance of Nature's abilities by relating human wants and needs to the living world's manifest accomplishments. People would be happy to develop effective antivenom serums for dangerous snakes, for instance; opossums have just such a serum, a unique peptide in their blood that renders rattlesnake venom harmless. In fact, many other species that show adaptations to snake venom, including peacocks, chickens, wood rats, and even other snakes, are the very species that bump into venomous snakes on a regular basis. People desperately need ways to capture carbon dioxide—I'm breathing through a device right now that's positively masterful at it (my lungs). How about shoes that don't slip on ice? Polar bears, arctic foxes, and penguins surely have strategies for dealing with this kind of issue.

The point is, maybe we aren't taught to think of Nature as relating to what humankind wants and needs to figure out, but that's exactly how many engineers have discovered we *should* think of Nature. In the words of material scientist Christopher Viney, "Nature is full of solutions looking for problems to solve." We need to learn to look at the natural world not just as something out the window and unconnected to our busy human lives, but more the way we scan through a cluttered kitchen drawer, looking for a tool to help us pry open a bottle or whatever it is we need to do. The answers are there. That's how Nature-inspired engineers look at the living world around us.

Perhaps we should be asking, then, how would Nature learn how to look at Nature in this new way?

ACTIVITY: Function Junction

This simple and effective schoolyard activity is a fun place to get started seeing Nature the way engineers do. Write down some general functional qualities, each on its own slip of paper, such as "stabilizes," "aerodynamic," "attaches," "detects," "orients," "communicates," "packs into a small space," "flexible but strong," and "creates conditions conducive to Life" (you can vary the competencies you write down, depending on the age of the students). Put the slips of paper in a hat and have small teams of students pick three to five slips. Then have students go into the schoolyard and find examples in Nature that exhibit the abilities written on their slips of paper.

For example, birds clearly exemplify "aerodynamic," as do floating dandelion seeds (in something of an opposite way), and perhaps, in a very broad sense, so do mushrooms pushing their way out of the ground. "Communicates" is on display not just in ants smelling pheromone trails of their pals but between the grass roots in the soil of the schoolyard, and even from the trees outside to the school children subconsciously enjoying their presence.

After students have had some time to scavenge about for examples in Nature that illustrate each ability, hold a "field trip," letting students take the rest of the class around to show everyone what they found and how it illustrates the functional quality listed on their pieces of paper. For a special touch, include a blank piece of paper in each group's small pile, so they can write down any abilities they discover in the schoolyard not already listed on their pieces of paper. (After I described this activity to him once in a taxi we were sharing, Richard Louv, the author of *Last Child in the Woods*, christened this exercise "Hunting and Gathering for Ideas.")

Gained in Translation

Notice that it really isn't difficult to make a connection between things in Nature and human types of needs and wants, like attaching things and communicating and packing stuff into small spaces. Making analogies between biology and technology is difficult not because the issues each addresses are different—they're remarkably similar—but because the *language* we use in each of these realms can be very different.

Consider any problem, say, electrical line loss. This is a feature of the power lines you see strung across the landscape. The longer electricity flows through these wires, the more energy is lost from electrical resistance—the collision of electrons with ions of the metal wire. Electrical line loss causes us to have to generate a lot more energy (e.g., by burning coal) just to get enough electricity to where we want it to go. How can we access biological information to help us consider new approaches to this problem? There may very well be models in Nature that could help us, but it is difficult to think of them while having the words *electrical line loss* in our minds. That's because biologists don't use these words to describe any phenomena in Nature.

Language matters. If someone declares their love in Chinese to someone who loves them back but speaks only Greek, these two poor souls may never get together. So, Nature-inspired engineers have to become good at *translating* challenges into terms that make biological ideas flow more easily, that is, into language that Nature can work with. If we translate "electrical line loss" instead into a challenge of "managing electrical resistance," all of the sudden biological models start to appear. How does Nature manage electrical resistance?

Our nerve cells have fibers that conduct electrical energy, for instance. Some of these fibers are covered in a sheath of fatty material called myelin, while other nerve fibers are unmyelinated. Perhaps this is a bio-

FUNCTION JUNCTION: Students can begin seeing solution-oriented designs in Nature through simple exercises done in the schoolyard.

logical model that can give us ideas of how to conduct electricity through power lines more efficiently? As one research paper concisely put it, "The 500-mm diameter unmyelinated giant axon of the squid requires 5,000 times as much energy and occupies about 1,500 times as much space as the 12-mm diameter myelinated nerve in the frog." (Interestingly, myelin increases electrical resistance in a nerve cell, but the result is an overall *improvement* in performance.) All of the sudden, because of a small modification in language, the natural world seems like it might have some relevant models for us to consider when thinking about the problem of electrical line loss in power lines, and to think about the problem perhaps in a very different way.

This translation step is often essential, and it's not hard to do. You just have to remember to do it. My kids put on their tennis shoes as quickly as possible, shoving their feet in without untying the laces, so that the first thing to rip on their shoes is always the once-stiff back heal. How is Nature going to help me improve the design of tennis shoes so this no longer happens? Nature doesn't wear tennis shoes! But if I translate my engineering challenge instead into finding materials that are "elastic and strong," all of the sudden Nature is brimming with possible models to help me—spider silk, cardiac muscle, microscopic jellyfish harpoons, the throat sacs of singing frogs, and on it goes.

Just like with poetry, a *good* translation matters, too. Nuance is important. For a thousand years people who wanted to fly like birds literally attached feathers to their arms and jumped off towers, flapping wildly to their death. The implicit translation of the challenge they were trying to address was, how does Nature fly? But that's pretty broad, and it led these unfortunate mavericks to zero in on the wrong aspect of the biological model. It wasn't until George Cayley realized that humans couldn't create enough power by flapping that he refined the question. How does a heavier-than-air object stay aloft without flapping? he wondered.

With this more precise translation of the challenge in mind, Cayley looked at birds and saw something that a millennia of would-be aviation pioneers missed: many birds stay aloft without flapping at all. *Soaring* birds became Cayley's biological inspiration, and he extracted a trove of insight from studying how birds managed to stay aloft through soaring alone. The fixed wings of modern aircraft are a direct consequence of the pivotal shift Cayley made in our understanding of the real challenges involved in human flight. Cayley's translation of the problem enabled the Wright brothers to come along and finally get humanity off the ground.

On the other hand, one can define a challenge too narrowly, too. Let's say a laundry company approaches you and asks for ideas on a better detergent for cleaning clothes. If you take their challenge at face value, you'll work on creating a better detergent. But is the challenge really about creating a better detergent, or is it to create a better way to keep clothes clean? You may think the difference is minor, but it isn't. If the challenge is really to find a better way to keep clothes clean, then suddenly there are biological models to consult that you may have ignored before. Hydrophobic leaves, for instance (from Chapter 5), keep themselves clean not with detergent but by using microscopic textures to which water can't adhere. The idea of modifying fabrics so that they become hydrophobic wouldn't have occurred to you if you thought you had to develop a new detergent. The point is, it's important to clarify the *real* challenge—the actual end goal you want to achieve, not necessarily the means—so that all available biological inspirations are on the table. You want the design solution space to be as large as possible, while still addressing the essential challenge.

ACTIVITY: Translation Challenge

Encourage your students to spend time thinking about an engineering challenge, learning about its context, and discussing it, before they rush off to discover biological models to inspire their solutions. Defining the challenge considerately, and playing with different possible interpretations of the challenge, will be worth the investment of time. The key is to try to identify the essence of the challenge and then to translate this into general functional terms. The well-known education philosopher John Dewey (1859–1952) put it succinctly when he said, "A problem well put is half solved."

TABLE 8.1

Examples of Design Challenges for Students to Translate
into General Functional Terms

Engineering challenge	Biological question in functional terms
It's so frustrating! I can never find the end on the roll of Scotch tape.	What in Nature *shows up* when torn or in sudden contact with air?
The coil radiator in my apartment has plenty of hot water going through it, but it doesn't seem to heat up my apartment.	What in Nature has a *high surface area*?
When I go jogging, first I'm too cold and then I'm too hot.	How does Nature *actively manage temperature*?
Car tires with the wrong air pressure can reduce the gas efficiency of cars. Plus, you just don't need a lot of contact area with the road except when braking suddenly.	What in Nature *spreads out with pressure*?
Commercial delivery trucks aren't very energy efficient, and half the time they travel without any packages even in them.	How does Nature make *large voluminous shapes aerodynamic*?

It's often helpful to give your students a list of, say, ten challenges and have them practice translating these into their essence, described by general functional terms. Table 8.1 gives a few examples to illustrate what this can look like. Nature may not go jogging, live in apartments, or drive delivery trucks, but it very well might make things that have a high surface area, dynamically manage temperature, and are simultaneously large, voluminous, and aerodynamic.

By stripping all the jargon and superficial context away from the initial description of an engineering challenge, you are removing the associations that hold functional fixedness in place. When all that remains of the description is the challenge in its most elemental physical form, we are finally speaking a common language with the world of biology. These generalized functional terms are vital to building a bridge between the living world (what's possible to achieve) and the technological world (what we want to achieve), across which helpful analogies can more freely travel.

Once students have defined the essence of their engineering challenges and translated them into general functional terms, the search for relevant biological models is on! Often, biological models at this point will just come to mind, because you've worked to remove as many barriers to making analogies as possible. What in Nature has a high surface area? Loads of things: tree canopies, plant roots, fungal mycelium, leaf epidermis, elephant skin, your stomach lining, and many more. The tails of squirrels, for instance, are a fascinating high-surface-area structure. Some squirrel species have been shown to use their tails as a decoy for pit vipers, which can find prey in the dark through special heat sensors. When confronted by a snake, some squirrels instantly route more blood into their tails. This radiates a conspicuous heat signature into the night, providing a stunningly clever foil should a viper strike.

Another thing your students can try is to go outside with their functional challenge now firmly in mind. Suddenly Nature is not an infinite, overwhelming spectacle but more like that kitchen drawer through which you rifle looking for examples of things with high surface area or what have you. Armed with specific purpose, your students will suddenly be much more efficient outside at hunting and gathering for ideas. You don't have to travel anywhere exotic to find completely ingenious insights, either. Continental Tire Company realized that cats are excellent at stopping on a dime. Their paws spread out when they have to stop short. The simple strategy led the company to redesign their tires, considered some of the safest on the market, to spread out when braking, bringing more rubber into contact with the road, exactly when you need it.

THE HEMOGLOBIN MOLECULE IN OUR BLOOD, represented here as a public sculpture, changes shape upon contact with oxygen, which alters its interaction with light and hence color—a potentially promising model for designing clear tape one can easily find the end of on a roll. The images show changes to the color of the sculpture's metal once exposed to the elements, at installation (left), after ten days (middle), and after one month (right).

Of course, first-hand discovery isn't the only way to develop biological inspiration: you can also learn from what others have discovered about Nature. We now live in a world where exploring biological information others have developed has never been easier. Students can go to the Internet, where, with a few judicious words typed into a search box (e.g., temperature + regulation + species), a world of information is zipped right to their eyes while they just sit there, the way burgers used to be skated to your car at drive-in diners. You can search the entire Internet for information or use narrower databases (see the Additional Resources section at the end of the chapter).

ACTIVITY: Tapping Into Human Resources

Another source of biological inspiration that many overlook comes from actual biologists, who have troves of potential information that doesn't appear on the Internet or make it into scientific papers. Once your students are ready with their well-defined and well-translated challenges, have them identify naturalists and biologists who work on related topics, and then have them craft an e-mail describing their project and asking for any ideas of biological models to consider for their challenge. If nothing else, you'll help develop your students' abilities to communicate clearly, politely, and strategically with others.

From Translation to Application

Once students have some biological models in mind, they can research the structures, behaviors, processes, and/or systems that define how these models work. Often, just knowing what features in Nature do is enough to inspire an innovative solution. For example, "large, voluminous yet aerodynamic shape" makes me think right away of whales. Looking at pictures of whales on the Internet, one set of images in particular catches my eye: a whale shark (technically not a whale but a shark that's converged on a whale body type). One image shows a whale shark feeding, with its mouth wide open and its body big and round. But the other image shows a whale shark when it is just traveling through the water and not eating; in this case, its body is remarkably flat. Right away, the idea hits me that, to improve the energy efficiency of commercial delivery vehicles, it would

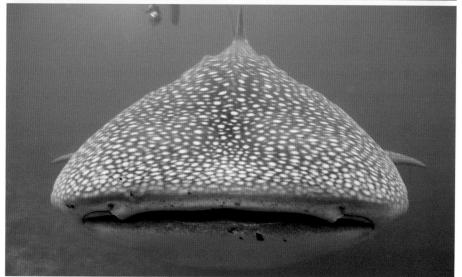

make sense if they *changed their shape* depending on what they were doing, redesigning them like popup campers: when full of packages, delivery vehicles could be big like they are normally, but traveling back to the depot empty after delivering their packages, they could compress, reducing their height, thus greatly improving their aerodynamics. Just think about the cost savings and cleaner air this one Nature-inspired change would create when applied to the hundreds of millions of delivery vehicles rumbling over the roads.

Ken Phillips spent his life working as a doctor, and in his retirement he developed a radical improvement to a technology that hadn't changed much since soldiers began using them in 900 B.C.: helmets. As Ken learned from his son, who worked as a writer for a motorcycle magazine, helmets can help against direct impacts from things like spiked clubs and 300-pound defensive tackles. But they do little to protect against rotational impact, which is most often what causes concussions and serious brain damage.

When our head is struck and our bodies stop moving, the brain inside our skulls keeps turning, causing veins to snap, like so much wet spaghetti, and brain tissue to tear, resulting in lesions and hemorrhaging. As motoring sportscaster Jeremy Clarkson said, "Speed has never killed anyone. Suddenly becoming stationary, that's what gets you." When Ken's son told him how common brain injury from rotation was in motocross, Ken found himself asking: "How does the human head protect against rotational injury?" It was the perfect biological model hiding in plain sight.

"The scalp is a very complex organ with all sorts of protective qualities," Ken thought to himself. "It is dense, fibrous, and well vascularized. It moves up to 15–20 millimeters, so there is 15–20 millimeters of friction-free movement over the scalp not imparting rotational force at all to the skull or brain." Why, he thought, does no one seem to make helmets with a movable membrane on them? "We prototyped it with just simple materials," Ken explained to me on the phone, "and immediately saw a 60 percent improvement in protection against rotational movement."

Thomas Edison famously said, "Genius is one percent inspiration, ninety-nine percent perspiration." One could mistakenly come away from this statement thinking that the ideation stage in developing a solution concept is not that important. But that would be wrong. Think about it: if you're 1 percent is off, then your 99 percent effort is wasted. If you get your initial compass heading wrong, you will spend all your time walking away from where you actually need to be. That 1 percent is vital to successful innovation, even if there's still more work to do.

FROM BIOLOGY TO CHALLENGE

While most of this chapter, indeed, this book, involves starting with an engineering challenge and then looking to the biological world for inspiring solution ideas, we can reverse this order: we can start by looking to the biological world for its impressive abilities, and then think up how these inspiring talents might drive technological innovation. John Crowe's work with water bears is a perfect example of this. As a high schooler, John first saw a water bear through a microscope and learned about their near-mythic powers. He then spent the rest of his life researching their amazing abilities and how we might apply their lessons to improve human life.

Water bears (sometimes called tardigrades or moss piglets) are microscopic animals with eight legs, each of which sports tiny but wickedly curved claws, a bit like a microscopic grizzly bear. If you see one through a microscope, it will likely be dog-paddling peacefully about, landing on a piece of moss, and piercing it with its straw-like mouth. You can literally see the green chloroplasts getting sucked inside water bears, with their translucent bodies, as they sip the plant juices down.

There are hundreds of species of water bears. They've been found at the top of mountains and at the bottom of the ocean, and everywhere in between. They're so common, you've no doubt drunk one in a glass of water at some point in your life. To delight your own eyes seeing one yourself, simply go outside and gather up a bit of moss. Pour some distilled water over it (i.e., not chlorinated), and then use an eyedropper to suck up some of the liquid and deposit it on a microscope slide. You'll very likely be in for a treat.

In the name of curiosity, researchers have harassed water bears more than a little bit. They've discovered these tiny wonders can withstand vast extremes of temperature (from –273°C, which is nearly absolute zero, to

151°C, which will cook a pizza), a dose of radiation more than a thousand times stronger than a human can withstand, and six times the pressure of the deepest ocean trench. Oh, and the vacuum of outer space, too. When times are tough, water bears go into a suspended state, during which they lose nearly all the water from their bodies and shrink down into an unrecognizable wrinkled dot. Miraculously, though, all they need to revive completely is a drop of rain, even after years and years have gone by. John recalled the first time he saw one revive: "It was sort of a mystical experience. Here was this creature that was completely dry—by some definitions dead. Then by adding water, you create life."

If drying out doesn't kill you first, most organisms die upon rehydrating, as their expanding tissues rub and stick together, ripping and tearing apart. As John put it, "Trying to revive a body that's been frozen is like trying to make a cow out of hamburger." So John wondered, why don't tardigrades leak after coming back to life? What he discovered is that as water bears dry themselves out, they replace their body's water with *sugar.* If you've ever tried to get dried sugar off of something, you know how rock hard it can get. In a dry tardigrade, sugar locks all the cells and tissues in place, like an internal cast. Then, when a raindrop finds them, the sugar just dissolves as though in a warm cup of tea. The water bear's body isn't chafed a bit, and it just ambles off, good as new.

What John realized is that the water bear's special sugar, called trehalose, could preserve more than just water bears. If trehalose could preserve water bears so well, then it could probably also preserve other kinds of organic tissue. He and his colleagues went to work figuring out how to get trehalose inside mammalian cells, and when they succeeded a few years later, John realized humans had just acquired the extraordinary abilities of water bears in a major way.

Blood platelets in hospitals have a shelf life, for instance, of three to five days. That's why hospitals and the Red Cross need to hold near-constant blood drives. But a platelet preserved with trehalose can last *months.* "If you get in a car accident," John told me at a conference, "the EMTs could open up your glove box, pull out a bandage with your *own* blood platelets preserved in it, and apply it to any wounds you may have." Several companies are working on this technology right now. It all started with admiring the abilities of one tiny little critter. And it all began in high school.

> ### ACTIVITY: Expanding Opportunity Consciousness
>
> This biology-to-challenge sequence works well with having an "opportunity consciousness," with no specific engineering challenge in mind to begin with. It also works especially well with younger students, whose sense of the challenges facing people and humankind in general may be less developed. For example, very young students can pick a biological inspiration that captures their interest or impresses them, and then design a superhero's gear, vehicle, or hideout to have these sorts of abilities (à la Spiderman). Or, to broaden the applications further, have students pick a favorite organism, pick their favorite activity, and then imagine how the organism's talents could improve the activity.

One teacher did this with a student who was having trouble making any progress in thinking like a Nature-inspired engineer. The student answered the first question (camel), the second question (football), and then, with a smile and the proverbial light bulb suddenly going off, the third question (helmets that contain water to keep footballers from getting thirsty on the field). The general format to this biology-to-challenge approach is, first, to discover Nature's genius (as discussed) and, second, to ask yourself, when do people need to do X? A fifth grader and his cat, described in the next section, provide the perfect example of just such an approach.

DESIGNING AND PRESENTING YOUR IDEAS

Once students begin to create with Nature inspiring their ideas, expect completely fresh approaches to innovation. There simply is no more fruitful approach to innovation than combining the strengths of the human mind with the world of biological ideas, the two most powerful creative forces on the planet.

ACTIVITY: Designing Ideas

Just as students can be quick to leap to solutions before they have bio-logical models to inspire them, they will be quick to leap to solutions now that they *do* have them. If they do the legwork, the bio-inspired design concepts will almost generate themselves.

Have students draw out their initial design concepts. Sometimes that's as far as your students may get, but this can be pretty impressive and demonstrate the kind of analogical reasoning so fundamental to Nature-inspired engineering. Remember, it's the cognitive processes that you really want evidence of, more than anything else.

For example, a drawing by New York third grader Eliza H. shows Eliza's grandmother, who has Alzheimer's, moving through her house. Eliza cleverly imagined her grandmother owned a pair of slippers that behaved like slugs, leaving a trail behind them, which her grandmother could use to find her way back to her bedroom or the kitchen. That simple drawing demonstrates a great deal: awareness of human challenges, the ingenious-ness of Nature, and solving challenges through analogical insight, not to mention heart-warming empathy.

Often further research into biological strategies is useful, to find out more about *how* Nature does what it does. This may inspire still larger and deeper solution possibilities for students to consider. Leaf-inspired solar cells weren't commercially competitive until they were redesigned to have a higher surface area like the heavily folded thylakoid membrane of leaf chloroplasts.

Other times, a biological model gives you enough to go on right away. I asked Dr. Phillips, for example, if the anatomy of the scalp and how it functioned helped inform the actual design of his helmet. "It inhibited it," he said decisively. The reason, Ken explained, was because deep study of the anatomy of the scalp revealed that the fibers in the scalp were unstretchable. So for a while they tried to mimic this by making an unstretchable mem-brane, but it was ineffective. Further study revealed that what stretches are muscles, which are attached to the face. But this of course is not really feasible in a helmet, so they went back and changed the design to include a stretchable membrane.

The point is to let natural models *inspire* human design but not entirely define it. Ideas are abstracted from Nature, not cut and pasted. During their application to human technologies, things often end up working somewhat or very differently than they do in the original biological models. The way turkey vultures twist their wings to stabilize themselves against lateral winds, Wilbur Wright's key insight that enabled the successful development of airplanes, is accomplished today by small flaps on airplane wings, called ailerons, which move up and down rather than twist. Sometimes only the very general idea of something in Nature is carried over into the technological application, like the value of vertical architecture from ants. This is one of the reasons this approach to engineering is called *Nature-inspired* rather than *Nature-based*, and it's also one of the reasons human creativity and cleverness are vital to the process.

ACTIVITY: Prototyping

It's great if, in addition to drawing their design concepts, your students can also prototype their design, or some aspect of it. In prototyping, a whole new set of skills, cognition, and rewards come into play. It doesn't need to look like a final product. A thoughtful three-dimensional mockup of a shape or mechanism in cardboard is a great elaboration to a design concept, no injection molded polycarbonate or 3D printing necessary.

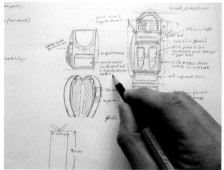 

SKETCHING AND PROTOTYPING have their own unique value in the process of engineering, helping clarify ideas and fostering the skill of communicating these ideas to others. It doesn't have to be fancy: a little cardboard and tape can go a long way.

For example, a group of high school students in France wanted to develop a sled concept for exploring polar regions, which could double as a shelter if the weather got rough. They found their inspiration, quite marvelously, in a roly-poly bug (also known as a pill bug, *Armadillidium vulgare*), the kind of creature you often find under your outdoor plant pots at home. (They're actually crustaceans, not insects, more closely related to lobsters than to beetles.) Pill bugs roll up when threatened, creating a protected inner area, perfect for transforming something flat into a shelter, and quickly. The students carefully measured the dimensions of the scales of a deceased pill bug, as well as how they slid over one another, and created a working prototype of their sled in cardboard and aluminum foil. To see this scale model roll up conveys the brilliance and efficacy of the design like nothing else could, as clear a validation of the value of prototyping as possible.

Inflation/deflation tube or pump

FUNCTIONAL PROTOTYPES ENABLE TESTING: A simple prototype of a key feature of the cat-inspired jacket—an air-filled plastic chamber—enabled the inventor to test air against other forms of insulation.

Of course, another terrific thing about prototypes is that they can then be tested. Sean, a fifth grader from Texas, noticed how his cat puffed up its fur on cold mornings. He learned that by doing this cats can trap more of their own body heat in their fur, keeping them warmer. Sean then came up with a design concept for a jacket inspired by his clever cat: on cold days one blows more air into the jacket, while on warmer days one simply deflates it. It's so simple, it's extraordinary no one thought of it before! It's also a terrific example of the biology-to-challenge sequence of designing. Using a heat lamp and thermometer, Sean then used a simple prototype of an air-filled plastic membrane and tested air against other types of insulation, such as polyester fiberfill. Air performed the best of all the insulation types he tested. Sean's ingenious cat-inspired jacket concept has recently been commercialized and is being sold.

ACTIVITY: Designing for Sustainability

For older students, have them use the Five to Thrive framework (see Chapter 6) to think about and evaluate their design's sustainability. Where do the materials for their innovations come from? What about the energy and chemistry required to process these materials? And where does it all go when people are through using it? Reflecting on these questions is good practice for engineers and can lead to both humility and further aspirations to improve a design, perhaps again with Nature's help.

ACTIVITY: Presenting Designs

Have students present their designs to the rest of their class, laying out the engineering challenge, providing background context, and explaining their design process. Have them use their drawings and prototypes, and demonstrate their idea in use. This is a good way for students to pull together all of their activities, to show their work from start to finish.

You can expand the audience for your students, having them present their ideas to parents, the rest of the school, the Chamber of Commerce, city council—any group that could benefit from the inspiration students have identified and applied.

You can even expand the design process by having your class team up with classrooms in other parts of the world via video conferencing to address a design challenge with Nature-inspired ideas. This would allow students to learn about other parts of the world and the issues people there face, design solution concepts, and share them together, connecting biology to design and community to community. In their presentations they can include this international viewpoint to expand the awareness of their audience, too. The possibilities are endless, and so are the rewards.

SUMMARIZING NATURE-INSPIRED DESIGN STEPS

To wrap things up, here are the steps involved in student-led projects using engineering inspired by Nature:

1. Identify engineering challenges and opportunities
2. Translate into essential functional terms
3. Discover biological models of interest
4. Design, test, and optimize

The framework of the process is that simple. And if you start with biology and apply Nature's ideas to an engineering opportunity (like John Crowe's water bears, or Sean's cat jacket), you just switch steps 1 and 3: students start with a biological model of interest (cat fur-puffing habit), translate its abilities into simple functional terms (manages temperature with air volume), identify an engineering challenge (temperature-regulating clothing), and then design, test, and optimize (blowup jacket).

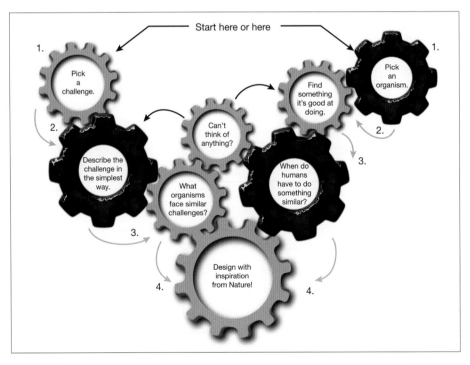

SCHEMATIC OF THE NATURE-INSPIRED ENGINEERING DESIGN PROCESS.

This chapter has discussed a lot of the theoretical ideas that relate to these steps in the process, but for your students, simply show them the framework early and then help mentor them through each step as needed. Here are some of the activities and approaches discussed thus far that support the steps in the design process:

- Identifying engineering challenges and opportunities
  - Keeping a Challenges and Opportunities journal
- Translating challenges into essential functional terms
  - Simple translation practice exercises
- Discovering promising biological models
  - Keeping a Nature's Talents journal
  - Writing a book report on a functional ability in Nature
  - Doing an original research project on Nature's functional abilities
  - Going outside with a challenge in mind (e.g., Function Junction)
  - Communicating with biologists about ideas

Any engagement with students about Nature-inspired engineering, whether for one semester or just one hour, should culminate in a student-led design project. Being able to apply what they've learned through their own initiative is the seminal test of having learned anything to begin with.

Moreover, the effort, even if not perfectly successful, is a valuable experience in a variety of ways. For one, the sense of empowerment students can feel in trying is reward itself. Difficulties in the process also help lay bare where students need help and where in the educational process more thought and refinement are needed.

In the end, you will have given students the opportunity to pull together everything they've learned to take their first steps in being Nature-inspired engineers themselves. More important, you'll have raised their aspirations for human technology and their appreciation for the fascinating animate world we are a part of. There is powerful transformative potential in having students participate in student-led Nature-inspired engineering projects. Just read what fifth grader Sean from Texas said after participating in the design contest in which he produced his cat-inspired jacket:

After I graduate high school, I would like to get an engineering degree. My goal is to solve some of the earth's problems before I finish high school. For example, when settlers first came to Texas, they burned wood and buffalo dung for fuel. They were unaware of all the oil beneath their feet. We may be that way right now. There may be potential energy sources all around us and we do not realize it. Using 3.8 billion years of natural solutions, the answer to energy that will not harm the environment may be all around us if we look. I plan to keep looking.

CONCLUSION

We return, at the end, to the question that began this book: how should we teach young people engineering? I've tried to make the case that a Nature-inspired approach is a distinctly worthwhile option for educators. I didn't start out as an educator myself. I was originally trained as an ecologist, getting my graduate degree from research I conducted while a Peace Corps volunteer in the Philippines, on the conservation needs of giant flying foxes. While I also gave presentations to local kids about biological diversity and led ecology camps, I began to realize that all the scientific knowledge in the world wouldn't fix humankind's negative impact on the natural world.

Shortly after returning to the United States, I learned for the first time about the exploding advances of technological innovation inspired by Nature. I was floored. Here I had gone into ecological research because I loved Nature and wanted to get away from the human-dominated world. And then Nature led me back into the human-built world full of hope. I realized that, as educators, the most useful thing we can do for humankind is give students the information and experiences that will nurture their aspirations and abilities for improving the world and living a more fulfilling life. A Nature-inspired approach to engineering education is an unparalleled means to pursue these goals.

To begin with, teaching kids engineering using a Nature-inspired approach is an opportunity to reconnect children with Nature in a powerful way that can last a lifetime. This is true both because Nature-inspired engineering is such an engaging avenue for exploring the wonders of the natural world, and because one can do so in school environments, as part of the routine school curriculum, that is, without having to rely on limited and expensive field trips. Schools are also where most kids spend most of their educational time, so you can reach virtually all children this way, no matter how asphalted or otherwise underprivileged their circumstances. All children can be reached by a Nature-inspired engineering education.

At the same time, a Nature-inspired approach to engineering is a great way to encourage kids to pursue their further education and careers. For one, Nature-inspired approaches to engineering are the way engineers today are being trained in colleges and universities. It's also a background favored by companies hiring these students. For those kids that may go on to pursue engineering or other STEM careers beyond secondary school, a Nature-inspired approach is one of the most likely paths to get these students college and career ready.

An equally important rationale is that Nature-inspired engineering can be thoroughly engaging for teachers as well as students. Many teachers I've met are "learner" types—people who thrive on learning interesting, new things. Nature-inspired innovation is a topic I've been working with for nearly fifteen years, and I still learn new, fascinating things constantly. What could be bigger than the *creative combination* of Nature and technology? This is an approach to engineering that you will never tire from, that will never go out of fashion, and that will keep you motivated and enthusiastic, crucial for your own quality of life, as well as vital to your students' success.

Today, a ten-year-old can search through the combined knowledge of several thousand years of humankind's recorded thought from free online databases, all the while eating a bowl of Cocoa Crunch at the kitchen table. That same ten-year-old can then invent something new using more sophisticated and powerful computer modeling tools on a home laptop than a NASA scientist in the 1980s could have dreamed of. The information for the design of the kid's new gizmo can then be sent via electric wire, satellites, and radio waves halfway around the world, in a matter of seconds, where the gadget can be mass produced from a 3D printer and then shipped around the globe to consumers, who pay for the item remotely, filling the kid's college bank account. As technology writer Pagan Kennedy has put it, "We are at a moment in history when the barriers to invention are falling as never before."

But where is all this technological potential taking us? That is a vitally important question. Engineers, designers, and architects affect our world like few others, through their powers of imagination and aspiration.

The successes of Nature-inspired engineering to date and common logic strongly suggest that the compass heading for continued human innovation will best be guided by how Nature works. Nature is the only example we have, after all, of a world thriving in perpetuity. Meanwhile, we ourselves are designed to find beauty, meaning, and motivation in Nature's infinitely intriguing phenomena. Without Nature's technological mentorship, without Nature's ingeniousness, efficacy, and enchantment, humankind will likely end up somewhere technologically that we don't want to be.

But with Nature's help, we could produce a human-built world that embodies "imagination itself," designed to work with the natural world instead of against it, and that functions to help all of humanity live to its fullest potential. Such a world will come about only through seeds of aspiration perennially planted in future generations.

You, as a teacher, are the most vital part of that process: without your work, there is no spark, there is no flame; there is only darkness. A Nature-inspired approach to engineering education can provide young people new ways to critically understand human technology, to view and value the natural world, and to gain the skills and aspirations vital to a healthy and enduring engineering practice for humankind.

I hope the very next thing you do after closing this book will be to *go outside*, where humankind's technological dreams are real and awaiting us.

Additional Resources

Teaching students the Nature-inspired engineering design process

The Center for Learning with Nature: https://www.learningwithnature .org/—see the ending lessons of any of the *Engineering Inspired by Nature* curricula, and choose the curriculum relevant to your students' ages.

See resources from The Biomimicry Institute: https://toolbox.biomimicry .org/

http://biomimicry.org/shop/biomimicry-challenge-high-school -curriculum/

Design challenges for young people

Participating in existing design challenges is a great way to get students as engaged as possible. A search of the Internet will reveal several; here are a couple good ones to consider:

FIRST Lego League: https://www.firstinspires.org/robotics/fll/global -innovation

The Biomimicry Institute's Youth Design Challenge: https://youthchallenge .biomimicry.org/

Intel's International Science and Engineering Fair: https://www.intel.com/ content/www/us/en/education/competitions/international-science-and -engineering-fair.html

Google's Science Fair: https://www.googlesciencefair.com/

See also the National Academies of Engineering's Grand Challenges for Engineering: http://www.engineeringchallenges.org/

Places to post student work

Students often put in their best work when they know it will be seen by people outside the classroom. In addition to having your students present their work broadly, you can also submit it for posting to The Center for Learning with Nature site:

https://www.learningwithnature.org/engineering-curricula/earth -innovators-gallery/

Resources for building your own approach to Nature-inspired engineering

The Center for Learning with Nature: www.LearningWithNature.org.

See also The Biomimicry Institute's resources: https://asknature.org /resource/sharing-biomimicry-with-young-people/#.W_xtfDhKipo; https://asknature.org/?s=&page=2&hFR%5Bpost_type_label%5D% 5B0%5D=Resources&is_v=1#.W_xwdThKipq

Communities of teachers using Nature-inspired approaches to teaching

Biomimicry Education Network: https://asknature.org/groups/bio mimicry-education-network/#.W_xr9ThKipp

Education Inspired by Nature (LinkedIn Group): https://www.linkedin .com/groups/8479896/

NOTES

Frontmatter

xi The illustration of a flea's feet on the acknowledgments page came from Robert Hooke's revolutionary book *Micrographia*, published in 1665. Here's how Hooke describes a louse in the book (Chapter 54):

> This is a Creature so officious, that 'twill be known to every one at one time or other, so busie, and so impudent, that it will be intruding it self in every ones company, and so proud and aspiring withall, that it fears not to trample on the best, and affects nothing so much as a Crown; feeds and lives very high, and that makes it so saucy, as to pull any one by the ears that comes in its way, and will never be quiet till it has drawn blood: it is troubled at nothing so much as at a man that scratches his head, as knowing that man is plotting and contriving some mischief against it, and that makes it oftentime sculk into some meaner and lower place, and run behind a mans back, though it go very much against the hair; which ill conditions of it having made it better known then trusted, would exempt me from making any further description of it, did not my faithful Mercury, my Microscope, bring me other information of it. (Published online by eBooks@Adelaide, n.d., The University of Adelaide Library, University of Adelaide, Australia; https://ebooks.adelaide.edu.au/h/hooke/robert/micrographia/index.html. Retrieved June 5, 2019.

Lest anyone imagine science and art are difficult to combine, let Hooke be a lesson to you!

xiv Poem by Walt Whitman, written in 1865, from *Leaves of Grass* (1881–1882).

xiv Quote by John Muir from *John of the Mountains: The Unpublished Journals of John Muir* (1938), 317. University of Wisconsin Press.

Introduction

1 Helms, M. E., Vattam, S., and Goel, A. 2008, January. Compound analogical design, or how to make a surfboard disappear. *Proceedings of the Annual Meeting of the Cognitive Science Society, 30*(30), 781–786.

1 Claes, J. M., Aksnes, D. L., and Mallefet, J. 2010. Phantom hunter of the fjords: Camouflage by counterillumination in a shark (*Etmopterus spinax*). *Journal of Experimental Marine Biology and Ecology, 388*(1–2), 28–32.

1 Harper, R. D., and Case, J. F. 1999. Disruptive counterillumination and its anti-predatory value in the plainfish midshipman *Porichthys notatus*. *Marine Biology, 134*(3), 529–540.

Chapter 1

5   Quote by Steve Jobs from Isaacson, Walter. 2011. Simon & Schuster. Page 539.

7   *Engineers use cognitive processes to solve design challenges; engineering in the rest of Nature is accomplished through the ever creative, ever optimizing, ever restless process of evolution.*

Though I personally speak from an evolutionist tradition and understanding, creationists also find Nature-inspired engineering every bit as valuable an approach to education and innovation. Some very notable Nature-inspired engineers are creationists, and many educators who are creationists use Nature-inspired engineering curricula in their classrooms. The point is, it doesn't matter whether you believe Nature's ingenious designs got this way through evolution or by a superintelligent being: in either case, the rationale to look to the natural world's ingenious designs for engineering inspiration is equally valid.

8   *His anatomical drawings of the human heart educate and inspire surgeons and medical students to this day.*

DiLonardo, M. J. 2015. Eleven beautiful examples of art inspired by science. MNN. com. Retrieved June 5, 2019. https://www.mnn.com/lifestyle/arts-culture/photos/11 -beautiful-examples-of-art-inspired-by-science/leonardo-da-vinci.

8   *The practice of looking to Nature for design inspiration continued to pick up steam in the 1800s, when Alexander Graham Bell, fascinated by the structure and function of the human ear, had an epiphany that changed modern communication as we know it.*

See Bell, A. G. 1908. The Bell telephone: The deposition of Alexander Graham Bell, in the suit brought by the United States to annul the Bell patents. American Bell Telephone Company, 29.

See also Bell, Alexander Graham. 1878. The telephone. A lecture entitled Researches in Electric Telephony, by Professor Alexander Graham Bell, delivered before the Society of Telegraph Engineers, October 31st, 1877. Edited by Frank Bolton and William Edward Langdon. E. & F. N. Spon.

10   *Another monumentally consequential example of Nature-inspired engineering comes from the origin of modern antibiotics, which Alexander Fleming discovered in 1928.*

Fleming, A. 1929. On the antibacterial action of cultures of a penicillium, with special reference to their use in the isolation of *B. influenzae*. *British Journal of Experimental Pathology, 10*(3), 226.

13   Percentages of students reporting an interest in engineering following a Nature-inspired engineering course.

Test conducted in 2014 by Tiffany Roberts, instructor, Credo High School, Rohnert Park, CA.

National averages from Munce, R., and Fraser, E. 2013. Where are the STEM students? MyCollege Options and STEMconnector. STEMconnector. https://www .dailyherald.com/assets/PDF/DA127758822.pdf. Retrieved June 5, 2019.

13   *This course has been, without a doubt, my most absolute favorite course we've had at school so far.*
Student course evaluations, 2014, Credo High School, Rohnert Park, CA.

14   *"I cannot tell you how excited I am to integrate this curriculum into my classes . . ."*
Mr. Brian Hoover, Technical Design Instructor, Hellgate High School, Missoula, Montana. Quoted with permission.

15   *A recent, large-scale study of one million students across the United States found that less than half of these young souls feel hopeful about the future.*

Gallup Student Poll. 2016. Engaged today—ready for tomorrow. Fall 2015 survey results. https://www.gallup.com/file/services/189863/GSP_2015KeyFindings.pdf. Retrieved June 5, 2019.

16 *A recent study—this is no joke—actually found incarcerated* prisoners *spend more time outside today than do our children!*

Martinko, Katherine. 2016, March 25. Children spend less time outside than prison inmates. *Treehugger* (blog). Retrieved June 7, 2019. https://www.treehugger.com/culture/children-spend-less-time-outside-prison-inmates.html

17 *Table 1.1. NGSS engineering performance expectations for K–12*

NGSS Lead States. 2013. *Next Generation Science Standards: For states, by states.* National Academies Press. https://www.nextgenscience.org/

20 *Here's how Sonia Dhingra, a wise high school sophomore, put it in a recent article in Scientific American.*

Dhingra, Sonia. 2018. What High School Engineering Taught Me, and How It Can Empower Other Girls. Scientific American Online (https://blogs.scientificamerican.com/voices/what-high-school-engineering-taught-me-and-how-it-can-empower-other-girls/?redirect=1). Retrieved May 29, 2019.

21 *The positive connections among student engagement, intrinsic interest, learning, and achievement (not to mention student satisfaction and happiness) are not only self-evident but also have been confirmed through extensive educational research.*

See, e.g., Ryan, R.M. and Deci, E.L., 2000. Self-determination theory and the facilitation of intrinsic motivation, social development, and well-being. American psychologist, 55(1), p. 68.

21 *In one study, for example, interest in engineering plummeted from a high of 63 percent in elementary school to 20 percent by the end of high school.*

Heiden, E. O., Cornish, D. L., Lutz, G. M., Kemis, M., and Avery, M. 2013. *Iowa STEM Monitoring Project: 2012–2013 summary report.* University of Northern Iowa, Center for Social and Behavioral Research.

21 *Nationwide student interest in engineering averages a measly 14 percent overall at the end of high school, and a scarce 2 percent for girls.*

Munce, R., and Fraser, E. 2013. Where are the STEM students? MyCollege Options and STEMconnector. STEMconnector. https://www.dailyherald.com/assets/PDF/DA127758822.pdf. Last accessed June 5, 2019.

21 *Only 14 percent of the professional engineering workforce in the United States is made up of women, for example, despite women making up half the population.*

Mark Crawford. 2012. Engineering Still Needs More Women. American Society for Mechanical Engineers. https://www.asme.org/career-education/articles/undergraduate-students/engineering-still-needs-more-women. Retrieved June 5, 2019.

Chapter 2

27 Thomas Edison quote, from *Wikiquote*, Thomas Edison. Retrieved June 5, 2019 from https://en.wikiquote.org/wiki/Thomas_Edison

28 *Its first recorded use in 1325 referred to someone who made mechanical weaponry.*

Oxford English Dictionary, as cited in *Wikipedia*. n.d. . Retrieved June 5, 2019 from Engineering: https://en.wikipedia.org/wiki/History_of_engineering

29 *But a few years ago, researchers Meredith Knight of Tufts University and Christine Cunningham of the Boston Museum of Science cleverly borrowed the well-known "draw a scientist" methodology.*

Knight, M., and Cunningham, C. 2004. Draw an engineer test (DAET): Development of a tool to investigate students' ideas about engineers and engineering. *ASEE Annual Conference and Exposition, 2004*, Session 2530.

30 *This activity likely exercises what today are seldom-used human abilities.*

Some interesting research related to this idea: Nakai, T., Nakatani, H., Hosoda, C., Nonaka, Y., and Okanoya, K. 2017. Sense of accomplishment is modulated by a proper level of instruction and represented in the brain reward system. *PloS One, 12*(1),e0168661. https://journals.plos.org/plosone/article?id=10.1371/journal.pone.0168661

32 *Peter Skillman, a designer credited with inventing the Marshmallow Tower Challenge, has conducted this activity with hundreds of people.*

Original Design Challenge. 2014, January 27. Peter Skillman marshmallow design challenge. YouTube. https://www.youtube.com/watch?v=1p5sBzMtB3Q.

33 *Steven Johnson's book.*

Johnson, S. 2011. *Where good ideas come from: The seven patterns of innovation.* Penguin UK.

34 *Inventors that aren't open to ideas from Nature either haven't been introduced to the idea or assume that what Nature has invented has little relevance.*

James Gordon highlights this theme, too:

> The break with the past that characterized the Industrial Revolution was considered indispensable to progress. Thus most engineers inhabited a world that was intellectually self-contained and self-sufficient. They drew little inspiration, or warning, from other branches of modern science such as medicine and biology. Plants and animals might indeed be successful in the evolutionary struggle, but engineers did not think that they had anything to learn from them. (James Gordon, *The Science of Structures and Materials*, 182)

37 *Charlie Chaplin once participated in a Charlie Chaplin look-alike contest.*

Poverty Bay Herald, Volume Xlvii, Issue 15302, 25 August 1920. https://paperspast.natlib.govt.nz/newspapers/PBH19200825.2.42. Accessed June 5, 2019.

But see also Skeptics Stack Exchange. https://skeptics.stackexchange.com/questions/9423/did-charlie-chaplin-lose-a-charlie-chaplin-look-alike-contest. Retrieved June 5, 2019.

Another good one: the world record for the loudest scream was by a woman who yelled the word "quiet!" She was a schoolteacher, and her yell reached 121.7 decibels—as loud as a jet engine or rock concert.

Belfast Telegraph Digital. https://www.belfasttelegraph.co.uk/news/northern-ireland/worlds-loudest-shout-belongs-to-northern-ireland-teacher-28559417.html. Retrieved June 5, 2019.

39 Toshi Fukaya quote, personal communication, August 1, 2018.

40 *This attachment is very strong.*

Irschick. D. J., Austin, C. C., Petren, K., Fisher, R. N., Losos, J. B., and Ellers, O. 1996 A comparative analysis of clinging ability among pad-bearing lizards. *Biological Journal of the Linnean Society, 59*, 21–35.

40   *A person with this ability could hang upside down from the ceiling.*

A bit of math was used to come up with this equivalency. In theory, a typical tokay gecko could support about 300 pounds (133 kilos).

Scientific American. How do gecko lizards unstick themselves as they move across a surface? https://www.scientificamerican.com/article/how-do-gecko-lizards-unst/. Retrieved June 5, 2019.

And it has 227 mm² of foot surface area.

Sun, W., Neuzil, P., Kustandi, T.S., Oh, S. and Samper, V.D., 2005. The nature of the gecko lizard adhesive force. Biophysical Journal, *89*(2), pp. L14–L17. https://www.ncbi.nlm.nih.gov/pmc/articles/PMC1366649/

If an average man had this ability, he could support over 155,000 pounds with his 120,000 mm² of hand and foot surface area.

Kaye, R., and Konz, S. 1986. Volume and surface area of the hand. *Proceedings of the Human Factors Society Annual Meeting, 30*(4), 382–384.

Birtane, M., and Tuna, H. 2004. The evaluation of plantar pressure distribution in obese and non-obese adults. *Clinical Biomechanics, 19*(10): 1055–1059.

This is approximately the weight of a space shuttle.

The Measure of Things. http://www.bluebulbprojects.com/MeasureOfThings/results.php?comp=weight&unit=lbs&amt=150000&sort=pr&p=1). Retrieved June 5, 2019.

40   *Geckos use interatomic forces.*

This is an area of active research and ongoing dispute (see below), which is why I generalized the mechanism involved. Regardless of the specific interatomic force you consider, the atoms of geckos' feet (more specifically the electrons) do "combine" (either by interaction, or transferring) with the atoms of the surface they are walking on. Note these are physical bonds, not ionic or covalent chemical bonds.

Izadi, H., Stewart, K. M. E., and Penlidis, A. 2014. Role of contact electrification and electrostatic interactions in gecko adhesion. *Journal of the Royal Society Interface, 11*(98): 20140371.

Autumn, K., Sitti, M., Liang, Y. A., Peattie, A. M., Hansen, W. R., Sponberg, S., Kenny, T. W., Fearing, R., Israelachvili, J. N., and Full, R. J. 2002. Evidence for van der Waals adhesion in gecko setae. *Proceedings of the National Academy of Sciences, 99*(19), 12252–12256.

40   *To answer this we have to peer very closely at a gecko's foot.*

Sun, W., Neuzil, P., Kustandi, T. S., Oh, S., and Samper, V. D. 2005. The nature of the gecko lizard adhesive force. *Biophysical Journal, 89*(2), L14–L17.

40   *Each individual attachment exerted by a frayed foot hair is weak.*

Here's a nice video of it: Autumn, K., Niewiarowski, P. and Puthoff, J. B. 2014. Gecko Adhesion as a Model System for Integrative Biology, Interdisciplinary Science, and Bioinspired Engineering: Video 3. *Annual Review of Ecology, Evolution, and Systematics.* Vimeo. https://vimeo.com/105308288. Retrieved June 5, 2019.

41   *Dead fish started floating up in a Manukau Harbor near Auckland, New Zealand.*

Jay Boreham. 2013. Dye spill stains Auckland harbour. http://www.stuff.co.nz/national/8868412/Dye-spill-stains-Auckland-harbour. Retrieved June 5, 2019.

42   *Twenty percent of all industrial water pollution comes from coloring textiles alone.*

Danielle LaRose. 2017. To Dye For: Textile Processing's Global Impact. https://www.carmenbusquets.com/journal/post/fashion-dye-pollution. Retrieved June 5, 2019.

41   *In Fort Myers, Florida, . . . a dye discharged accidentally from a hospital turned the Caloosahatchee River red.*
      NBC2 News. Dye spill turns Fort Myers waterway red. http://www.nbc-2.com/story/34504528/dye-spill-turns-fort-myers-waterway-red. Retrieved June 5, 2019.

41   *Toms River, New Jersey, has disproportionately high cancer rates.*
      Alexander Nazaryan, 2013. A Town Plagued by Water. New Yorker Magazine. https://www.newyorker.com/tech/elements/a-town-plagued-by-water. Retrieved June 5, 2019.

42   *In China, seventy-two toxic chemicals are known to come from the textile industry.*
      Danielle LaRose. 2017. To Dye For: Textile Processing's Global Impact. https://www.carmenbusquets.com/journal/post/fashion-dye-pollution. Retrieved June 5, 2019

42   *It's still used extensively in cosmetics and hair dye today.*
      David Suzuki Foundation. The Dirty Dozen: Coal Tar Dyes. https://davidsuzuki.org/queen-of-green/the-dirty-dozen-coal-tar-dyes/. Retrieved June 5, 2019.

42   *Other pigments and dyes, such as many used in textiles and plastics, include heavy metals.*
      Halimoon, N., and Yin, R. G. S. 2010. Removal of heavy metals from textile wastewater using zeolite. *Environment Asia, 3,* 124–130.

44   *L'Oréal has produced cosmetics based on structural color.*
      Luke, S.M. and Vukusic, P., 2011. An introduction to biomimetic photonic design. Europhysics news, *42*(3), pp. 20–23. https://www.europhysicsnews.org/articles/epn/pdf/2011/03/epn2011423p20.pdf

44   *A Japanese company has produced stunningly iridescent textiles by layering nylon together.*
      Transmaterial. 2010. http://transmaterial.net/morphotex/. Retrieved June 5, 2019.

51   *Research shows that teacher enthusiasm is a big determinant of student interest and success.*
      Keller, M., Neumann, K., and Fischer, H. E. 2013. Teacher enthusiasm and student learning. , 247–249 in Hattie, J. and Anderman, E.M. eds., 2013. International guide to student achievement. Routledge.
      Patrick, B. C., Hisley, J., and Kempler, T. 2000. "What's everybody so excited about?": The effects of teacher enthusiasm on student intrinsic motivation and vitality. *Journal of Experimental Educational, 68*(3): 217–236.

Chapter 3

58   *When you look at the Eiffel Tower . . . compressive forces are streaming down the structure . . . as if it were made of straws and someone at the top were pouring water on them.*
      Thanks to Roma Agrawal for this terrific analogy, from Built: The Hidden Stories Behind our Structures. 2018. Bloomsbury.

59   *We can use a mildly stretchy material to observe this tension and compression in bending, and a kitchen sponge works perfectly.*
      Thanks to Mario Salvadori for this terrific demonstration, from Salvadori, M. 1990. *Why buildings stand up: The strength of architecture.* Norton.

65   *And with this simple activity using a physical model of corrugation to investigate materials, shape, and strength, you've also simultaneously covered a slew of engineering design components involving shape and function in the Next Generation Science Standards.*
      In K-2, for example, the NGSS is explicit about examining the connection between shape

and function. One performance expectation (K-2-ETS1-2) involves developing "a simple sketch, drawing, or physical model to illustrate how the shape of an object helps it function as needed to solve a given problem," with lots of additional connections to the supporting three dimensions.

66 *According to the American Society of Civil Engineers, nearly 10 percent of the 600,000+ bridges in the United States alone are considered "structurally deficient."*
   2017 Infrastructure Report Card. American Society of Civil Engineers. https://www .infrastructurereportcard.org/cat-item/bridges/. Retrieved on June 5, 2019.

68 *This object made of chalk less than a third of millimeter thick is very unlikely to give way.*
   Sun, C. J., Chen, S. R., Xu, G. Y., Liu, X. M., and Yang, N. 2012. Global variation and uniformity of eggshell thickness for chicken eggs. *Poultry Science, 91*(10), 2718–2721.
   Strength of eggs: Ruth Milne, The Royal Society. 2017. The strength of eggs. https://phys .org/news/2017-01-strong-egg.html. Retrieved June 5, 2019.

76 *Add up the surface area of all the leaves on a mature broadleaf tree, such as an oak, and you get an area equivalent to one entire side of a professional basketball court.*
   Calculated from data in Monk, C. D., Child, G. I., and Nicholson, S. A. 1970. Biomass, litter and leaf surface area estimates of an oak-hickory forest. *Oikos,* Jan. 1: 138–141.

77 J. E. Gordon quote, In Delta Willis, 1996. Naturally Inspired. Natural History Magazine. https://www.questia.com/magazine/1P3-9284713/naturally-inspired. Retrieved June 5, 2019.

79 *Another way to scale the tree curve to any size desired is to use a method developed by Claus Mattheck.*
   Mattheck, C., Kappel, R., and Sauer, A. 2007. Shape optimization the easy way: the "method of tensile triangles." *International Journal of Design and Nature and Ecodynamics, 2*(4), 301–309. https://www.witpress.com/Secure/ejournals/papers/JDN020 4001f.pdf
   Mattheck, C., Kappel, R., and Kraft, O. 2008. Meaning of the 45-angle in mechanical design according to nature. *WIT Transactions on Ecology and the Environment, 114.* Reprinted in *Design and nature IV: Comparing design in nature with science and engineering,* edited by C. A. Brebbis and A. Carpi. WIT Press, 2010, Vol. 4, p. 139. https://www.witpress.com/Secure/elibrary/papers/DN08/DN08015FU1.pdf
   Mattheck, C., and Bethge, K. 1998. The structural optimization of trees. *Naturwissenschaften, 85*(1), 1–10.
   Mattheck, C. 2006. Teacher tree: The evolution of notch shape optimization from complex to simple. *Engineering Fracture Mechanics, 73*(12), 1732–1742.

80 *Tests done by Mattheck showed that using a tree-curve fillet reduces stress concentrations over quarter-circle fillets in notches by a whopping 57 percent!*
   Mattheck, C., and Kubler, H. 1997. *Wood—The internal optimization of trees.* Springer, 37.

Chapter 4

85 Antoine de Saint-Exupery quote from Terre des Hommes. 1939. Page 60. CreateSpace Independent Publishing Platform.

88 Von Meyer quote from von Meyer, G. H. 2011. The classic: The architecture of the trabecular bone (tenth contribution on the mechanics of the human skeletal framework). *Clinical Orthopaedics and Related Research, 469*(11), 3080.

88 On the influence of bone trabaculae on Culmann's engineering approach, the story is that

Culmann popped in to see Dr. von Meyer when von Meyer was dissecting a bone. Upon seeing the trabaculae of the bone, Culmann remarked, "That's my crane!"

Thompson, D. W. 1942. *On growth and form*. 977. Cambridge University Press.

Dr. von Meyer wrote that Culmann's "drawing of a modified bent crane was drafted under the supervision of Mr. Prof. Culmann, to approximately imitate the organization of the upper femur. " I don't think he meant that Culmann intended to imitate the femur, only that the stress lines Culmann drew coincidentally did imitate the femur.

von Meyer, G. H. 2011. The classic: The architecture of the trabecular bone (tenth contribution on the mechanics of the human skeletal framework). *Clinical Orthopaedics and Related Research, 469*(11), 3079.

Skedros, J.G. and Brand, R.A., 2011. Biographical sketch: Georg Hermann von Meyer (1815–1892). Clinical Orthopaedics and Related Research®, *469*(11), p. 3072. https://www.ncbi.nlm.nih.gov/pmc/articles/PMC3183195/

88   *This mesh-work approach to creating larger structures is the same approach engineers take in aligning metal struts . . . , for example, in the iconic metal latticework of the Eiffel Tower.*
Analysis of the weight and material of the Eiffel Tower adapted from a great article by Aatish Bhatia: Bhatia, A. 2015. What Your Bones Have In Common With The Eiffel Tower. Wired. https://www.wired.com/2015/03/empzeal-eiffel-tower/. Retrieved June 5, 2019.

90   Leonardo da Vinci quote from Da Vinci, Leonardo. *The Notebooks of Leonardo Da Vinci*, Vol. 2. 1970. Dover, 126.

91   *One of the . . . most significant applications of bone-inspired lightweighting is employed in a computer-assisted design or CAD program.*
In the 1990s, Jeff Brennan was a graduate student studying biomedical engineering under Noboru Kikuchi at the University of Michigan. They began to translate growth patterns observed in bones into mathematical formulas. Today, the Michigan-based Altair software company, where Brennan is now an executive, uses these algorithms in their famous OptiStruct CAD program.

91   *And that's a short list.*
For some great case studies, see Altair. n.d. Altair's Leadership in optimization. Retrieved June 5, 2019.from https://www.altair.com/optimization/

91   *Boeing alone used Altair's software to redesign 150 separate components of its 787 Dreamliner.*
Tom McKeag. The Biomimicry Column. 2014. https://www.greenbiz.com/blog/2014/08/05/how-nature-inspires-us-save-resources-shape-optimization. Retrieved June 5, 2019.

91   *With Altair's software, Airbus was able to drop the weight of its A380 by . . . 1,100 pounds.*
Altair. n.d. https://www.altair.com/optimization/. Retrieved June 5, 2019.

91   *Altair estimates its software saves 1.3* billion *pounds of material annually.*
Altair. 2009. https://www.altair.com/NewsDetail.aspx?news_id=10331. Retrieved June 5, 2019.

91   *Altair estimates its software . . . prevents nearly 1.8* billion *pounds of carbon dioxide a year from entering the atmosphere.*
GreenBiz. 2014. https://www.greenbiz.com/blog/2014/08/05/how-nature-inspires-us-save-resources-shape-optimization. Retrieved June 5, 2019.

91   *Using Altair's software, the medical device company Medtronic redesigned heart stents.*
Nikolsky, E., Gruberg, L., Pechersky, S., Kapeliovich, M., Grenadier, E., Amikam, S., Boulos, M., Suleiman, M., Markiewicz, W., and Beyar, R. 2003. Stent deployment

failure: Reasons, implications, and short- and long-term outcomes. *Catheterization and Cardiovascular Intervention*s, *59*(3), 324–328.

92   *The . . . software allowed Medtronic to reduce the buildup of mechanical stress in stents by . . . 71 percent.*
    Reducing Medical Stent Stress by 71%. n.d. https://www.altair.com/pd/customer-story/medtronic%2freducing-medical-stent-stress-by-71%25. Retrieved June 5, 2019.

92, 94   The drawings of the tape dispenser are from teacher Simone Ferdinand, as part of homework given during a teacher training by The Center for Learning with Nature.

Chapter 5

98   Elisabeth Tova Bailey quote from Bailey, E. T. 2016. *The sound of a wild snail eating*. Text Publishing, 90.

100   Charles Darwin quote, retold in Bailey, E. T. 2016 *The sound of a wild snail eating*. Algonquin., 98–99

99   *While snail mucus is used in locomotion . . . , it simultaneously serves additional purposes.*
    Ng, T., Saltin, S. H., Davies, M. S., Johannesson, K., Stafford, R., and Williams, G. A. 2013. Snails and their trails: The multiple functions of trail=following in gastropods. *Biological Reviews, 88*(3), 683–700.

107   *As the snail travels, muscle contractions flow across the snail's foot.*
    Lai, J. H., del Alamo, J. C., Rodríguez-Rodríguez, J., and Lasheras, J. C. 2010. The mechanics of the adhesive locomotion of terrestrial gastropods. *Journal of Experimental Biology, 213*(22), 3920–3933. http://jeb.biologists.org/content/jexbio/213/22/3920.full.pdf

108   *A bulletproof vest soaked in a shear-thickening fluid dissipates just as much ballistic energy as plain Kevlar but requires one-third less the thickness.*
    Lee, Y. S., Wetzel, E. D., and Wagner, N. J. 2003. The ballistic impact characteristics of Kevlar® woven fabrics impregnated with a colloidal shear thickening fluid. *Journal of Materials Science, 38*(13), 2832 (Table 3).

108   *Such armor in fact now exists, as well as kneepads that floor installers use . . . and more.*
    Lang, N., Pereira, M. J., Lee, Y., Friehs, I., Vasilyev, N. V., Feins, E. N., Ablasser, K., O'Cearbhaill, E. D., Xu, C., Fabozzo, A., and Padera, R. 2014. A blood-resistant surgical glue for minimally invasive repair of vessels and heart defects. *Science Translational Medicine, 6*(218), 218ra6–218ra6.
    Wikipedia. n.d.. Retrieved June 5, 2019. from https://en.wikipedia.org/wiki/Dilatant #Applications

109   E. E. Cummings quote from his 1938 introduction to *New Poems*, from Bob Schwartz, 2018. Always the beautiful answer. https://bobmschwartz.com/2018/05/10/always-the -beautiful-answer/

113   *Some plants, known as superhydrophobic . . . , have what seems like a magical force field against water droplets.*
    Texture-based water repellency was discovered first in studies of the lotus plant. Key early papers include the following:
        Barthlott, W., and Neinhuis, C. 1997. Purity of the sacred lotus, or escape from contamination in biological surfaces. *Planta, 202*(1), 1–8.
        Neinhuis, C., and Barthlott, W. 1997. Characterization and distribution of water-repellent, self-cleaning plant surfaces. *Annals of Botany, 79*(6), 667–677.

120   *Studies have found correlations between perfluorinated compounds and a variety of health issues, including ADHD in children, hormone disruptions, increased cholesterol levels, birth defects, heart disease, and cancer.*

Webster, G. 2010, October. Potential human health effects of perfluorinated chemicals (PFCs). National Collaborating Centre for Environmental Health. http://www .ncceh.ca/sites/default/files/Health_effects_PFCs_Oct_2010.pdf

122   *The seed of a dandelion . . . is very light.*

Pappus weight calculated from data in Hale, A. N., Imfeld, S. M., Hart, C. E., Gribbins, K. M., Yoder, J. A., and Collier, M. H. 2010. Reduced seed germination after pappus removal in the North American dandelion (*Taraxacum officinale*; Asteraceae). *Weed Science, 58*(4), 420–425.

123   *Dandelion seeds couple their mechanism of abscission (detachment) with their mechanism of dispersal (wind).*

Tackenberg, O., Poschlod, P., and Kahmen, S. 2003. Dandelion seed dispersal: The horizontal wind speed does not matter for long-distance dispersal—it is updraft! *Plant Biology, 5*(5), 451–454.

Without these updrafts, a dandelion seed would settle to the ground at a rate of about 0.4–0.65 meters per second.

Andersen, M. C. 1993. Diaspore morphology and seed dispersal in several wind-dispersed Asteraceae. *American Journal of Botany, 80*(5), 487–492.

Azuma, A. 2007. Flight of seeds, flying fish, squid, mammals, amphibians and reptiles. *Flow Phenomena in Nature, 1,* 88.

123   *This is loosely referenced as Bernoulli's principle.*

Wikipedia. n.d. Retrieved June 5, 2019. https://en.wikipedia.org/wiki/Bernoulli%27s _principle

125   *This "ramps" the flowing air upward, constricting it so that it speeds over the wing more quickly than the air flowing unimpeded beneath the wing.*

John S. Denker. See How It Flies. n.d. Retrieved June 5, 2019. http://www.av8n.com/ how/htm/airfoils.html

126   *Its downward angle . . . is 12 percent, an optimum amount to cause the seed to descend a minimum amount necessary to create lift.*

Azuma, A., and Okuno, Y. 1987. Flight of a samara, *Alsomitra macrocarpa. Journal of Theoretical Biology, 129*(3), 263–274.

126   *As a result of this very shallow angle of attack, the seed descends as little as 0.3 meters per second.*

Rate of descent is 0.3–0.7 meters per second: Azuma, A. 2007. Flight of seeds, flying fish, squid, mammals, amphibians and reptiles. *Flow Phenomena in Nature, 1,* 88.

126   *The swept-back shape of the wings improves both the stability of the seed, including yaw . . . and pitch . . . the swept-back wings effectively make more of the glider covered by horizontal wings, nose to tail, which stabilizes the glider against pitch.*

Quora. 2016. Retrieved June 5, 2019. https://www.quora.com/How-does-sweepback -improve-lateral-stability-of-an-aircraft

Stack Exchange Aviation. n.d. Retrieved June 5, 2019. https://aviation.stackexchange .com/questions/9287/how-does-wing-sweep-increase-aircraft-stability

126   *The Javan cucumber seed has served as an inspiration both for human-made gliders and tailless airplanes.*

Bio-aerial locomotion. 2011. Retrieved June 5, 2019. http://blogs.bu.edu/biolocomotion /2011/09/25/gliding-vine-seeds/

See also Azuma, A. 2007. Flight of seeds, flying fish, squid, mammals, amphibians and reptiles. *Flow Phenomena in Nature, 1*, 88.

See also Alexander, D. E. 2004. *Nature's flyers: Birds, insects, and the biomechanics of flight.* JHU Press, 50–51.

127   *Cayley solved the problem at the same time, noting that the tapered backend shape of trout and ducks helped reduce the vacuum's formation.*

Cayley, G. 1810. On aerial navigation. *Nicholson's Journal of Natural Philosophy*, March: 10.

127   *The genius of a helicopter seed is to* use *pressure drag to suck itself upward, against gravity, and thus delay descent.*

Lentink, D., Dickson, W. B., Van Leeuwen, J. L., and Dickinson, M. H. 2009. Leading-edge vortices elevate lift of autorotating plant seeds. *Science, 324*(5933), 1438–1440.

Chapter 6

135   Carina Moeller and colleagues quote from Moeller, C., Sauerborn, J., de Voil, P., Manschadi, A. M., Pala, M., and Meinke, H. 2014. Assessing the sustainability of wheat-based cropping systems using simulation modelling: sustainability = 42? *Sustainability Science, 9*(1), 1–16.

136   *There are roughly 13,000 active mines around the globe, from which humans currently extract about 68 billion tons of material out of Earth's crust in a year.*

Number of active mines: The National Institute for Occupational Safety and Health. Statistics: All Mining. n.d. Retrieved June 5, 2019. https://www.cdc.gov/niosh/mining/ statistics/allmining.html

Humans mine approximately 17 billion tonnes (metric tons) of minerals each year, which includes all fossil fuels.

Reichl, C., Schatz, M., and Zsak, G. 2014. World mining data. *Minerals Production Inter-national Organizing Committee for the World Mining Congresses, 32*(1), 24.

This doesn't include bauxite or components of concrete (rock, sand, calcium carbonate). To this we can add 300 million tonnes of bauxite.

Wikipedia. n.d. Retrieved June 5, 2019. https://en.wikipedia.org/wiki/List_of_ countries_by_bauxite_production

And, 44.2 billion tonnes of concrete (40 billion tonnes world aggregate market.

http://www.freedoniagroup.com/World-Construction-Aggregates.html

Plus 4.2 billion tonnes of cement (calcium carbonate).

Freedonia. 2015. Retrieved June 5, 2019. http://www.freedoniagroup.com/World -Cement.html

This makes for a grand total of 61.5 billion tonnes.

136   *Ten cubic miles of material [removed from the Earth's crust], every year . . . you can pack 16,000 Great Pyramids of Giza.*

A total of 68 billion tons of material (or 61.5 billion tonnes) is extracted from Earth's crust each year, which equals 136 trillion pounds. Most of this is crushed stone for use as aggregate in concrete. Concrete aggregate weights about 100 pounds per cubic foot.

Kamran Nemati. 2015. Retrieved June 5, 2019. http://courses.washington.edu/ cm425/aggregate.pdf

Divide 136 trillion pounds by 100 pounds, and it thus occupies 1,360,000,000,000 cubic feet, which equals about 39 billion cubic meters, or about 40 cubic kilometers, or about 10 cubic miles; 1 cubic kilometer is about 400 Great Pyramids of Giza.

> The Measure of Things. n.d. Retrieved June 5, 2019. http://www.bluebulbprojects .com/MeasureOfThings/results.php?amt=1&comp=volume&unit=ckm&searc hTerm=1+cubic+ki

So 16,000 Great Pyramids of Giza of stuff is mined out of the earth each year.

136 *Manufacturing all of this material into the things humans make . . . releases some 9.5 billion tons of carbon dioxide into the atmosphere each year, plus 10 million tons of toxic chemical effluent.* Global carbon dioxide emissions were 45 billion tons in 2017.

> USA Today. Global carbon dioxide emissions reach record high. 2017. Retrieved June 5, 2019. https://www.usatoday.com/story/news/world/2017/11/13/global -carbon-dioxide-emissions-reach-record-high/859659001/

And, 21 percent of global greenhouse gas emissions come from manufacturing (hence 9.5 billion tons come from industry).

> Environmental Protection Agency. Greenhouse Gas Emissions. n.d. Retrieved November 15, 2018. https://www.epa.gov/ghgemissions/global-greenhouse-gas -emissions-data

Some 10 million tons of toxic chemicals are released into the environment from industry each year.

> Worldometers. n.d. Retrieved November 15, 2018. http://www.worldometers.info/ view/toxchem/

137 *Cancer rates are expected to more than double in the next couple of decades.*

> CNN. 2014. WHO: Imminent global cancer 'disaster' reflects aging, lifestyle factors. Retrieved November 15, 2018. https://www.cnn.com/2014/02/04/health/who -world-cancer-report/index.html

137 *Half of the species on Earth are projected to go extinct by the end of the century.*

> The Guardian. 2017. Biologists think 50% of species will be facing extinction by the end of the century. Retrieved June 5, 2019. https://www.theguardian.com/ environment/2017/feb/25/half-all-species-extinct-end-century-vatican-conference

137 *We add 300 million tons of plastic . . . to the planet each year.*

> United Nations. n.d. Retrieved November 15, 2018. https://www.unenvironment.org/ interactive/beat-plastic-pollution/

137 *Less than 10 percent of it gets recycled.*

> National Geographic. Planet or Plastic? 2017. Retrieved June 5, 2019. https://news .nationalgeographic.com/2017/07/plastic-produced-recycling-waste-ocean-trash -debris-environment/

137 *By 2050, there will literally be more plastic in the ocean than fish*

> Neufeld, L., Stassen, F., Sheppard, R., and Gilman, T. 2016. The new plastics economy: Rethinking the future of plastics. In *World Economic Forum.*, 7.

137 *The fish we eat today already contain plastic bits and fibers.*

> Rochman, C. M., Tahir, A., Williams, S. L., Baxa, D. V., Lam, R., Miller, J. T., Teh, F. C., Werorilangi, S., and Teh, S. J. 2015. Anthropogenic debris in seafood: Plastic debris and fibers from textiles in fish and bivalves sold for human consumption. *Scientific Reports*, 5, 14340.

138 *Engineers . . . rarely if ever have classes about biological sustainability or environmental science.*

Dr. Mariappan Jawaharlal, professor of mechanical engineering, California State Polytechnic University, Pomona, personal communication, 2014.

140 *The leads are sandwiched between two slabs of wood before being cut into individual pencils.*

Since the wood-encircled graphite, as a type of coal, comes from ancient vegetation heated and compressed over time, pencils in cross section are like a "before" and "after" of geological forces.

Photo essay of the pencil making process: General Pencil Company. n.d. Retrieved June 5, 2019. https://www.generalpencil.com/how-a-pencil-is-made.html

The Library of Economics and Liberty. A deep exploration of the pencil making process: Read, L. E. 1958. I, pencil. Retrieved June 5, 2019. https://www.econlib.org/library/Essays/rdPncl.html

More about pencils can be found at the following websites:

Stationery Wiki. n.d. Retrieved June 5, 2019. https://stationery.wiki/Pencil#cite_note-Petroski-33

Chemical and Engineering News. 2001. Retrieved June 5, 2019. http://pubs.acs.org/cen/whatstuff/stuff/7942sci4.html

Popular Mechanics. Jonathan Schifman. 2016. Retrieved June 5, 2019. https://www.popularmechanics.com/technology/a21567/history-of-the-pencil/

140 *Trees like red cedar (*Juniperus virginiana*) were preferred for pencil wood until about the 1920s, when overharvesting of old growth reduced the large-diameter trees available. In England during World War II, wood for pencils became so scarce that owning a rotary pencil sharpener was actually made illegal, in an attempt to reduce waste. Today, wood for pencils comes from trees like incense cedar (*Calocedrus decurrens*), found in the Sierra Nevada foothills and mountains of California.*

Pencils.com. n.d. Retrieved June 5, 2019. https://pencils.com/pages/the-history-of-the-pencil

How Products Are Made. n.d. Retrieved June 5, 2019. http://www.madehow.com/Volume-5/Eraser.html

Nice video about pencil history: Ted.com. Caroline Weaver. Why the pencil is perfect. n.d. Retrieved June 5, 2019. https://www.ted.com/talks/caroline_weaver_why_the_pencil_is_perfect/transcript?language=en

141 *Attempts to certify the sustainable management of forests for pencil wood production exist, but they are imperfect, with some operations still clearing old-growth forests, using toxic herbicides in plantations, and so on.*

Worldwatch Institute. Life-Cycle Studies: Pencils. n.d. Retrieved June 5, 2019. http://www.worldwatch.org/node/6422

William Harris. n.d. How Stuff Works. Manufacturing of aluminum. Retrieved June 5, 2019: https://science.howstuffworks.com/aluminum2.htm

141 *It wasn't until 1858, some three hundred years after the pencil was invented, that someone first attached an eraser to a pencil.*

Wikipedia. n.d. Retrieved June 5, 2019. https://en.wikipedia.org/wiki/Eraser#History

Pencil paint:

Carey Brothers. 2015. On the house. Retrieved June 5, 2019. http://onthehouse.com/three-main-ingredients-in-paint/

Gabrielle Hick. 2017. Artsy.net. Retrieved June 5, 2019. https://www.artsy.net/article/artsy-editorial-little-known-reason-pencils-yellow

Ethyl acetate, used in pencil lacquer, is also used by entomologists researching insects because it effectively asphyxiates them.

Wikipedia. n.d. Retrieved June 5, 2019. https://en.wikipedia.org/wiki/Ethyl_acetate

141   *Whether the idea of attaching eraser to a pencil could be patented went all the way to the Supreme Court.*

How products are made. n.d. Retrieved June 5, 2019. http://www.madehow.com/Volume-5/Eraser.html

143   Thomas Paine quote from Paine, T. 1794. *Age of Reason*, pt. 1, sec. 8.

144   For more about the *IPAT* equation, see Wikipedia. n.d. Retrieved June 5, 2019. https://en.wikipedia.org/wiki/I_%3D_PAT

145   The Five to Thrive framework was developed by the author; see, for example, the following: Green Teacher. 2013. Retrieved June 5, 2019. https://greenteacher.com/concrete-without-quarries/

Engineering Inspired by Nature curriculum (middle/high school version), at The Center for Learning with Nature: www.LearningWithNature.org

147   The entire Materials Without Mining part of the chapter is published with credit to "Brainy Coral," in *Engineering Inspired by Nature* curriculum. © Sam Stier.

147   *Nature makes every living thing—230 billion tons . . . out of thin air.*

Nature produces about 105 billion tonnes of carbon in carbon-based products each year.

Field, Christopher B., Behrenfeld, Michael J., Randerson, James T., and Falkowski, P. 1998. Primary production of the biosphere: Integrating terrestrial and oceanic components. *Science, 281*(5374), 237–240.

See also Niklas, K. J. 1992. *Plant biomechanics: An engineering approach to plant form and function.* University of Chicago Press.

This only measures the carbon component, so the actual tonnage is much higher, because it involves other elements. Since vegetation is roughly 50 percent carbon by weight and 50 percent other elements (primarily hydrogen and oxygen), we could double the above number to approximately 210 billion tonnes of net primary products, or 230 billion tons.

Note too this is net primary productivity, not gross (i.e., minus the energy to produce it). Also, this is only *primary* production, and doesn't include all the secondary, tertiary, and so forth, products made out of fixed carbon (e.g., herbivores, carnivores, decomposers).

147   *More than 90 percent of a solid tree comes from CO2 . . . , with another 7 percent coming from rain (H2O), and the remainder . . . from the soil.*

"Dry (moisture-free) wood is about 48–50% carbon, 38–42 percent oxygen, 6–7% hydrogen and a number of other elements, such as nitrogen and sulfur in very small percentages." These percentages are based on weight.

Jeff Howe. 2011. What do Trees and People have in Common? - Lots! Dovetail Partners. Retrieved June 5, 2019. http://www.dovetailinc.org/reports/Commentary+What+do+Trees+and+People+have+in+Common+-+Lots%21++_n358?prefix=%2Freports

148   *Whereas atmospheric compounds are about three nanometers apart on average, the diameter of an entire glucose molecule is only a single nanometer wide.*

Quora. n.d. How far apart are air molecules at standard temperature and pressure (on average)? Retrieved June 5, 2019. https://www.quora.com/How-far-apart-are-air -molecules-at-standard-temperature-and-pressure-on-average

Cell biology by the numbers. n.d. Retrieved June 5, 2019. http://book.bionumbers.org/ how-big-are-biochemical-nuts-and-bolts/

More about glucose and its global significance: Wikipedia. n.d, Retrieved June 5, 2019. https://en.wikipedia.org/wiki/Glucose

148 *If you weighed the air extending above your head to the top of Earth's atmosphere, it would weigh in at a tonne (a metric ton, over two thousand pounds).*

Physics.org. n.d. Retrieved June 5, 2019. http://www.physics.org/facts/air-really.asp

148 *The total weight of Earth's atmosphere is . . . 6 quadrillion tons.*

Physlink.com. n.d. Retrieved June 5, 2019. http://www.physlink.com/Education/ AskExperts/ae328.cfm

148 *The airy carbon Nature spins into the world's vegetation then proceeds to nurture everything else.*

The exception are lithoautotrophs, microbes (mostly bacteria) that make their tissues powered not with sunlight, but with minerals they actively decompose and organisms that feed on them. In terms of biomass, these food chains are small compared to vegetative-based food chains.

See, for example, Ramos, J. L. 2003. Lessons from the genome of a lithoautotroph: Making biomass from almost nothing. *Journal of Bacteriology, 185*(9), 2690–2691.

149 *The carbon in us (about 18 percent of our body mass) isn't anything we fixed ourselves but comes completely from the atmosphere, via carbon first sequestered by plants or phytoplankton, transferred to our bodies when we eat salad, grass-eating cows, or plankton-eating fish.*

Wikipedia. n.d. Retrieved June 5, 2019. https://en.wikipedia.org/wiki/Composition_ of_the_human_body

149 N. J. Berrill quote from Berrill, N. J. 1958. *You and the universe.* Dodd, Mead, 18–19.

Why carbon is such a good molecule for making stuff in Nature:

MadSci Network. Dan Berger, Faculty Chemistry/Science, Bluffton College. 2011. Retrieved June 5, 2019. http://www.madsci.org/posts/archives/2001 -06/993247450.Ch.r.html

Socratic. n.d. Retrieved June 5, 2019. https://socratic.org/questions/why-is-carbon -important-for-forming-complicated-molecules

Scientific American. S.E. Gould. 2012. Retrieved June 5, 2019. https://blogs .scientificamerican.com/lab-rat/shine-on-you-crazy-diamond-why-humans -are-carbon-based-lifeforms/

150 *To date, over 9 million distinct carbon-containing chemical compounds are known. In contrast, there are but half a million inorganic (noncarbon) ones.*

Ouellette, R. J., and Rawn, J. D. 2014. *Organic chemistry: Structure, mechanism, and synthesis.* Elsevier, 31.

151 *In its mildest forms, shortages of industrial raw materials cause economic disturbances; in its worst forms, such shortages result in physical conflict.*

Henckens, M. L. C. M., Van Ierland, E. C., Driessen, P. P. J., and Worrell, E. 2016. Mineral resources: Geological scarcity, market price trends, and future generations. *Resources Policy, 49,* 102–111.

Prior, T., Giurco, D., Mudd, G., Mason, L., and Behrisch, J. 2012. Resource depletion, peak minerals and the implications for sustainable resource management. *Global Environmental Change, 22*(3), 577–587.

Alao, A. 2007. *Natural resources and conflict in Africa: The tragedy of endowment.* University Rochester Press.

Dinar, S. ed. 2011. *Beyond resource wars: Scarcity, environmental degradation, and international cooperation.* MIT Press.

Shields, D., and Šolar, S. 2011. Responses to alternative forms of mineral scarcity: Conflict and cooperation. In S. Dinar, ed. *Rethinking environmental conflict: Scarcity, degradation and the development of international cooperation*, 239–285. MIT Press.

150 *Bulk mining of Earth's surface to create physical products, our approach, is an utter anomaly across the millions of species we share this planet with.*

Though the vast majority of new material Nature fabricates comes from carbon dioxide, a relatively small number of species do fabricate new materials from other compounds, such as sponges, which precipitate silicon dioxide out of seawater to build their skeletons. In addition, a comparatively small number of species make some things by bulk extraction of materials from Earth's surface, such as burrows or the mounds of termites. The former do not actually comprise new material, however but the absence of it, and the latter, which use soil for walls, are new material only insofar as the addition of saliva changes soil's mechanical behavior. Nonetheless, the vast majority of new material fabricated by Nature is sourced from air.

151 *Day-to-day, mines are problematic in terms of their impact on water quality . . . and a host of other issues.*

Warhurst, A., 1992, February. Environmental management in mining and mineral processing in developing countries. In Natural Resources Forum (Vol. 16, No. 1, pp. 39–48). Oxford, UK: Blackwell Publishing Ltd.

Young, J. E. 1992. Mining the earth. Worldwatch Paper 109. Worldwatch Institute.

Kitula, A. G. N. 2006. The environmental and socio-economic impacts of mining on local livelihoods in Tanzania: A case study of Geita District. *Journal of Cleaner Production, 14*(3–4), 405–414.

Palmer, M. A., Bernhardt, E. S., Schlesinger, W. H., Eshleman, K. N., Foufoula-Georgiou, E., Hendryx, M. S., Lemly, A. D., Likens, G. E., Loucks, O. L., Power, M. E., and White, P.S. 2010. Mountaintop mining consequences. *Science, 327*(5962), 148–149.

Saviour, M. N. 2012. Environmental impact of soil and sand mining: A review. *International Journal of Science, Environment and Technology, 1*(3), 125–134.

Dudka, S., and Adriano, D. C. 1997. Environmental impacts of metal ore mining and processing: A review. *Journal of Environmental Quality, 26*(3), 590–602.

Müezzinoğlu, A. 2003. A review of environmental considerations on gold mining and production. Critical Reviews in Environmental Science and Technology. *33*: 45–71.

Ochieng, G. M., Seanego, E. S., and Nkwonta, O. I. 2010. Impacts of mining on water resources in South Africa: A review. *Scientific Research and Essays, 5*(22), 3351–3357.

152 *To make [plastic], we pump crude oil and natural gas from the Earth's crust, 4 percent . . . is transformed within . . . oil refineries into the feedstock for crinkly grocery bags, slick nylon track suits, and glittery cell phone cases. . . . 300 million tons of plastic get made each year.*

British Plastics Foundation. Oil Consumption. 2014. Retrieved June 5, 2019. http://www
.bpf.co.uk/press/oil_consumption.aspx

Wassener, B. 2011. Raising Awareness of Plastic Waste. New York Times. Retrieved
June 5, 2019. https://www.nytimes.com/2011/08/15/business/energy-environment/
raising-awareness-of-plastic-waste.html

152 Mark Herrema quote from Zhou, L. 2015. Creating Plastic From Greenhouse Gases.
Smithsonian Magazine. Retrieved June 5, 2019. https://www.smithsonianmag.com/
innovation/creating-plastic-from-greenhouse-gases-180954540/

Learn more about Newlight Technologies: Barnes, G. 2017. 5 Green Startups Working
To Make Our World A Better Place. Retrieved June 5, 2019. https://www.snapmunk
.com/5-green-startups-working-to-make-our-world-a-better-place/

Another very cool thing about the plastics Newlight Technologies creates is that, in addition to making them from the greenhouse gas CO_2, it can also make them from
methane (CH_4). Methane is at least 23 times more powerful at trapping heat than
CO_2. Thus, when plastics are made from methane, a very powerful greenhouse gas
is removed from our atmosphere. Moreover, when methane-based plastics degrade,
they degrade back into not methane but CO_2. The methane is thus permanently
transformed into a much less dangerous greenhouse gas.

154 *We mine over 4.5 billion tons of limestone out of the earth every year.*
Freedonia Group. n.d. Retrieved June 5, 2019. http://www.freedoniagroup.com/World
-Cement.html

154 *After locating a deposit, we blow the limestone up with dynamite and then transport the material
to a cement factory, where we then cook the limestone at about 1500°C (2732°F).*
Cement Production. Science Direct. n.d. Retrieved June 5, 2019. https://www
.sciencedirect.com/topics/engineering/cement-production

154 *In fact, making cement accounts for about 7 percent of all the CO2 humans release into the atmo-
sphere each year.*
Cement Industry Federation. n.d. Retrieved June 5, 2019. http://www.cement.org.au/
SustainabilityNew/ClimateChange/CementEmissions.aspx

154 *Calera partnered with a coal-fired power plant . . . [and] built an apparatus that bubbled seawater and the gases, leaving the power plant together, and* voila!*, powdered limestone was the
result! Tons of it, no cooking required.*
Calera.com. n.d. Retrieved June 5, 2019. http://www.calera.com/beneficial-reuse-of-co2/
process.html
California Air Resources Board. n.d. Retrieved June 5, 2019. https://www.arb.ca.gov/cc/
etaac/meetings/102909pubmeet/mtgmaterials102909/basicsofcaleraprocess.pdf

155 The paper Dona Boggs read on how corals are able to precipitate calcium carbonate out of
seawater: Cohen, A. L., and McConnaughey, T. A. 2003. Geochemical perspectives on
coral mineralization. *Reviews in Mineralogy and Geochemistry, 54*(1), 151–187.

156 *Specifically, the stony corals . . . collect calcium ions (Ca2+) and carbonate ions (CO32–) from
seawater, and expel . . . H+ ions, . . . increasing the rate of calcium carbonate formation some 100
times over geological processes.*
Madin, K. 2009. Ocean Acidification. Woods Hole Oceanographic Institute. Retrieved
June 5, 2019. https://www.whoi.edu/oceanus/feature/ocean-acidification-a-risky
-shell-game/

159   The entire Power without Pollution part of the chapter is published with credit to "Largesse of Leaves," in the *Engineering Inspired by Nature* curriculum. © Sam Stier.

159   *Early hominids used fire hundreds of thousands of years ago to transform food in ways that made it easier to eat and to harden tools and weapons that made it easier to catch food.*
      Wikipedia. n.d. Retrieved June 5, 2019. https://en.wikipedia.org/wiki/Control_of_fire_by_early_humans

159   *Later, fire was used to manufacture things like pigments . . . , glue . . . , and pottery.*
      Science Daily. 2011. Oldest pigment factory dates back 100,000 years. Retrieved June 5, 2019. https://www.sciencedaily.com/releases/2011/10/111019154507.htm
      Chodosh, S. 2018. Popular Science. Retrieved June 5, 2019. https://www.popsci.com/oldest-pigments-colors
      Science Daily. 2017. How Neanderthals made the very first glue. Retrieved June 5, 2019. https://www.sciencedaily.com/releases/2017/08/170831093424.htm

159   *Eighty-seven percent of humankind's energy use comes from fossil fuels.*
      Wikipedia. n.d. Retrieved June 5, 2019. https://en.wikipedia.org/wiki/World_energy_consumption

159   *Scientists began warning of climate change due to CO2 emissions from burning fossil fuels as early as 1965.*
      Peterson, T. C., Connolley, W. M., and Fleck, J. 2008. The myth of the 1970s global cooling scientific consensus. *Bulletin of the American Meteorological Society, 89*(9), 1325–1338.

160   *Air pollution from coal directly kills over 13,000 people every year and results in 20,000 heart attacks, in the United States alone.*
      Union of Concerned Scientists. n.d. The Hidden Costs of Fossil Fuels. Retrieved June 5, 2019. https://www.ucsusa.org/clean-energy/coal-and-other-fossil-fuels/hidden-cost-of-fossils

160   *Children raised near facilities that burn fossil fuel are at much higher risks for low birth weight, depressed IQ, asthma, attention deficit disorder, and other issues that will debilitate them for the rest of their lives.*
      ClimateNexus. n.d. The Localized Health Impacts of Fossil Fuels. Retrieved June 5, 2019. https://climatenexus.org/climate-issues/health/the-localized-health-impacts-of-fossil-fuels/

160   *Mercury spewed from power plants burning coal has made as many as a third of fish species unsafe to for human consumption.*
      Burger, J., and Gochfeld, M. 2011. Mercury and selenium levels in 19 species of saltwater fish from New Jersey as a function of species, size, and season. *Science of the Total Environment, 409*(8), 1418–1429.

160   *Other changes to the ocean have resulted in the staggering loss of 40 percent of the world's phytoplankton since the 1950s.*
      Minogue, K. 2010. Science. Critical Ocean Organisms Are Disappearing. Retrieved June 5, 2019. https://www.sciencemag.org/news/2010/07/critical-ocean-organisms-are-disappearing

160   *Global changes from greenhouse gas emissions can quickly become irreversibly catastrophic, from self-generating, "runaway" global warming—when, for example, the frozen peat soils of the northern hemisphere, which hold trillions of tons of methane, begin warming. Indeed, researchers have documented recent surges of methane coming from the Arctic.*

Wikipedia. n.d. Retrieved June 5, 2019. https://en.wikipedia.org/wiki/Runaway_green house_effect

161 *The natural world uses far more energy than humankind.*

Adesina, O., Anzai, I. A., Avalos, J. L., and Barstow, B. 2017. Embracing biological solutions to the sustainable energy challenge. *Chem, 2*(1), 20–51.

161 *The next gasp or sigh you take comes straight from phytoplankton, which produce 50–85 percent of the oxygen found in our atmosphere.*

EarthSky. 2015. How much do oceans add to world's oxygen? Retrieved June 5, 2019. http://earthsky.org/earth/how-much-do-oceans-add-to-worlds-oxygen

See also Stier, S. 2017, January 6. Seeing the devastation of climate change in the ruins of Aleppo. *Los Angeles Times.* https://www.latimes.com/opinion/op-ed/la-oe-stier -climate-change-and-syrian-civil-war-20170106-story.html

161 *The lizard's high-performance skin is designed with precision grooves and channels that capitalize on water's restless hydrogen bonds, drawing the cooling liquid up and over the outside of its body and then straight into its mouth.*

Sherbrooke, W. C., Scardino, A. J., de Nys, R., and Schwarzkopf, L. 2007. Functional morphology of scale hinges used to transport water: Convergent drinking adaptations in desert lizards (*Moloch horridus* and *Phrynosoma cornutum*). *Zoomorphology, 126*(2), 89–102.

Sherbrooke, W. C. 1993. Rain-drinking behaviors of the Australian thorny devil (Sauria: Agamidae). *Journal of Herpetology,* Sept 1: 270–275.

162 *A pine cone releases its seeds with scales that raise all by themselves, even if detached from the tree: contracting in dry weather with angled fibers, the scales lift themselves like garage doors, at just the right season for dispersal.*

Dawson, C., Vincent, J. F., and Rocca, A. M. 1997. How pine cones open. *Nature, 390*(6661), 668.

163 *Using these detergents, clothing can be washed just as well at 60°F with the enzymes as at 90°F without them. At these cooler temperatures, in the United States alone, we could wash all our laundry without dumping 70,000 pounds of CO2 into our atmosphere, equivalent to the annual electricity use of almost 4 million homes.*

Delaware Online. 2014. Retrieved June 5, 2019. https://www.delawareonline.com/ story/delawareinc/2014/03/06/dupont-agriculture-sustainability-procter—gamble -enzyme-technology/6119485/

Mars, C. 2016. Retrieved June 5, 2019. https://www.cleaninginstitute.org/assets/1/Page/ Cold-Water-Wash-Technical-Brief.pdf

Reed, S. 2018. Fighting Climate Change, One Laundry Load at a Time. The New York Times. Retrieved June 5, 2019. https://www.nytimes.com/2018/01/01/business/ energy-environment/climate-change-enzymes-laundry.html

Dr. Frances Arnold's work on renewable fuels using enzymes and directed evolution:

Woo, M. 2012. NASA. Retrieved June 5, 2019. https://climate.nasa.gov/news/659/ researcher-tries-directed-evolution-to-craft-better-biofuels/

Chang, K. 2018. Use of Evolution to Design Molecules Nets Nobel Prize in Chemistry for 3 Scientists. The New York Times. Retrieved June 5, 2019. https://www.nytimes.com/2018/10/03/science/chemistry-nobel-prize.html

164 *When a similarly bumpy leading edge was tested on fan blades, they were a whopping 20 percent more energy than straight-edged blades.*

Howle, L. E. 2009. Whalepower Wenvor blade: A report on the efficiency of a whale-power corp. 5 meter prototype wind turbine blade. BelleQuant, LLC. http://www.whalepower.com/drupal/files/PDFs/Dr_Lauren_Howles_Analysis_of_WEICan_Report.pdf

164   *Applying the whale-inspired tubercle shape on computer fans increases their efficiency by 12 percent or more.*

Dewar, S. 2011. Tech Briefs. Retrieved June 5, 2019. https://contest.techbriefs.com/2011/entries/electronics/1736

164   *Just cooling down computers eats up some 4 percent of* all *electricity use worldwide.*

Computers and the Internet use approximately 5–10 percent of the world's electricity.

Science Daily. 2016. World should consider limits to future internet expansion to control energy consumption. Retrieved June 5, 2019. https://www.sciencedaily.com/releases/2016/08/160811090046.htm

Mills, M. 2013. The Cloud Begins with Coal. Retrieved June 5, 2019. https://www.tech-pundit.com/wp-content/uploads/2013/07/Cloud_Begins_With_Coal.pdf?c761ac

Cooling system uses about 60 percent of a computer's total energy.

Dewar, S. 2011. Tech Briefs. Retrieved June 5, 2019. https://contest.techbriefs.com/2011/entries/electronics/1736

164   *By arranging wind turbines in patterns inspired from schools of fish, positive interference from turbine turbulence can actually increase efficiencies of turbine arrays, by as much as five times, a staggering amount.*

McMahon, J. 2016. Small Turbines Can Outperform Conventional Wind Farms, Stanford Prof Says, With No Bird Kill. Retrieved June 5, 2019. https://www.forbes.com/sites/jeffmcmahon/2016/04/29/stanford-small-wind-arrays-can-outperform-conventional-wind-farms-with-no-bird-kill/#735ba86f592a

164   *Engineers drawing inspiration from this ability of leaves have designed ever more economical "artificial leaves," similarly capable of producing hydrogen fuel out of water, sunshine, and metal catalysts.*

Nocera, D. G. 2012. The artificial leaf. *Accounts of Chemical Research*, 45(5), 767–776.

165   *The U.S. Navy has succeeded in converting seawater—with its dissolved CO2 and hydrogen from the water—into* jet fuel.

Science Daily. 2014. Scale model WWII craft takes flight with fuel from the sea concept. Retrieved June 5, 2019. https://www.sciencedaily.com/releases/2014/04/140409075907.htm

Science Daily. 2016. Proven one-step process to convert CO2 and water directly into liquid hydrocarbon fuel. Retrieved June 5, 2019. https://www.sciencedaily.com/releases/2016/02/160222220828.htm

Al Sadat, W. I., and Archer, L. A. 2016. The O_2-assisted Al/CO_2 electrochemical cell: A system for CO_2 capture/conversion and electric power generation. *Science Advances*, 2(7), e1600968.

165   *The quartzite sand that today's photovoltaic cells are made of must be mined and then cooked to create the electrical-grade silicon used in solar panels.*

Xakalashe, B.S. and Tangstad, M., 2012. Silicon processing: from quartz to crystalline silicon solar cells. Chem Technol, (March), pp. 6–9. Retrieved June 5, 2019. https://pyrometallurgy.co.za/Pyro2011/Papers/083-Xakalashe.pdf

165   *Cooking quartzite sand at 2000°C results in a lot of CO2 being released into the air . . . it takes a solar panel an average of three years just to pay back that carbon debt, that is, to create enough clean electricity to compensate for the CO2 released into the atmosphere during its manufacture. From then on, solar panels are vastly superior to burning coal to create electricity.*

Mother Nature Network. n.d. How much CO2 does one solar panel create? Retrieved June 5, 2019. https://www.mnn.com/green-tech/research-innovations/blogs/how-much-co2-does-one-solar-panel-create

165   *There are significant toxic by-products from the manufacturing of conventional solar panels.*

Silicon Valley Toxics Coalition. 2009. Toward a Just and Sustainable

Solar Energy Industry. Retrieved June 5, 2009. http://svtc.org/wp-content/uploads/Silicon_Valley_Toxics_Coalition_-_Toward_a_Just_and_Sust.pdf /

166   *From the late 1950s to the early 1970s, what began as a way to study photosynthesis became the idea of developing a different kind of solar cell, based on the way plants capture sunlight and use it to create a flow of electrons.*

Gerischer, H., Michel-Beyerle, M. E., Rebentrost, F., and Tributsch, H. 1968. Sensitization of charge injection into semiconductors with large band gap. *Electrochimica Acta, 13*(6), 1509–1515.

Tributsch, H., and Calvin, M. 1971. Electrochemistry of excited molecules: Photoelectrochemical reactions of chlorophylls. *Photochemistry and Photobiology, 14*(2), 95–112.

Tributsch, H. 1972. Reaction of excited chlorophyll molecules at electrodes and in photosynthesis. *Photochemistry and Photobiology, 16*(4), 261–269.

166   *A pivotal innovation in the early 1990s mimicked another part of the leaf, the thylakoid membrane.*

O'Regan, B., and Grätzel, M. 1991. A low-cost, high-efficiency solar cell based on dye-sensitized colloidal TiO_2 films. *Nature, 353*(6346), 737.

167   *An engaging way to have students get their hands into the engineering and innovation of Nature-inspired clean energy is to have them build their own dye-sensitized solar cell.*

Smestad, G. P., and Gratzel, M. 1998. Demonstrating electron transfer and nanotechnology: A natural dye-sensitized nanocrystalline energy converter. *Journal of Chemical Education, 75*(6), 752.

169   The entire Benign by Design part of the chapter is published with credit to "Ascendant Cities," in the *Engineering Inspired by Nature* curriculum. © Sam Stier.

169   *At one o'clock in the morning of Dec. 3, 1984, in the Indian city of Bhopal . . .*

Wikipedia. n.d. Retrieved June 5, 2019. https://en.wikipedia.org/wiki/Bhopal_disaster

Broughton, E. 2005. The Bhopal disaster and its aftermath: A review. *Environmental Health, 4*(1), 6. https://www.ncbi.nlm.nih.gov/pmc/articles/PMC1142333/

169   *Databases documenting the chemicals we synthesize or isolate now have an astonishing tens of millions of entries—an average of 4,000 new entries per day.*

Binetti, R., Costamagna, F. M., and Marcello, I. 2008. Exponential growth of new chemicals and evolution of information relevant to risk control. *Annali-Istituto Superiore di Sanità, 44*(1), 13. http://www.hepatitis.iss.it/binary/publ/cont/ANN_08_04%20Binetti.1209032191.pdf

169   Quote by Philippe Grandjean and Philip Landrigan is from Grandjean, P. and Landrigan, P.J., (2014). Neurobehavioural effects of developmental toxicity. The lancet neurology, *13*(3), 330–338.

For more information on their work on associations between common manmade chemicals and effects on children, see the following:

Martinko, K. 2015. Treehugger. Retrieved June 5, 2019. https://www.treehugger.com/health/children-have-become-unwitting-chemical-sentinels-us.html

Hamblin, J. 2014. The Toxins That Threaten Our Brains. The Atlantic. Retrieved June 5, 2019. https://www.theatlantic.com/health/archive/2014/03/the-toxins-that-threaten-our-brains/284466/

Grandjean, P., and Landrigan, P. J. 2006. Developmental neurotoxicity of industrial chemicals. *Lancet, 368*(9553), 2167–2178.

170   *People worldwide now lose an average of over two and half years of their life spans because of toxins produced by human industry and dumped into the air.*

The Washington Post. n.d. How many years do we lose to the air we breathe? Retrieved June 5, 2019. https://www.washingtonpost.com/graphics/2018/national/health-science/lost-years/?utm_term=.a049bacae5ca

Air Quality Life Index. n.d. Retrieved June 5, 2019. https://aqli.epic.uchicago.edu/reports/?fbclid=IwAR19IL-b7ZNtwL_DEm3EpPx1UQaMPlV5gQ8tkDuRNqPpDgmYo3inbARDC70

170   *It's important to clarify to students that Nature makes and uses toxic chemicals too.*

Wilcox, C. 2016. *Venomous: How Earth's deadliest creatures mastered biochemistry.* Scientific American/Farrar, Straus and Giroux.

172   Description of Dr. Kaichang Li's work can be found at Huang, J., and Li, K. 2016. Development and characterization of a formaldehyde-free adhesive from lupine flour, glycerol, and a novel curing agent for particleboard (PB) production. *Holzforschung, 70*(10), 927–935

172   *The plywood . . . is competitive in both performance and cost, and you can now buy it at the largest home building supply store chains.*

PureBond Plywood. n.d. Retrieved June 5, 2019. http://purebondplywood.com/ Biomimicry Case Study. n.d. The Biomimicry Institute. Retrieved June 5, 2019. http://toolbox.biomimicry.org/wp-content/uploads/2016/03/CS_PureBond_TBI_Toolbox-2.pdf

172   *Consider the development of cities, which can degrade, separate, and gobble up the habitat of wildlife populations.*

Swenson, J. J., and Franklin, J. 2000. The effects of future urban development on habitat fragmentation in the Santa Monica Mountains. *Landscape Ecology, 15*(8), 713–730.

Dickman, C. R. 1987. Habitat fragmentation and vertebrate species richness in an urban environment. *Journal of Applied Ecology,* 337–351.

172   *Wolves used to howl across the island of Manhattan.*

A terrific resource to explore related to this: Wildife Conservation Society. n.d. Retrieved June 5, 2019. https://welikia.org/

172   *Bison used to roam throughout grasslands now paved over in Dallas, Texas.*

Wikipedia. n.d. Retrieved June 5, 2019. https://en.wikipedia.org/wiki/American_bison#/media/File:Extermination_of_bison_to_1889.svg

172   *Grizzly bears used to romp across the Hollywood hills of Los Angeles.*

Wikipedia. n.d. Retrieved June 5, 2019. https://en.wikipedia.org/wiki/Grizzly_bear#/media/File:Ursus_arctos_horribilis_map.svg

172 *Urban sprawl has already wiped out millions of acres of habitat around the world, and it's set to get much worse, much faster.*

   Radeloff, V. C., Hammer, R. B., and Stewart, S. I. 2005. Rural and suburban sprawl in the US Midwest from 1940 to 2000 and its relation to forest fragmentation. *Conservation Biology, 19*(3), 793–805.

   Miller, M. D. 2012. The impacts of Atlanta's urban sprawl on forest cover and fragmentation. *Applied Geography, 34*, 171–179.

   Robinson, L., Newell, J. P., and Marzluff, J. M. 2005. Twenty-five years of sprawl in the Seattle region: Growth management responses and implications for conservation. *Landscape and Urban Planning, 71*(1), 51–72.

   See also: Poon, L. 2018. Mapping the 'Conflict Zones' Between Sprawl and Biodiversity. Retrieved June 5, 2019. https://www.citylab.com/environment/2018/02/mapping -the-conflict-zones-between-sprawl-and-biodiversity/553301/

   The Dirt. 2018. New Maps Show How Urban Sprawl Threatens the World's Remaining Biodiversity. Retrieved June 5, 2019. https://dirt.asla.org/2018/02/06/new-maps -show-how-urban-sprawl-threatens-the-worlds-remaining-biodiversity/

173 *There are more ants on the planet than people. A single colony of ants may contain millions of individuals in it. . . . The Earth's biomass of ants is higher than the biomass of humans.*

   Holldobler, B., and Wilson, E. O. 1994. *Journey to the ants: A story of scientific exploration.* Belknap Press.

   There is some uncertainty about this with regards to ants, primarily because we don't have very good estimates of the number of ants on the planet. But it really is beside the point. Humans have a lower biomass than other groups of species on the planet, and yet these species' presence on the planet is generally considered good for the planet. In other words, it is not population size that is directly responsible for humankind's negative impact on the planet.

173 *Using plaster and liquid metal, Tschinkel . . . has cast actual nests of several ant species, excavated them out of the ground, and revealed to the world the outsized efforts of these diminutive architects.*

   Florida State University. n.d. Retrieved June 5, 2019. https://www.bio.fsu.edu/faculty .php?faculty-id=tschinkel

174 *The Burj Khalifa . . . is one of the tallest buildings in the world, about half a mile tall. It can house 5,000 people with a footprint of only two acres.*

   Civil and structural engineering media. 2014. Retrieved June 5, 2019. https:// csengineermag.com/article/standing-tall-with-very-good-posture/

   Some say 12,000 people: Thought Co. n.d. Quick Facts on Burj Dubai/Burj Khalifa. Retrieved June 5, 2019. https://www.thoughtco.com/facts-on-burj-dubai-burj -khalifa-2353671

175 *People in urban areas spend an increasing amount of time in their cars, commuting. What happens to our quality of life when we live, work, shop, and go out to lunch all in the same building?*

   Lyons, G., and Chatterjee, K. 2008. A human perspective on the daily commute: costs, benefits and trade-offs. *Transport Reviews, 28*(2), 181–198.

   Christian, T. J. 2012. Trade-offs between commuting time and health-related activities. *Journal of Urban Health, 89*(5), 746–757.

175   *Roads and pavement create major issues because of runoff, which can pollute waterways.*

Barrett, M. E., Zuber, R. D., Collins, E. R., Malina, J. F., Charbeneau, R. J., and Ward, G. H. 1995. A review and evaluation of literature pertaining to the quantity and control of pollution from highway runoff and construction. CRWR Online Report 95-5. Retrieved June 5, 2019. file:///C:/Users/samstier/Documents/crwr_onlinereport95-5.pdf.

Revitt, D. M., Lundy, L., Coulon, F., and Fairley, M. 2014. The sources, impact and management of car park runoff pollution: A review. *Journal of Environmental Management, 146*, 552–567.

176   *What's possible through vertical agriculture?*

Despommier, D. 2011. The vertical farm: Controlled environment agriculture carried out in tall buildings would create greater food safety and security for large urban populations. *Journal für Verbraucherschutz und Lebensmittelsicherheit, 6*(2), 233–236.

Besthorn, F. H. 2013. Vertical farming: Social work and sustainable urban agriculture in an age of global food crises. *Australian Social Work, 66*(2), 187–203.

176   *What are the physical and mental advantages of having large outdoor recreation and wilderness areas easily accessible to everyone?*

There is a large and fascinating body of research around this topic. See, for example, the following:

Maller, C., Townsend, M., Brown, P., and St Leger, L. 2002. Healthy parks, healthy people: The health benefits of contact with nature in a park context: A review of current literature. Parks Victoria, Deakin University Faculty of Health and Behavioural Sciences.

Hartig, T., van den Berg, A. E., Hagerhall, C. M., Tomalak, M., Bauer, N., Hansmann, R., Ojala, A., Syngollitou, E., Carrus, G., van Herzele, A., and Bell, S. 2011. Health benefits of nature experience: Psychological, social and cultural processes. In *Forests, trees and human health*. Nilsson, K., Sangster, M., Gallis, C., Hartig, T., De Vries, S., Seeland, K., & Schipperijn, J. (Eds.). Springer, 127–168.

176   *At the density of Paris, all of humankind could actually live on an area covering no more than the states of Louisiana, Mississippi, and Alabama.*

de Chant, T. 2011. If the world's population lived in one city . . . Retrieved June 5, 2019. https://persquaremile.com/2011/01/18/if-the-worlds-population-lived-in-one-city/

177   *Self-healing roads, inspired by the way living tissue like skin heals itself. Adding pockets of a liquid substance within the concrete or asphalt that hardens in contact with air allows it to repair cracks by itself.*

Jonkers, H. M. 2007. Self healing concrete: A biological approach. In *Self healing materials*. R. Hull R.M. Osgood, Jr. J. Parisi H.Warlimont, eds. Springer, 195–204.

178   *Due to its washboard texture, the skin of sharks turns out to be difficult for bacteria to colonize. By mimicking this texture in a plastic film applied to surfaces in hospitals, bacteria can be controlled without relying on chemicals to kill them. Destroying microbes with antibiotics inadvertently breeds resistant bacteria, which already kill hundreds of thousands of people every year.*

Levy, S. B., and Marshall, B. 2004. Antibacterial resistance worldwide: Causes, challenges and responses. *Nature Medicine, 10*(12s), S122.

Chung, K. K., Schumacher, J. F., Sampson, E. M., Burne, R. A., Antonelli, P. J., and Brennan, A. B. 2007. Impact of engineered surface microtopography on biofilm formation of *Staphylococcus aureus*. *Biointerphases, 2*(2), 89–94.

See also Sharklet Technologies. n.d. Retrieved June 5, 2019. https://www.sharklet.com/

179 *Inspired by the tardigrade's example, researchers are now able to use trehalose to preserve biological material without refrigeration, with huge implications for blood platelet availability, vaccine spoilage, and organ transplantation.*

See Cellphire. n.d. Retrieved June 5, 2019. www.cellphire.com

Kanojia, G., Have, R. T., Soema, P. C., Frijlink, H., Amorij, J. P., and Kersten, G. 2017. Developments in the formulation and delivery of spray dried vaccines. *Human Vaccines and Immunotherapeutics, 13*(10), 2364–2378.

Iwai, S., Kikuchi, T., Kasahara, N., Teratani, T., Yokoo, T., Sakonju, I., Okano, S., and Kobayashi, E. 2012. Impact of normothermic preservation with extracellular type solution containing trehalose on rat kidney grafting from a cardiac death donor. *PLoS One, 7*(3),e33157.

179 *One study found that, if Stanford University's 350 labs all stored their biological samples using the water-bear-inspired technology instead of refrigeration, the university would save $1.6 million and avoid emitting 1,800 tonnes of CO2, every year.*

Sustainable Stanford. 2009. Room Temperature Biological Sample Storage. Retrieved June 5, 2019. https://www.sigmaaldrich.com/content/dam/sigma-aldrich/docs/Sigma -Aldrich/General_Information/1/biomatrica-and-stanford.pdf

179 *A concept with wide applicability to the improved performance of human-made places is biophilia.*

Fromm, E. 1973. *The anatomy of human destructiveness.* Holt, Rinehart and Winston.

Wilson, E. O. 1992. *Biophilia.* Harvard University Press

179 *People tend to position their beds so that they are as far as possible from the bedroom door, while still being able to see it.*

Spörrle, M., and Stich, J. 2010. Sleeping in safe places: An experimental investigation of human sleeping place preferences from an evolutionary perspective. *Evolutionary Psychology, 8*(3), 147470491000800308.

See also the Genius of Place: Hooker, G. 2017. Retrieved June 5, 2019. https://asknature .org/collections/genius-of-place/#.XPhjHBZKipo

180 *Designing buildings to have lots of natural sunlight and fresh air is one simple example, which research has shown makes people happier, healthier, and more productive.*

Kellert, S. R., Heerwagen, J., and Mador, M. 2011. *Biophilic design: The theory, science and practice of bringing buildings to life.* Wiley.

Hall, E. T. 1966. *The hidden dimension.* Doubleday.

Lindenmeyr, R. 2017. Biophilic Design Is Coming to a Building Near You. Retrieved June 5, 2019. https://www.ecolandscaping.org/04/sustainability/biophilic-design -coming-building-near/

180 *The robotic tree, with its actuators and other mechanisms, bends and moves and sways, as though in direct contact with the weather outdoors. In this way, the inhabitants of a building are kept in implicit contact with the outdoors, through an artistic engineered object/system.*

See, for example, Anthony Howe. n.d. Retrieved June 5, 2019. https://www.howeart .net/

182 *The entire Infinitely Useful part of the chapter is published with credit to "Counsel of Mycelium," in the* Engineering Inspired by Nature *curriculum.* © Sam Stier.

182 *Engineers have created biodegradable electronics, wind turbines, and even cars.*

Jung, Y. H., Chang, T. H., Zhang, H., Yao, C., Zheng, Q., Yang, V. W., Mi, H., Kim,

M., Cho, S. J., Park, D. W., and Jiang, H. 2015. High-performance green flexible electronics based on biodegradable cellulose nanofibril paper. *Nature Communications, 6,* 7170.

Sanandiya, N. D., Vijay, Y., Dimopoulou, M., Dritsas, S., and Fernandez, J. G. 2018. Large-scale additive manufacturing with bioinspired cellulosic materials. *Scientific Reports, 8*(1), 8642.

Irimia-Vladu, M., Głowacki, E. D., Voss, G., Bauer, S., and Sariciftci, N. S. 2012. Green and biodegradable electronics. *Materials Today, 15*(7–8), 340–346. https://www.sciencedirect.com/science/article/pii/S1369702112701396.

Tan, M. J., Owh, C., Chee, P. L., Kyaw, A. K. K., Kai, D., and Loh, X. J. 2016. Biodegradable electronics: Cornerstone for sustainable electronics and transient applications. *Journal of Materials Chemistry C, 4*(24), 5531–5558.

The Verge. n.d. Retrieved June 5, 2019. https://www.theverge.com/2016/4/6/11380818/toyota-setsuna-wood-concept-car-family-heirloom

183   *The average person in the United States produces 4.4 pounds of garbage a day.*

Environmental Protection Agency. Municipal Waste. n.d. Retrieved June 5, 2019. https://archive.epa.gov/epawaste/nonhaz/municipal/web/html/

183   *Worldwide, humankind produces some 2.2 billion tons of solid waste annually.*

World Bank. 2019. Solid Waste Management. Retrieved June 5, 2019. http://www.worldbank.org/en/topic/urbandevelopment/brief/solid-waste-management

184   *Some plastics that manufacturer's claim will "decompose" simply break into smaller pieces of plastic.*

Weinberger, H. 2014. KQED Science. Biodegradable Plastics: Too Good to Be True? Retrieved June 5, 2019. http://ww2.kqed.org/quest/2014/06/12/biodegradable-plastics-too-good-to-be-true/

188   A video of Lilian van Daal's work can be found on YouTube: YouTube. 2017. Retrieved June 5, 2019. https://www.youtube.com/watch?v=Z5NvIT_oIN8

189   Many thanks to Sherry Ritter for inspiring the concept for the Closing the Loop activity.

Chapter 7

197   This chapter is published with credit to "The Acumen of Ants," in the *Engineering Inspired by Nature* curriculum. © Sam Stier.

197   Chapter title inspired from the following article: *The Economist.* 2010, August 12. Riders on a swarm. https://www.economist.com/science-and-technology/2010/08/12/riders-on-a-swarm

197   Quote by Aristotle quote from *Metaphysics*, bk. 8, pt. 6. http://classics.mit.edu/Aristotle/metaphysics.8.viii.html

198   *The development of computers has a long, complicated history, but at the very beginning there was Claude Shannon.*

See, for example, Waldrop, M. M. 2001. *The dream machine: JCR Licklider and the revolution that made computing personal.* Viking Penguin.

200   *As entomologist Jean-Louis Deneubourg figured out, the key is how ants work together.*

Verhaeghe, J. C., and Deneubourg, J. L. 1983. Experimental study and modelling of food recruitment in the ant *Tetramorium impurum* (Hym. Form.). *Insectes Sociaux, 30*(3), 347–360.

Deneubourg, J. L., Pasteels, J. M., and Verhaeghe, J. C. 1983. Probabilistic behaviour in ants: A strategy of errors? *Journal of Theoretical Biology, 105*(2), 259–271.

Classic article by Jean-Louis Deneubourg and colleagues on ants self organization. Goss, S., Aron, S., Deneubourg, J. L., and Pasteels, J. M. 1989. Self-organized shortcuts in the Argentine ant. *Naturwissenschaften, 76*(12), 579–581.

202 Marco Dorigo quote from Miller. 2010. *The smart swarm: How understanding flocks, schools, and colonies can make us better at communicating, decision making, and getting things done.* Avery, 13.

204 *Today, a growing number of companies manage their delivery logistics.*
Stier, S. 2014. *Engineering inspired by Nature: A high school engineering curriculum.* The Center for Learning with Nature.

204 Description of Barilla's use of ant-inspired software is from *The Economist.* 2010, August 12. Riders on a swarm. https://www.economist.com/science-and-technology/2010/08/12/riders-on-a-swarm.

205 Description of Air Liquide's use of ant-inspired software is from Miller, P. 2010. *The smart swarm: How understanding flocks, schools, and colonies can make us better at communicating, decision making, and getting things done.* Avery, 20–26.

205 Torsten Reil quote from Stacey, Nic, dir. 2010. *The secret life of chaos.* Documentary. Retrieved June 5, 2019. https://www.dailymotion.com/video/xv1j0n. Quote begins on 52:00.

206 *Aggregated slime molds are able to solve many kinds of challenges.*
Sanders, L. 2010. Wired. Retrieved June 5, 2019. https://www.wired.com/2010/01/slime-mold-grows-network-just-like-tokyo-rail-system/
Slime mold solves maze: Nakagaki, T., Yamada, H., and Tóth, Á. 2000. Intelligence: Maze-solving by an amoeboid organism. *Nature, 407*(6803), 470. https://www.researchgate.net/profile/Toshiyuki_Nakagaki/publication/238823756_Intelligence_Maze-Solving_by_an_Amoeboid_Organism/links/5481d4550cf2e5f7ceaa5a0f/Intelligence-Maze-Solving-by-an-Amoeboid-Organism.pdf

208 Stephen Regelous quotes from Miller, P. 2010. *The smart swarm: How understanding flocks, schools, and colonies can make us better at communicating, decision making, and getting things done.* Avery, 182.

210 Michael Fellows and Ian Parberry quote from Fellows, Michael R., and Parberry, I. 1993. SIGACT trying to get children excited about CS. *Computing Research News, 5*(1), 7. http://archive.cra.org/CRN/issues/9301.pdf

214 *In a large space in the schoolyard or gym, imagine a square or rectangle.*
Stier, S. 2014. *Engineering inspired by Nature: A high school engineering curriculum.* The Center for Learning with Nature.

Chapter 8

221 Alison Gopnik quote from Berger, W. 2014. *A more beautiful question: The power of inquiry to spark breakthrough ideas.* Bloomsbury, 43.

222 Origin of the word *tinker* from *Wikipedia.* n.d. Retrieved June 5, 2019. https://en.wikipedia.org/wiki/Tinker

223 *Romeo and Juliet* quote from act 2, scene 2, lines 33–49.

224 Elliott, T. (2016). The Sydney Herald. It's hip to be Square: What Twitter CEO Jack Dorsey did next. Retrieved June 5, 2019. https://www.smh.com.au/lifestyle/its-hip-to-be-square-what-twitter-ceo-jack-dorsey-did-next-20160308-gnd5sd.html

224 *Researchers . . . have studied the way animals shed water to design more efficient laundry machines.*

Dickerson, A. K., Mills, Z. G., and Hu, D. L. 2012. Wet mammals shake at tuned frequencies to dry. *Journal of the Royal Society Interface, 9*(77), 3208–3218. https://pdfs .semanticscholar.org/d87e/7e00a5416c7d948961a5f69230b357c1335c.pdf

225 *Perhaps we can use inductive reasoning to try to derive general principles for how to do Nature-inspired engineering, and then from this develop ways to teach it to children.*

This is standard practice, for example,

> If you delve into the history of cancer cures, squirt guns, and smoke detectors, you'll find startling similarities in the way that they came into existence. So if we can observe the techniques that have led lots of inventors to success, we might extrapolate what methods work best. (Kennedy, P. 2016. *Inventology: How we dream up things that change the world.*Mariner Books, x)

A lot has been written about the ideation phase of invention. See, for example, the following:

Ashton, K. 2015. *How to fly a horse: The secret history of creation, invention, and discovery.* Anchor.

Kennedy, P. 2016. *Inventology: How we dream up things that change the world.* Mariner Books. Weber, R. J., Moder, C. L., and Solie, J. B. 1990. Invention heuristics and mental processes underlying the development of a patent for the application of herbicides. *New Ideas in Psychology, 8*(3), 321–336.

227 *Owls, uniquely, have tiny serrations along the forward and aft parts of their primary flight feathers. This doesn't eliminate the wings' turbulence but it does cut it up into smaller vortices, too small for us to hear.*

R. R. Graham. 1934. The silent flight of owls. *Journal of the Royal Aeronautical Society, 286*, 837–843.

Sarradj, E., Fritzsche, C., and Geyer, T. 2011. Silent owl flight: Bird flyover noise measurements. *AIAA Journal, 49*(4), 769–779.

229 Eiji Nakatsu quote from personal correspondence—I began an e-mail correspondence with Eiji in 2016, and the quotes are from things that Eiji wrote and shared with me. Eiji visited my bio-inspired design class at Otis College in 2017.

229 The engineering jokes in the book come from around the Internet, for example, Reddit. r/EngineeringStudents. What's your favorite engineering joke? Retrieved June 5, 2019. https://www.reddit.com/r/EngineeringStudents/comments/1y730h/whats_your_favorite _engineering_joke/

230 *Famous stories of responsive design are everywhere, from the demand and subsequent development of the disposable diaper to the upside down, squeeze-type plastic ketchup bottle.*

Madhavan, G. 2015. *Think like an engineer.* Oneworld, 159–160.

230 *When the best-selling Toyota RAV4 SUV was first launched in the United States, it didn't have any cup holders.*

Liker, J. K., Hoseus, M., and Center for Quality People and Organizations. 2008. *Toyota culture.* McGraw-Hill.

230 *Huzaifah Khaled did his own social science.*

Hui, M. 2017. A vending machine for the homeless just launched in the U.K., and will soon debut in U.S. cities. The Washington Post. Retrieved June 5, 2019. https://www .washingtonpost.com/news/inspired-life/wp/2017/12/30/a-vending-machine-for -the-homeless-just-launched-in-the-u-k-and-will-soon-debut-in-u-s-cities/?utm_ term=.373bffdef50a

231   *Architect Bill McDonough quips in his excellent TED talk that it took humans 5,000 years to put wheels on luggage.*
      Ted.com. 2005. Retrieved June 5, 2019. https://www.ted.com/talks/william_mcdonough _on_cradle_to_cradle_design?language=en

232   *During their final commutes together, they explored their next move.*
      Xavier, J. 2014. Retrieved June 5, 2019. https://www.bizjournals.com/sanjose/news/2014 /01/08/netflixs-first-ceo-on-reed-hastings.html

234   *They can give a slower song a bluesy feel, but in a faster song they can add a sense of urgency (car horns often contain seventh notes).*
      TalkBass.com. 2015. Retrieved June 5, 2019. https://www.talkbass.com/threads/car -horns-in-the-key-of-f.1142036/

240   *When we observe something in Nature, we actually begin a process that has many similarities to the physical and cognitive processes involved in the act of reading written language. Our visual system . . . comes equipped with a high-focus area for our eyes . . . , as well as a parafoveal region, and still further a peripheral region.*
      Wolf, M., and Stoodley, C. J. 2008. *Proust and the squid: The story and science of the reading brain.* Harper Perennial, 147–148.

240   *Looking at Nature and reading are so similar because reading, a newly acquired cultural ability, co-opts much the same visual and cognitive systems we evolved to observe the natural world.*
      Dehaene, S. 2009. *Reading in the brain: The new science of how we read.* Penguin.

242   *When I was growing up, the human appendix was considered just a vestigial organ that served no purpose, for example, not the vital reservoir of gut microbes it's now understood to be.*
      See e.g., https://www.sciencealert.com/your-appendix-might-serve-an-important-biolog ical-function-after-all-2

246   *Mark Changizi . . . hypothesized that this behavior might actually serve a purpose in helping us grip slippery things.*
      Changizi, M., Weber, R., Kotecha, R., and Palazzo, J. 2011. Are wet-induced wrinkled fingers primate rain treads? *Brain, Behavior and Evolution, 77*(4), 286–290.
      Fast motion of fingers pruning: YouTube. 2014. Retrieved June 4, 2019. https://www .youtube.com/watch?v=1H-J_j0ae00

246   *Kyriacos Kareklas and colleagues . . . devised a test in which subjects with smooth fingers trans-ferred wet marbles from one bowl into another, while other subjects with fingers wrinkled by soaking in water attempted the same.*
      Kareklas, K., Nettle, D., and Smulders, T. V. 2013. Water-induced finger wrinkles improve handling of wet objects. *Biology Letters, 9*(2), 20120999.

249   *My favorite is an activity Joe Cornell relays in* Sharing Nature With Children, *which I call "Find Your Tree."*
      Cornell, J. 2009. *Sharing nature with children.* Dawn Publications.

249   *By the time children reach about five years of age, they will have asked about 40,000 [questions].*
      Harris, P. L. 2012. *Trusting what you're told: How children learn from others.* Harvard University Press.

250   George de Mestral quote from Jenkins, C. H. 2011. *Bio-inspired engineering.* Momentum Press, 000.

251   *In 1632, Galileo described butterflies flitting about the rafters in the cabin of a moving ship.*
      Galileo. 1632. *Dialogue concerning the two chief world systems.* Translated by Stillman Drake. Repr., University of California Press, 1953, 186–187.

For a great related article about analogies, imagination, and education (this time about Albert Einstein), see Isaacson, W. 2015. The Light-Beam Rider. *The New York Times*. Retrieved June 5, 2019. https://www.nytimes.com/2015/11/01/opinion/sunday/the-light-beam-rider.html

252   The use of Japanese honeybees is my Nature-inspired adaptation of a well-known analogy from Gick, M. L., and Holyoak, K. J. 1980. Analogical problem solving. *Cognitive Psychology, 12*(3), 306–355.

252   About Japanese giant hornets and Japanese honey bees: Wikipedia. n.d. Retrieved June 5, 2019. https://en.wikipedia.org/wiki/Japanese_giant_hornet

254   History of Bernie Sadow's inspiration for rolling luggage from Sharkey, J. 2010. Reinventing the Suitcase by Adding the Wheel. Retrieved June 5, 2019. https://www.nytimes.com/2010/10/05/business/05road.html

254   *Dr. Annick Bay wondered if fireflies might hold secrets for improving the energy efficiency of LED lights.*
Bay, A., André, N., Sarrazin, M., Belarouci, A., Aimez, V., Francis, L. A., and Vigneron, J. P. 2013. Optimal overlayer inspired by *Photuris* firefly improves light-extraction efficiency of existing light-emitting diodes. *Optics Express, 21*(101), A179–A189.

255   *The term* functional fixedness *was coined by psychologist Karl Duncker in 1945.*
Duncker, K., and Lees, L. S. 1945. On problem-solving. *Psychological Monographs, 58*(5), i.

257   *Opossums have . . . a unique peptide in their blood that renders rattlesnake venom harmless. In fact, many other species . . . show adaptations to snake venom, including peacocks, wood rats, and even other snakes.*
Domont, G. B., Perales, J., and Moussatche, H. 1991. Natural anti-snake venom proteins. *Toxicon, 29*(10), 1183–1194.

260   Quote from research paper on giant squid axons from Morell P, Quarles RH. The Myelin Sheath. In: Siegel GJ, Agranoff BW, Albers RW, et al., editors. Basic Neurochemistry: Molecular, Cellular and Medical Aspects. 6th edition. Philadelphia: Lippincott-Raven; 1999.https://www.ncbi.nlm.nih.gov/books/NBK27954/

262   Dewey, J. 1938. *Logic—The theory of inquiry.* Read Books, 108.

263   Continental tire safety information from Consumer Reports, 2012. Retrieved June 5, 2019. https://www.bostonglobe.com/business/2012/12/30/consumer-reports-michelin-and-continental-tires-top-ratings/DZKLJZqrRFNySIyZNiqIbM/story.html

266   *Rotational impact . . . is most often what causes concussions and serious brain damage.*
Kleiven S. Why Most Traumatic Brain Injuries are Not Caused by Linear Acceleration but Skull Fractures are. Front Bioeng Biotechnol. 2013;1:15. https://www.ncbi.nlm.nih.gov/pmc/articles/PMC4090913/
More on Ken Phillips's helmets: YouTube. 2009. Retrieved June 5, 2019. https://www.youtube.com/watch?v=GZIE2XoxaFE

267   *[Water bears] can withstand vast extremes of temperature . . . , a dose of radiation more than a thousand times stronger than a human can withstand, and six times the pressure of the deepest ocean trench . . . and the vacuum of outer space.*
Dean, C. 2015. The Tardigrade: Practically Invisible, Indestructible 'Water Bears'. Retrieved June 5, 2019. https://www.nytimes.com/2015/09/08/science/the-tardigrade-water-bear.html
Wikipedia. n.d. Retrieved June 5, 2019. https://en.wikipedia.org/wiki/Tardigrade

268 John Crowe quote from Holder, K. 2004. Just add water. *UC Davis Magazine* 22(1). http://magazinearchive.ucdavis.edu/issues/fall04/feature_1.html

272 *Air performed the best of all the insulation types he tested.*
nudown. n.d. Retrieved June 5, 2019. https://www.nudown.com/technology/

277 Pagan Kennedy quote from Kennedy, P. 2016. *Inventology: How we dream up things that change the world.* Mariner Books., xiii.

IMAGE CREDITS

Cover

Flying fish drawing. George Shaw. 1789–1813. *The Naturalists' Miscellany or Coloured Figures of Natural Objects*. Acquired from rawpixel.com. CC BY 4.0. https://www.flickr.com/photos/vintage_illustration/44024563441/in/album-72157700183515885/ courtesy of the Biodiversity Heritage Library (https://www.biodiversitylibrary.org/).

Wooden cog. Public domain image. https://pixabay.com/en/gear-wood-transmission-mechanics-2353700/

Octopus drawing. Public domain image. https://pixabay.com/en/octopus-vintage-squid-animal-ocean-875511/

Technical drawing. Courtesy of Isaín Calderón. Public domain image. https://pixabay.com/en/blueprint-project-plan-design-2432266/

Snake illustration on spine. Courtesy of Casey Kanode. Public domain image.

Title font by Kimberly Geswein.

Frontmatter

Illustration of flea feet. Robert Hooke. 1665. *Micrographia*. Public domain image from the National Library of Wales: https://commons.wikimedia.org/wiki/File:HookeFlea01.jpg.

Alfred Smee. 1872. *My Garden, Its Plan and Culture Together With a General Description of Its Geology, Botany, and Natural History*, 426. Public domain image from Internet Book Archive Images:https://www.flickr.com/photos/internetarchivebookimages/20131359843/

Introduction

Gulper eel (*Eurypharynx pelecanoides*). M. L. Valliant. 1883. A Wonder from the Deep-Sea. *Popular Science Monthly, 23,* 76. Public domain image from https://commons.wikimedia.org/wiki/File:PSM_V23_D086_The_deep_sea_fish_eurypharynx_pelecanoides.jpg.

Illustration of porcupine. *Zoological Lectures Delivered at the Royal Institution in the Years 1806–7*, illustrated by George Shaw. Public domain image. Acquired from rawpixel.com. CC BY 4.0. https://www.rawpixel.com/image/378074/illustration-porcupine-zoological-lectures-delivered-royal-institution-years-1806-7-illustrated

Chapter 1

Ladybug. © Power & Syred. Used with permission.

Julian Stier looking at an inchworm. © Sam Stier.

Chapter numbers and opening letters by Kimberly Geswein.

Leonardo da Vinci sketches. Courtesy Вера Мошегова. Public domain image. https://pixabay.com/en/collage-leonard-da-vinci-2231082/

Airplane. Public domain image. https://pixabay.com/en/a380-span-aileron-wing-gross-66217/

Turkey vulture courtesy of Ståle Freyer. Public domain image. https://pixabay.com/photos/turkey-vulture-turkey-buzzard-1805821/

Images of researchers (clockwise from top left):
Dr. Frank Fish, courtesy of Frank Fish and West Chester University
Dr. Paula Hammond, courtesy of Paula Hammond and © Len Rubenstein, photographer.
Dr. Zhenan Bao courtesy of Zhenan Bao and Linda A. Cicero/Stanford News Service
Dr. John Dabiri, courtesy of John Dabiri and Robert Whittlesey, photographer.
Lilian van Daal courtesy of Lilian van Daal and Luna Maurer.
Dr. Kaichang Li, courtesy of Kaichang Li and Oliver Day.

Figure 1.11. National averages from Munce, R., and Fraser, E. 2013. Where are the STEM students? MyCollege Options and STEMconnector. Local school data collected by Tiffany Roberts. Graph by author.

Spear point. Used with permission from Vincent Mourre/Inrap,

Cell phone. Courtesy of Jan Vašek. Public domain image. https://www.maxpixel.net/Apps-Iphone-Smartphone-Mobile-Phone-Apple-Inc-410311

Spolia Atlantica. Bidrag til Kundskab om Klump- eller Maanefiskene (Molidae). 1898. Steenstrup, J. Japetus Sm. (Johannes Japetus Sm.), 1813–1897 Lütken, Chr. Fr. (Christian Frederik), 1827–1901.

Chapter 2

Scanning electron micrograph of gecko foot (*Tarentola mauritanica*). © Power & Syred. Used with permission.

Gecko. Public domain image. https://pixabay.com/en/gecko-lizard-tokhe-reptile-247316/

Person climbing skyscraper. Used with permission from Elliot Hawkes and Eric Eason, Biomimetic and Dexterous Manipulation Lab.

Students deconstructing copy machine. Used with permission from Elizabeth Collins-Adam.

Deconstructed typewriter. © Sam Stier.

Children making spaghetti tower. Used with permission from Diane Bradford.

Bison. Public domain image. Courtesy of National Park Service/Jacob W. Frank.

Mangrove trees. Public domain image. https://pixabay.com/en/australia-mangroves-plant-695197/

Student teachers making spaghetti tower. Used with permission from Dr. Douglas Williams.

Cat claws. Public domain image. https://commons.wikimedia.org/wiki/File:Claw.jpg

Cat-inspired thumb tack images. Used with permission from Toshi Fukaya.

Stickbot robot. Used with permission from Mark Cutkosky, Stanford University.

Butterfly images (left to right, top to bottom):
Images 1–4 used with permission from Jan Gräser.
Image 5, © Sam Stier.
Image 6, Used with permission from Radislav A. Potyrailo, GE Research, Niskayuna, NY, USA.

Cosmetics. Public domain image. https://www.pexels.com/photo/woman-makeup-beauty-lipstick-3123/

Watch and structural color screen illustration. © Sam Stier. Thank you to Qualcomm for providing the watch.

Sun icon. Public domain image. http://www.publicdomainfiles.com/show_file.php?id=13488928811745

Cell phone icon. Public domain image. https://www.goodfreephotos.com/vector-images/mobile-cellphone-vector-clipart.png.php

Sao Paolo skyline. Public domain image. https://www.maxpixel.net/Urban-Brazil-Landscape-City-Sao-Paulo-Metropolis-903974

Coral reef. Jim Maragos/U.S. Fish and Wildlife Service. Public domain image. https://digitalmedia.fws.gov/digital/collection/natdiglib/id/12445/rec/6

Nested figures. © Sam Stier

Plant illustration Palm drawing. *Rhapis excelsa*, 1892, author unknown. Public domain image. https://commons.wikimedia.org/wiki/File:Rhapis_excelsa_drawing.jpg

Chapter 3

Person in tree courtesy of Rob Mulally. Public domain image. http://www.peakpx.com/594270/man-laying-on-brown-wooden-tree-branch.

Tree. Used with permission from Robert Couse-Baker.

Children experiencing tensile force. © Sam Stier.

Sponge "beam." © Sam Stier.

I-beam illustration. © Sam Stier.

Dandelion. © Sam Stier.

Building. Used with permission from Andrew Leonard.

Fig tree. Used with permission from Peter Woodard.

Student with hand in sock. © Sam Stier.

Scallop shell illustration, 1896. Public domain image. https://commons.wikimedia.org/wiki/File:PSM_V49_D563_Scallop_shell.jpg

Corrugated paper holding up book. © Sam Stier.

Collapsed bridge. Kevin Rofidal/U.S. Coast Guard. Public domain image. https://commons.wikimedia.org/wiki/File:Image-I35W_Collapse_-_Day_4_-_Operations_%26_Scene_(95)_edit.jpg

Author's son standing on eggs. © Sam Stier.

Author's son demonstrating the setup for using the photoelastic effect. © Sam Stier.

Plastic showing force lines. © Sam Stier.

Plastic model of notch, with photoelasticity. © Sam Stier

Cracks in sidewalk. © Sam Stier.

De Havilland aircraft. Public domain image. https://commons.wikimedia.org/wiki/File:Comet_Prototype_at_Hatfield.jpg

Making a quarter-circle fillet in plastic. © Sam Stier.

Quarter-circle fillet in plastic. © Sam Stier.

Base of tree. Karen Arnold. Public domain image. https://www.publicdomainpictures.net/en/view-image.php?image=54319&picture=tree-trunk.

Method of tensile triangles, drawn from Claus Mattheck. © Sam Stier.

Base of tree. Karen Arnold. Public domain image. Modified with tensile triangles by Sam Stier.

Tree curve fillet modeled in plastic. © Sam Stier.

Snake illustration. *Sibon argus*, from E. D. Cope. 1875. *On the batrachia and reptilia of Costa Rica: With notes on the herpetology and ichthyology of Nicaragua and Peru.* Public domain image. https://commons.wikimedia.org/wiki/File:Sibon_argus.jpg

Chapter 4

X-ray. By Nick Veasey. Used with permission.

Broken glass. Public domain image courtesy of Paul Barlow.

Spiderweb. Used with permission from Chen-Pan Liao.

Julian Stier listening to bones © Sam Stier

Trabecular bone structure. Science Photo Library/Alamy Stock Photo. Used with permission.

Eiffel Tower. Public domain image.

Illustrations using the Eiffel Tower by Sam Stier, adapted from Aatish Bhatia. What Your Bones Have In Common With The Eiffel Tower. Wired Magazine. 2015.

Skateboard images. Used with permission from Seth Astle. sethastle.com

Tape dispenser illustrations. Used with permission from Simone Ferdinand.

Tape dispenser with photoelastic effect. © Sam Stier.

Chapter 5

Seed. Used with permission from T. R. Shankar Raman. Creative Commons Attribution-Share Alike 4.0 International. https://commons.wikimedia.org/wiki/File:Spinning Sal.jpg

Duck illustration. Public domain image. https://commons.wikimedia.org/wiki/File:Duck_ of_Vaucanson.jpg

Snail on carpet. Used with permission from Thales Carvalho.

Snail with trail. Used with permission from Dan Alcantara.

Street paving. Public Domain Image courtesy of National Park Service.

Viscosity versus shear graphic. © Sam Stier.

Snail poem in the shape of a snail. © Sam Stier

Small snail on hand. Public domain image by Maria Godfrida.

Silly Putty. © Sam Stier

Snail climbing grass. Public domain image by Tanja Richter. https://pixabay.com/photos/ slug-snail-grass-molluscs-animal-412694/

Underside of snail. Used with permission from Jak O'Dowd. Illustrations added by author.

Snail on tire. Public domain image.

Astronaut suit. Public domain image. https://pixabay.com/photos/space-suit-astronaut -isolated-nasa-1848839/

Lotus. Public domain image. https://pixabay.com/en/gorgeous-beautiful-lotus-huashan -2352806/

Water drops on wax paper. © Sam Stier.

Sunita Williams with water droplet in space. Public domain image. NASA. Still from You Tube.com video.

Student placing drop on plant. Used with permission from Diane Bradford.

Water drops on leaf. Public domain image. https://pixabay.com/en/dew-pearl-rain -leaf-drop-of-water-3284680/

Mars Rover images. Public domain image. NASA. https://en.wikipedia.org/wiki/Cleaning_event

Sandpaper and glass with water drops. © Sam Stier

Drop contact angles illustration. © Sam Stier.

Drop on rough surface illustration. © Sam Stier.

Computer graphic of drops, close-up on leaf surface. Used with permission from William Thielicke.

Cotton fabric treated and untreated. © Sam Stier.

Wilber (left) and Orville Wright investigating aviation with a kite. 1901. Public domain image. https://wright.nasa.gov/airplane/kite00.html

Collapsing building. Public domain image by Joe Kniesek. https://pixabay.com/photos/house-trash-ruin-concrete-3466731/

Dandelion. Public domain image. https://pixabay.com/en/dandelion-floating-flower-nature-1931080/

Airplane sketch. Public domain image by Sierra Papa; adapted by author. https://pixabay.com/vectors/airplane-jet-turbine-high-flight-2098593/

Car with streamlines. Used with permission from Rob Bulmahn.

Javan cucumber seed soaring over jungle. Used with permission from Adrian Davies.

Javan cucumber seed. Used with permission from Scott Zona.

Flying wing. Public domain image. https://commons.wikimedia.org/wiki/File:B-2_first_flight_071201-F-9999J-034.jpg

Sycamore Maple seed. Used with permission from Helmut Kobelrausch.

Falling sycamore seed. Used with permission from Adrian Davies.

Student testing glider. Used with permission from Diane Bradford.

Flying squirrel. Used with permission from Dr. Angela Freeman.

People gliding. Used with permission from Graham Hall.

Turtle illustration. *Chelus fimbriatus*, courtesy of R. Mintern, 1885. Public domain image. https://commons.wikimedia.org/wiki/File:Chelus_fimbriatus.jpg

Chapter 6

Bird nest. Public domain image by Fran Urquhart.

Composite city/leaf image. Leaf. Public domain image by Alan Cabello. https://www.pexels.com/photo/shallow-focus-photography-of-person-holding-green-leaf-990349/. City. Public domain image. https://pxhere.com/en/photo/655644

Paddle wheel bucket mining. Public domain image. https://pixabay.com/en/paddle -wheel-bucket-wheel-excavators-1051962/

Smokestacks. Public domain image by Nikola Belopitov. https://pixabay.com/en/ pollution-smoke-environment-smog-2043666/

Shopping. Public domain image by Senior Airman Nichelle Anderson.

Landfill. Used with permission from Michelle Cortens.

Linear production image. © Sam Stier.

Icons in linear production image. Used with permission by Anastasia Grebneva, Community Manager (icons8.com).

Linear production image font. KG HAPPY used with permission from Kimberly Geswein.

Five to Thrive graphic © Sam Stier.

Icons in Five to Thrive graphic. Used with permission by Anastasia Grebneva, Community Manager (icons8.com).

Arrows in Five to Thrive graphic. Used with permission from Ralph Hogaboom.

Five to Thrive image font. KG HAPPY used with permission from Kimberly Geswein.

Origins of the atoms in a glucose molecule. © Sam Stier.

Quarry blast. Courtesy of CSIRO. Creative Commons Attribution 3.0 Unported. https:// commons.wikimedia.org/wiki/File:CSIRO_ScienceImage_2878_Blasting_in_an_open _cut_mine.jpg

Quarry in the landscape. Used with permission from Christina Belton.

Los Angeles. Courtesy of Alina. Public domain image. https://www.pexels.com/photo/ architecture-blooming-california-city-420744/

Coral reef. Used with permission from Malcolm Browne.

Students gathering car exhaust and conducting lab. Used with permission from Elizabeth Collins-Adams, Dona Boggs, and Tiffany Roberts.

Glass sea sponge. Courtesy of NOAA. Public domain image. https://oceanexplorer.noaa.gov/ okeanos/explorations/ex1708/dailyupdates/media/sept10-3.html

Cavemen diorama. Courtesy of Nathan McCord/U.S. Marine Corps. Public domain image. https://commons.wikimedia.org/wiki/File:Diorama,_cavemen_-_National_Museum_of _Mongolian_History.jpg

Steel making. Public domain image. https://nara.getarchive.net/media/molder-1st-class -deem-e-ott-skims-slag-from-a-pot-of-molten-steel-as-molders-ce5459

Thorny lizard. Used with permission from Stuart Phillips.

Trees in sunlight. Public domain image. https://pixabay.com/en/redwoods-tree-sunlight -california-1455738/

WhalePower Tubercle Wind Turbine. Used with permission by Frank Fish and WhalePower.

Fish school. Courtesy of NOAA. Public domain image. https://toolkit.climate.gov/tool/oceanadapt

Flexible dye-sensitized solar cell. Used with permission from Armin Kübelbeck.

Swiss Tech Convention Center. Used with permission from Michel Mégard. Wikimedia Commons, MHM55 [CC BY-SA 4.0 (https://creativecommons.org/licenses/by-sa/4.0)]

Teachers assembling a dye-sensitized solar cell. © Sam Stier.

Dye-sensitized solar cell diagram. © Sam Stier.

Spider with prey. Public domain image. https://pixabay.com/en/spider-jumping-spider-outdoor-2743549/

Toxic waste. Public domain image. https://commons.wikimedia.org/wiki/File:Pollution_of_the_Snohomish_river,_Everett,_Washington_State._-_NARA_-_552248.jpg

PureBond plywood with mussel-inspired adhesives. © Sam Stier

Urban sprawl: suburban Honolulu. Public domain image.

Anthill. Used with permission from Luke Jones.

Ant nest. Used with permission from Dr. Walter Tschinkel and Charles Badland, Florida State University.

Forest with skyscrapers. Public domain image. Adapted by Sam Stier.

If humans lived at the density of Paris graphic. © Sam Stier, adapted from the work of Tim De Chant Mapping program from mapchart.net: https://mapchart.net/usa.html

Shark skin scanning electron micrograph. Used with permission from Pascal Deynat.

Bacteria on shark-inspired surface. Reproduced from Chung, K. K., Schumacher, J. F., Sampson, E. M., Burne, R. A., Antonelli, P. J., and Brennan, A. B. 2007. Impact of engineered surface microtopography on biofilm formation of *Staphylococcus aureus. Biointerphases, 2*(2), 89–94, Figure 5. With the permission of the American Vacuum Society.

Water bear. Used with permission from Willow Gabriel and Bob Goldstein, UNC Chapel Hill.

Wooden car. Public domain image. https://commons.wikimedia.org/wiki/File:Wooden_roadster_Susiandjames._Spielvogel.JPG

Biodegradable electric circuit. Used with permission from Dr. Shaoqin Sarah Gong

Biodegraders on leaf. Used with permission from Dr. Simon Park. https://exploringtheinvisible.com/

Styrofoam mountain. With permission from Shanti Hess.

Teachers at workshop doing egg drop activity. © Sam Stier.

Conifer. © Sam Stier.

Chair. Lilian van Daal. Used with permission.

Setup for "Closing the Loop" activity. © Sam Stier.

Mushroom illustration. *The Illustrated Dictionary of Gardening—A Practical and Scientific Encyclopaedia of Horticulture*, edited by George Nicholson, circa 1885. Public domain image. https://olddesignshop.com/2013/07/free-vintage-image-mushrooms-page-and-clip-art/

Chapter 7

Leaf. Public domain image by Antonio Doumas. https://pixabay.com/en/ply-black-and-white-nature-natural-3810946/

Flock of birds. Public domain image. https://pixabay.com/en/birds-swarm-flock-of-birds-sky-2189476/

Ant trail diagram. Courtesy of Johann Dréo. Creative Commons Attribution-Share Alike 3.0 Unported. https://commons.wikimedia.org/wiki/File:Aco_branches.svg

Slime mold (*Stemonitis sporangia*) close-up. Public domain image. https://www.flickr.com/photos/usgsbiml/14531373586

Slime mold on log. Used with permission from Björn Sothmann.

Slime mold solving maze. Public domain image. https://commons.wikimedia.org/wiki/File:Slime_mold_solves_maze.png

Following a string with smell alone. © Sam Stier.

"Simple Rules Game" schematic. © Sam Stier.

Setup for "Algorithm Search Game." © Sam Stier.

Collective robots. Used with permission from Marco Dorigo, IRIDIA, Université Libre de Bruxelles.

Fish. Public domain. https://pixabay.com/en/america-american-animal-fish-ocean-2028122/

Chapter 8

Macaca silenus illustration from The Natural History Museum of London, c. 1862. Hardwicke Collection, image taken by author.

Students drawing. © Sam Stier

Dog shedding water. Public domain image. https://pixabay.com/en/dog-shaking-image-sch%C3%BCttelnder-dog-672845/

Laundry machine. Public domain image.

Owl feather. Used with permission from Eiji Nakatsu.

Owl. Public domain image. https://pixabay.com/en/eurasian-eagle-owl-flying-owl-1574166/

Pantograph illustrations. Used with permission from Eiji Nakatsu and JR-West and the Railway Technical Institute.

Bullet train pantograph. © Sam Stier

Experiment device for train model testing. Used with permission from Eiji Nakatsu, and the Railway Technical Institute, Train Launcher Facility.

Bullet train with Eiji Nakatsu. Used with permission from Eiji Nakatsu.

Burdock seed. Used with permission from Richard Wheeler.

Velcro. © Sam Stier

Water fountain. Used with permission from Brendan Riley.

Park bench. Public domain image. https://pixabay.com/fr/photos/banc-nature-art-contem porain-2299496/

Snowed-in house. Public domain image. https://pixabay.com/fr/photos/neige-nature-maison -arbres-hiver-2590494/

Refrigerator made of snow. Courtesy of Neal Costello.

Trout leaping. Used with permission from Kim Taylor/Warren Photographic.

Twisty tree. © Sam Stier

Flamingos. Public domain image. https://pixabay.com/en/pink-flamingos-birds-wild -wildlife-1763885/

Kestrel Stier standing on one leg. © Sam Stier

Teachers doing the "Find Your Tree" activity. © Sam Stier.

Graph of questions asked over time. From Berger, W. 2014. *A more beautiful question: The power of inquiry to spark breakthrough ideas.* Bloomsbury, 44. Adapted from an analysis done by the Right Questions Institute of data from the U.S. Dept. of Education's 2009 *Nation's Report Card.*

Bee ball and thermal image. Used with permission from Dr. Masato Ono, Tamagawa University, Tokyo.

Analogy graphic. © Sam Stier

Gas cap. © Sam Stier.

Function junction activity. © Sam Stier

Hemoglobin sculpture. Used with permission from Julian Voss-Andreae "Heart of Steel (Hemoglobin)", 2005. Weathering (CorTen) steel and glass, height 5' (1.50 m).

FedEx Truck. Public domain image.

Whale shark, mouth open. Used with permission from Kazuto Ushioda.

Whale shark, mouth closed. Public domain image by Simone Saponetto. https://pixabay.com/ en/whale-shark-maldives-sea-363623/

Drawing of slug slippers. © Sam Stier, adapted from drawing by Eliza H.

Sketch of backpack. Used with permission from Hannah Perner-Wilson.

Prototype of backpack. Used with permission from Hannah Perner-Wilson.

Cat in snow. Public domain image. https://pixabay.com/en/black-cat-dacha-animals-2233386/

Jacket. © Sam Stier, adapted from drawing by Sean D.

Design process graphic. © Sam Stier.

Gear style 1 (smooth). Public domain image. https://pixabay.com/en/sprocket-gear-gear-wheel-machine-153306/

Gear style 2 (metal). Courtesy of gadgetscode. Commercial free. https://openclipart.org/detail/168010/gear

Spiderweb. Johannes Plenio. Public domain image. https://pixabay.com/en/nature-cobweb-spider-dew-grid-3102765/

INDEX

Note: Italicized page locators refer to illustrations; tables are noted with *t*.